frankie

The Autobiography of
FRANKIE DETTORI

with JONATHAN POWELL

CollinsWillow
An Imprint of HarperCollinsPublishers

First published in hardback in 2004 by
CollinsWillow
an imprint of HarperCollins*Publishers*
London

Revised and updated in paperback in 2005

A CIP catalogue record for this book is
available from the British Library

ISBN 0 00 717687 2

Typeset in PostScript Minion by
Rowland Phototypesetting Ltd, Bury St Edmunds, Suffolk

Printed and bound in Great Britain by Clays Ltd, St Ives plc

The HarperCollins website address is www.harpercollins.co.uk

PHOTOGRAPHIC ACKNOWLEDGEMENTS

All photographs provided courtesy of Frankie Dettori with the exception of
the following: **Associated Press**: p11 (centre left), p18 (bottom left),
p27 (bottom), p28 (centre and bottom), p30 (centre). **Empics**: p5 (top and
centre right), p7 (centre), p9 (top), p11 (top and bottom right), p14 (top),
p24 (bottom left and right), p30 (bottom), p31 (bottom). **Getty Images**:
p14 (bottom right) p20 (right inset), p22 (centre left and bottom),
p23 (centre left and bottom), p27 (top left and right, centre), p28 (top),
p30 (top), p31 (top). **Mirrorpix**: p8 (all), p18 (centre right), p22 (centre
right), p25 (top). **PA Photos**: p14 (centre). **Topham/PressNet**: p18 (bottom
right). **Trevor Jones**: p5 (centre left and bottom), p6 (top), p7 (top),
p17, p18 (top), p20 (main and left inset), p21 (inset), p22 (top), p23 (top
left and right), p31 (centre left and right).

*To my dad Gianfranco
who never doubted that I would make it
as a jockey, even when I was not sure.
A thousand thanks.*

Acknowledgments

So many friends have had a part to play in the telling of this story. My thanks to all of them. From my earliest days in England Val and Dennis Sykes, Luca Cumani, and my first pals in Newmarket Colin Rate and Andy Keates all brought back great memories. In addition Cuthie Suttle, Richard Cross, Bruce Raymond and Arthur Taylor willingly helped with useful tales from the past.

Later Barney Curley and John Gosden recalled some of the dark days when my career was at the crossroads. They were the ones whose backing set me on the path to my first championship after a roller-coaster ride. Mattie Cowing, my agent for so many fruitful years, is sadly no longer with us but his widow Rita helped remind me of our happy partnership. Ian Balding and Simon Crisford have played key roles, too, in my autobiography.

Ray Cochrane and Pete Burrell seem to have been around since my first fumbling attempts as an apprentice. I owe so much to Ray, not least my life, and I thank him again for recalling that horrible day at Newmarket when we both feared we were about to die. Now that he is retired from riding he is doing a terrific job booking my rides. Pete clearly relished relating the great deals he has made on my behalf, and the ones that got away.

I could not have attempted this marathon without the enthusiasm and energy of Jonathan Powell who managed to dig up so many tales of my misspent youth that I had forgotten. I never sit still for long and admit I was often elusive, but over a period of months Jonathan kept persevering until every question was answered. By then I felt like an orange that had been squeezed dry.

My greatest thanks go to my lovely wife Catherine who builds me up when I am down and brings me back to earth on the days when I am heading for the stars. I could not manage my crazy daily schedule without her total support. Together we have five beautiful children. They are my finest achievement.

Frankie Dettori

Contents

CONTENTS

one

I Knew I Was Going to Die

Death came calling with terrifying suddenness on a bleak summer's day in 2000. It happened as Ray Cochrane and I were taking off in a small plane from Newmarket racecourse on the sort of routine flight to the races that had been part of my daily schedule for the past fifteen years.

One moment we were sitting side by side in the rear seats as our Piper Seneca bumped alarmingly along the grass runway on that wet and windy June morning. The next I knew with horrible certainty that I was about to die as our little plane, fatally damaged on take-off, struggled to reach a height of perhaps 100 feet before plunging towards Devil's Dyke, a huge ancient bank and ditch that lies between the July track and the main course at Newmarket.

White smoke was already streaming from a crippled engine, and there were the first signs of flickering flames as our doomed aircraft tilted crazily onto its right side, hampered from the lack of full power when we needed it most. In front of us our pilot Patrick Mackey was fighting manfully at the controls to keep

1

us in the air long enough to avoid the dyke on our way down, but his task was impossible from the moment the right-wing engine propeller gouged into the ground just before lift-off.

Not too many people in full health know beyond doubt that they have only a few seconds to live. Ray was icy calm as we waited for the impact that would end it all. Next to him I wasn't so controlled.

'We're going to die mate, we've had it!' I screamed.

So many people have asked me what it was like to stare death in the face. It's impossible to explain because it all seemed to happen so quickly. I was certain that it was all over, finished, as if somebody had pressed a button to end my life. I was also terrified that it was going to hurt like hell, but my main feeling was one of disappointment at the waste of it all, that I would never see my wife Catherine and little boy Leo again.

The left wing tip was just about vertically above the other wing as we dived towards the bank and the ground rushed up to meet us. If we'd crashed nose first onto the dyke we would all have been killed instantly, no question – smashed to pieces like flies on a car windscreen.

By some miracle Patrick nearly managed to clear the dyke – until the extreme tip of the right wing clipped the top of the bank. This sent us cartwheeling into the ground on the other side of the ditch. The noise of the impact seemed to last forever.

It was a nightmare sound I'll never forget.

At a time like this you have no control over your fate. If the plane had ended upside down we would all have been trapped in the wreckage and burned to death. There would have been no escape as more than sixty gallons of aviation fuel ignited. Even though we settled the right way up, the force of the impact left Ray unconscious for a few seconds, and I was out of it too.

When we came to our senses we were still strapped in our seats, with the passenger door on my left squashed in on top of me. No escape route there. In front of us poor Patrick was slumped unconscious over the controls, flames were coming from the engines and the horrible smell of fuel was overpowering. I was already aware of a dreadful pain in my right leg. There was also so much blood on my face from deep cuts on my forehead that I thought I'd been blinded. Ray immediately took charge, thank goodness, or I wouldn't be here to tell the tale.

Spotting that the tiny door used to stow baggage immediately behind my seat was ajar, he kicked the rest of it out, then squeezed forward again to undo my seat belt, dragged me backwards and pushed me out of the narrow opening. The drop onto the ground was probably no more than eighteen inches but I landed on my injured ankle and immediately began screaming from the pain, unable to move.

Lying in a heap near the remains of the tail plane, I was still far from safe.

Terrified that I could be trapped by the flames at any moment, I cried out to Ray for help as he was turning back to try to save Patrick. When he heard me he came back, pushed himself through the broken hatch and dragged me thirty yards or more to safety just as the fire was really starting to take hold.

Then he immediately rushed back determined to rescue Patrick, but by the time he reached the wreckage flames were beginning to appear underneath the plane. Ray should have given up at that point but he was unbelievably brave. Showing total disregard for his own safety, he forced open the pilot's door on the right-hand side, leaned in, reached towards Patrick and was just about to release his belt when there was a whoosh and the whole lot went up.

Driven back by the ferocity of the inferno and already suffering from burns, Ray then struggled round to the other side of the plane to have another go through the hatch that had provided our escape. By now the first rescuer had appeared, a racecourse worker, who was begging Ray at the top of his voice to get away from the flames, yet still he persisted.

The last image I have of this incredible rescue attempt was of Ray taking off his jacket and trying to use it to beat out the flames, then collapsing in tears of rage, overcome with guilt at being unable to save Patrick, before crawling over to comfort me.

We lay huddled together in an advanced state of shock, like two small refugees silhouetted by the fire. Then the cavalry began to arrive. Soon we were both trussed up and on our way by helicopter to Addenbrooke's Hospital in Cambridge. The last thing we wanted after our ordeal was to be flying again so soon, but we were in no condition to argue.

As we lay in emergency, shocked, hurting and distressed, neither of us knew quite how badly we were injured. I remember thinking: Why go on as a jockey? What's the point? I had a lovely wife and a bouncy little son. There was so much more to life than racing. Why not jump off the treadmill and take things easy for a change?

Then I began to realise that God had saved me. I was going to die and he spared me. Why? Obviously it wasn't my time. And because my life almost ended far too soon, I decided there and then that I was going to make the most of it the second time around.

two

Against the Odds

As a small boy I wanted to be a petrol pump attendant when I grew up. Well, the price of petrol was very high then. It seemed like a rewarding career. Later I fancied myself as a professional footballer, but it was my destiny to become a jockey. My dad Gianfranco was champion jockey thirteen times in Italy and also won lots of big races in England, but he didn't sit on a horse until he was twenty and stumbled into racing by chance after he left the family home in Sardinia to seek fame and fortune on the mainland.

His father Mario, my grandfather, had an iron will. He stood little more than 5ft 2in tall and came from a family who were often penniless. He was a man's man – tough, stubborn, hard as nails – and could be an absolute bastard. We all called him Super Mario and you will soon understand why. He was doing odd building jobs, earning money where he could – sometimes in the mines at Carbonia – when Italy became involved in the Second World War in June 1941 as an ally of Germany.

Soon the Germans were everywhere in Sardinia with several

army barracks, but at least there was no fighting on the island. Once my grandfather joined the Italian Army he was based full-time in barracks, which was a bit of a problem because his wife Apollonia lived thirty miles away from the camp. He used to tell me stories of how he cycled over to see her whenever he was free. Since the tyres on the bicycle were old and worn, his journey would often be interrupted by punctures which he mended with the crudest of equipment.

Mario's love for my grandmother cost him dear. When he failed to return to camp in time one Monday morning he was put on a charge and locked in a cell for a month. The second time it happened they tied him to a pole in the middle of a courtyard and left him there for several days, maybe a week. Ants creeping all over his body made him so itchy that they nearly drove him mad. In desperation he shook the pole so hard that it broke and came crashing down and he was put in a cell once more. You might think that he had learned his lesson by then, but the Dettoris are resolute in matters of the heart. Once he'd completed his sentence he rushed off for a reunion with my grandmother and failed to return to barracks before the curfew yet again.

This time there was no escaping serious punishment. Mario was immediately sent to the front at Montecassino early in 1944, where one of the fiercest battles of the war was raging around the famous monastery – which was eventually destroyed by Allied bombers after months of heavy fighting. It came at the point in the war when the Allies were trying to drive the Germans out of Italy. Casualties were horribly high in the battle for Montecassino, south of Rome. It was a bloodbath. Mario told me he spent six months crouching in the trenches there and escaped with no more than a small scratch on his arm from a stray bullet.

The way he told it to me years later, rain fell for weeks on end and the only way he managed to keep himself from sinking into the mud at night was by sleeping on a lilo in the trenches. He smoked incessantly, and quickly learned never to put his head above the parapet – for the very good reason that those who did immediately came under fire, often with fatal results.

Once Italy was liberated by the Allies, Mario returned home to Sardinia and started working in the local mines at Carbonia which supplied coal for much of the mainland. Since he was a builder he had the perilous job of erecting a barrier with bricks and cement at great speed to stop fire spreading whenever it broke out. This required great skill and courage because he was obviously the last man out when a fire started. Mining was much more primitive then and he saved quite a few lives.

My grandparents had six children, all boys, but one died at birth. Pepe was the oldest followed by Gianfranco, Salvatore, Sandro, and finally Sergio. Eventually Mario left the mines and began his own building business, though there were months at a time when he was unemployed. As the boys grew up and left school they all began working for him. My dad remained at school until he was sixteen, which was like going to university in those days in such a poor community.

My dad was pretty cute and soon realised there was more to life than toiling away for his father for ten hours or more a day, mixing cement for the modest reward of just a bowl of pasta with beans and a roof over his head. After months of hard labour he couldn't see any sort of future. So, one day, with huge blisters on his hands, he hurled his bucket and shovel into a well and informed my grandfather that he was leaving home. Mario's response was typical: as my dad walked away he heard Mario shouting that he needn't bother to return.

Gianfranco just about had the price of a ticket for the ferry that took him to the mainland. He headed for Rome and stayed with one of his brothers until he found a job washing plates in a restaurant. Soon he moved on to a second restaurant where he lived in the cellar with his sparse belongings. These he kept on a shelf to avoid the attention of rats. When it poured with rain one night, the cellar flooded and everything he owned was swept away.

Dad was left with nothing, but you are resilient at that age and all he cared about at the time was chasing the girls and smoking cigarettes. He was just exploring life and worked like hell to pay for his fun. He switched from washing dishes to selling fruit and veg at a market stall. This also involved making home deliveries, a job that offered unexpectedly exciting perks from some of the housewives he met on his daily rounds.

My dad was smart, had a bit of charm and an easy smile. He was hungry for life and kept moving on, looking for a break. One of the stall holders was a policeman who also owned three trotting horses, stabled at Tor di Valle racecourse in Rome. Soon Dad began looking after these three horses, even though at first, he didn't have a clue what to do with them. He learned by asking and watching other lads at nearby stables, and within a week he was quite efficient at attaching the horses to the sulky, which is the little chariot used in trotting. He was also feeding the horses and mucking them out twice a day, throwing out the manure, adding fresh straw, and brushing around their stables.

He did this all by himself in return for an unlimited supply of cigarettes, as many packs as he could puff his way through. He was small, stocky, extremely fit and bright enough to realise that there wasn't much money in looking after trotting horses. Some friends suggested he switch to the Capannelle, then the home of Italian horse racing. So he turned up there, offered his services to the first trainer he met, and at the age of eighteen signed up as an apprentice for five years – even though he'd never sat on a horse in his life. It was the start of an odyssey that would make him the most successful jockey in the history of Italian racing.

In those days an apprentice in racing was not much more than a slave, expected to do all the hard, dirty, dangerous and menial jobs for minimal reward. In the first few months he toiled away, cleaning out stables, sweeping the yard, and feeding the horses without so much as climbing onto their backs. The opportunity he craved came in the most unlikely circumstances. The adjoining stable at the Capannelle housed a lunatic race-horse called Prince Paddy. My dad says it was so mad that no-one dared go near it. The only way they could brush its coat with any degree of safety was with a long-handled broom. When the man who trained and looked after this crazy horse became ill with flu, no-one wanted to risk handling the beast in his absence.

That's where my dad stepped in. He must have been mad too, because in addition to grooming Prince Paddy he decided to ride him at exercise. Young, fearless, and frustrated at the way things were turning out, he ended up begging to ride the one horse in the place that terrified everyone who came near it. People at the track feared the worst when he led the beast out of the stable and jumped onto its back. They all assumed it would be only a matter of time before my dad was sent crashing to the ground. Instead the pair hacked round together at a gentle pace as though they'd done it a thousand times before. It was the same when they teamed up again the next morning.

So that was how my dad started in racing. Eventually he partnered Prince Paddy every day, got his licence and rode the horse in his first race. To general amazement they won. My dad had experienced a very tough upbringing and believes the hunger and anger inside fired his ambition. By the time he reached twenty-one he had managed only five winners, three of them on Prince Paddy – yet within four years he was champion of Italy. Once he got there he was never going to throw it away. He was the best. No question.

Three of his brothers followed him into racing. Sergio became a very successful jockey too, with upwards of 1,500 winners and still rides a little bit while concentrating on his new career as a trainer. Sandro was also a jockey and is still involved as head lad to a trainer in Pisa. Pepe worked for years as a groundsman for the Italian Jockey Club. Salvatore was the outrageous one of the family. I don't recall ever meeting him – which is a shame because everyone says he was a lovely bloke. He was strong as an ox but never really channelled his energy in the right direction. Instead he became an alcoholic and died in 1996 when he choked on his own vomit.

As a young jockey my dad was so disciplined that he was in bed at nine every evening, his jodhpurs laid out nearby without a single crease in them, ready for an early start in the morning. You could say he was single-minded to the point of obsession, and who could blame him. For years he'd been toiling away in filthy jobs for meagre reward, and unlike a lot of young jockeys with easy money in their pockets he wasn't in a hurry to throw it all away.

It was the time of Molvedo, who followed in the hoofbeats of the mighty Ribot a few years earlier by winning Europe's greatest race, the Prix de l'Arc de Triomphe, for Italy. Initially Dad was second jockey to Ribot's rider Enrico Camici. He learned much from Camici, but when he became champion he forged a strong alliance with the trainer Sergio Cumani in Milan – which, by then, was becoming the centre of Italian racing.

My parents married after a whirlwind romance that began when my father visited a travelling circus in Milan. His Saturday nights were spent with his friends either at the cinema or at the Circo Russo – which stretched to a pair of camels, a few monkeys, three or four lions and a resident clown. That evening he chose the circus, chiefly because it was next to the racecourse, and was immediately captivated by a gorgeous young girl in

12

the ring with long black hair all the way down to her calves. She had a variety of roles that evening, including trapeze artist, contortionist, juggler and balancing athletically on the backs of two horses, one leg on each, with reins in her hands as they cantered side by side around the tight circus ring. She was also tied to a rotating wheel of fortune while some idiot wearing a headband threw knives at her!

Sitting in the front row, smartly turned out in a suit and tie, his brand new Vespa parked outside the big top, my dad couldn't take his eyes off this girl. For him it was a case of love at first sight. My mother's name is Iris Maria, but everyone calls her Mara. She was only sixteen that fateful night, like a rose about to bloom, and Dad made a point of meeting her afterwards. She had spent her entire life on the move with the rest of the family in the circus which originally came from Russia. They lived like a travelling band of gypsies. My dad pursued her relentlessly, swept her off her feet, and they were married a few short months later in 1963.

They were like two pigeons cooing at each other for sure. Theirs was a grand passion, but it was not an easy marriage because my mum had only known life on the road with the circus. She hardly ever attended school because she was always moving on to the next venue. As a result she can hardly read or write. We never did discover the identity of her father, but my grandmother Secondina, who never married, was one of two sisters who suffered terrible injuries to their legs when a caravan toppled over onto them when they were young children. Her sister was called Terzilla and their elder brother Primo.

They all lived a nomadic life, earning peanuts and living in caravans as the circus rolled on from town to town each week.

My uncle Claudio was the resident clown. With a big belly and white tee-shirt he's the spitting image of Onslow from the TV programme *Keeping Up Appearances*. Claudio was offered a house by his local council, but he was so used to life on the road that he turned it down to continue living in his own spartan caravan.

Once my parents married, my mother's days as a trapeze artist were over. She was totally fearless then, but now she can't bear to travel to England to see me because she's frightened of driving through the Channel Tunnel and even more terrified of flying. It's got to the stage where she won't even go up an elevator in a department store. So I keep in touch by phone and try to visit her whenever I am in Italy.

My sister Alessandra (who we call Sandra) was born in 1965. I followed five years later. Dad wanted my name to be as similar as possible to his. At first he considered calling me Gianfranco too, but eventually decided that if I became a jockey then Gianfranco Dettori junior was too much of a mouthful. So Lanfranco it was, although everyone in England has been calling me Frankie for years. I've inherited my suppleness and athleticism from my mother – and, of course, the agility and balance to carry out my trademark flying dismount. From my dad came the drive and desire to make it to the top.

By the time I was born on 15 December 1970 my parents' marriage was virtually over. I learned much later that at the time of my birth my father was away riding that winter in

Australia and he was already involved with Christine, who eventually became my stepmother. They had met that August when he was riding in Deauville. From the start she shared his ambition and he must have known that his marriage to my mother was coming to an end even before I was born.

One of the problems was that my mother hated horseracing. To her it is a stupid pastime. She is a lovely person, beautiful, though completely down to earth, and having given up the nomad's life she couldn't settle to domesticity. She never really understood what drove my father – and later me – to devote our lives to making horses run as fast as they possibly can. He would come home full of himself explaining that he'd won the big race, and she'd reply 'What race?' In those days it was important for him to have someone who could share and enjoy his achievements and my mum couldn't do that.

Nor did she appreciate the strict disciplines involving my father's weight, so he could never be sure his supper would be on the table each evening at 6.30 after a long day's work. My father was so single-minded in his pursuit of success that he became more and more well-known and eventually my mum was being left behind. She loved him for who he was, not for the fact that he was the most famous jockey in Italy. By becoming so successful he needed somebody to take him further, and perhaps my mum wasn't educated enough to take the next step with him. She preferred to retain her simple lifestyle as a housewife and couldn't cope with the fame that came with all his high-profile winners. I don't blame her for that. It's just the way she is.

The truth is that my parents probably married too early. They parted after six years and were quickly divorced. I don't really remember them being together at all. After the split Sandra and I stayed with our mother in Milan. Dad lived no more than half a mile away with Christine but we didn't see too much of him in the early days because he was so busy as a jockey. Then when I was five my parents had a summit meeting and decided that we should move in with him. It came down to economics. Mum felt he was much better placed to look after us and give us a decent start in life, but she made it clear she would always be there for us if we needed her.

The switch to living with my dad was tough for me, even tougher for my sister, and toughest of all for Christine. When you are so young you love your mother and it was only natural that we should hate the person who took her place. I wanted to hate Christine, and at first I did my best to make her life a misery. Looking back now I realise that I was totally unfair to her, yet I have to admit she brought me up brilliantly. I really respect what she did for me in the most trying circumstances.

I'm sure she made mistakes, too but it must be every woman's nightmare to have to take over two unfriendly children who are not your own. Poor Christine must have been biting her lip every minute of the day. She was unbelievably strict, but I understand now that she was teaching us the right way even though we didn't want to be told at that age – or in my case, at any age. It was: make your bed; clean your teeth; you must have a bath; get up when I tell you, blah, blah, blah. I might as well have been in the army. I had to be in bed early every night and my sister followed half an hour later. At least we had a break at the weekend when we went to stay with our mum. For me those were precious visits because I could sleep in until lunchtime if I wanted and could do pretty much what I liked. Then it would be back to reality with Christine on Sunday evening.

It was even more distressing for Sandra who had lived with mum until she was eleven. I'm sure the breakdown of our parents' marriage affected her more than me. She didn't take kindly to being told by Christine what to do every minute of the day. She tried to fight the system and became quite rebellious – but she was usually the loser and would end up in tears as we went to bed in the little cottage next to Dad's house.

My mother eventually set up home with a cool guy called Salvatore. He was good looking, a bit of a hippy, and has always treated me like his own son. They are still together to this day. Mum doesn't miss the glamour of life with my dad one bit. Far from it. She's happily set in her ways, enjoys looking after Salvatore, and works as a cleaner for a wealthy family in Milan. She is a natural house woman, absolutely obsessed by dusting, cleaning, ironing and washing. In some ways she is a servant woman, born to be a slave to society because she is in her element doing these things. Every Monday she goes right round the house until everything is spotless. That makes her the happiest woman in the world.

Soon after I moved in with Dad and Christine, he took me off for a few riding lessons. It didn't appeal to me one bit, partly perhaps because I was so small. Ponies held no interest for me. I was always waking up early in the mornings and often Dad would find me playing in the dining room when he came down. Soon he bought me jodhpurs, boots and a riding jacket. Then came the first time he took me with him in the morning to the stables of Sergio Cumani, the trainer who provided him with hundreds of winners during their rewarding association.

Once the racehorses had been exercised the lads would sometimes lift me onto the back of one that was tired and just walking round the yard while it cooled off. Being so light I'd cling to the mane while one of the lads held my leg just in case. Sergio would move among the horses after exercise, feeding them lots of sugar lumps. So this was my first experience of riding racehorses.

I also had an early insight into the demands on international jockeys. In addition to riding in Italy and sometimes France, Dad began to make frequent trips to England and occasionally Ireland. This followed the decision by Carlo d'Alessio, a Roman lawyer for whom he rode in Italy, to keep a select team of horses at Newmarket with Henry Cecil – who would become champion trainer countless times in the years ahead.

This development followed the appointment of Luca Cumani, Sergio's son, as Cecil's assistant. Years later Luca would play a pivotal role in my development as a jockey. Sergio trained for d'Alessio in Italy and had been in charge of the two-year-old colt Bolkonski when his first year's campaign ended with an easy victory ridden by my dad in the Premio Tevere at Rome early in November 1974. That prompted d'Alessio to send the colt to Cecil. It proved to be an inspired decision even though

Bolkonski was beaten on his debut in England in the Craven Stakes at Newmarket – often considered to be a trial for the 2,000 Guineas. Just over a fortnight later my dad rode him to victory at 33–1 in the Guineas, one of the five English Classics for three-year-olds that are the cornerstone of the racing calendar. Grundy, the horse he beat that day, went on to be one of the great horses of that decade.

My father's first Classic success in England was overshadowed by an ugly dispute over pay between the stable lads and trainers, which overflowed into bitter confrontation at Newmarket on Guineas' weekend. The night before the race some of the strikers stole a bulldozer, crashed it through a fence and damaged the track. On the day of the race striking lads formed a picket line while others joined forces at the start in an attempt to disrupt the Guineas. When the horses were almost all loaded in the stalls the strikers promptly sat down right across the course. A delay followed while police sought to restore order.

Eventually the runners formed a line just in front of the stalls and the starter let them go by waving a flag. My dad settled Bolkonski towards the rear of the pack before producing him with a timely run which gained the day by half a length over Grundy. Shortly after Bolkonski prevailed, Tom Dickie, the lad who'd looked after the horse from January until he joined the dispute, was carried shoulder high in front of the grandstand by his fellow strikers under heavy police escort.

Bolkonski extended his year of excellence by winning at Royal Ascot and Glorious Goodwood for my father, before an unexpected defeat at Ascot in September. By then the combination of Cecil, d'Alessio and Dettori were convinced that they had another potential champion on their hands in Wollow, who won all four of his races as a two-year-old.

Dad ended 1975 as the champion jockey of Italy once more with the added bonus of fourteen winners from forty-two rides in England. He briefly toyed with the idea of basing himself in England for a season, but it was a bit late in his career to be making significant changes and his commitments in Italy prevented the idea ever getting off the ground. He has always regretted that lost chance to ride full-time against the best jockeys in this country. That thinking influenced his choice of England as the starting point for my own career as a jockey ten years later.

The spring of 1976 saw Wollow continuing the good work by landing the 2,000 Guineas for the Italian connection for the second year running. There was then a brief hiccup on my dad's first foray at Epsom Downs, the home of the English Derby. Hopes were high that Wollow could complete the Guineas–Derby double. He started a red-hot favourite at 11–10 but ran out of stamina in the final quarter mile and finished only fifth behind Lester Piggott on Empery. Dad gained a further Classic success on Pampapaul in the Irish 2,000 Guineas at the Curragh in May 1977, where he beat Lester on the future Derby winner The Minstrel by a short head.

three

Lost in My Father's Shadow

In the late 1970s my father was flying as a jockey. He was the undisputed champion of Italy and increasingly gaining recognition abroad, but to me he was little more than a ghost – a distant, cold, intimidating figure. Life was still pretty tough for the rest of us at the Dettori home in Milan. There were many weeks during the height of the season when I saw him perhaps once in seven days. Usually he left before I was up and returned long after I'd gone to bed, and twice a week he set off at dawn to ride in Rome.

Towards the end of each summer he would be so far ahead of the other jockeys in the battle for the championship that he'd take a short break from domestic racing with a holiday abroad, followed by a few engagements riding in international events around the world. Then he tended to go away for the winters.

I'd often stay with my Godmother, Teresa Colangeli, who acted as my second mum and looked after me in the winter when Dad was away. She was married to a trainer called

Vincenzo. When he died fifteen years ago she took over the training licence and is still doing well with her team of horses in Varese. One of her owners, Giuseppe Molteni, is the most successful amateur rider in Italy – and probably the world – with close on a thousand winners. He won three races in a week as recently as February 2004, and still rides out every day at the age of 74. Teresa provided a refuge when I needed one most and was always generous with her time and support. I still speak to her when I can because she has played a big part in my life.

On the days that my father *was* around when I came home after school, he was a grim, forbidding figure. It was a bit like finding Roy Keane or Graeme Souness in your kitchen. At least he greeted me with a smile and a kiss, but after that he would pop upstairs to change into his shorts, come back down again, watch the news on television without saying a word, then retreat behind his newspaper for the rest of the evening as he studied the form for the next afternoon's card.

Conversation wasn't encouraged. If I suggested doing something, Christine's stock reply would be that he was racing the following day so please don't bother him. I can't say it upset me much because I was used to it. His riding always came first and you could see that he was a man with a mission. If things became tricky because I stepped out of line, Sandra did her best to protect me. If necessary she would lie for me, but he could be very rough with her. She was the one who bore the brunt of it. I can remember one incident when he made her kneel in a tray of salt which was an incredibly painful punishment. That kept me quiet for a while because I didn't fancy the same fate.

He was very wrong in the way he treated us as youngsters but he didn't know any different. That was how he'd been brought up too, so he was simply sticking to the same rules. Many years later he admitted to me that no-one taught him how to be a father. Now he is as nice as pie and we get on famously.

Most nights Sandra and I used to cry ourselves to sleep. My sister is very strong-willed and by the time she was fourteen she was determined to run away. She told me of her plans to escape back to mum. Sure enough, one day after school she didn't come home. When my dad realised what had happened he was furious and there was the most terrific row in the kitchen that night as I was going to bed. The upshot was that I was suddenly on my own with Dad and Christine. This proved to be the turning point in my life. In all my time at school Dad had never come to collect me at the end of the day, but the very next afternoon there he was leaning out of the driving seat of a horsebox near the school gates, waiting for me. I can still remember the excitement I felt the moment I spotted him. I dashed up to the lorry, climbed into the front seat and gave him a big kiss.

He promised me a big surprise and he wasn't kidding. We set off through the streets of Milan until we pulled up a few miles away beside a field that contained three ponies, two that were bay and a palomino. The choice was mine and I had no hesitation in picking the palomino with its white face, mane and tail. For me it was love at first sight. We took the pony home and put her in a field with stabling belonging to a farmer barely a hundred yards from our house.

Looking back now, I think my sister's sudden departure acted like an electric shock on my father. He realised he'd lost his daughter and was frightened of losing me, too. So he bought the pony to keep me happy. It's funny how things work out in life. If my sister hadn't run away and my dad hadn't bought that pony called Silvia, I might never have become interested in racing. Up until that point I had hated racing, chiefly because I found it so boring. Instead I spent all my time playing football at school and in my spare time. Once I had the pony I had to start looking after it and soon I was taking all my mates from school to watch me riding it round the field pretending to be a jockey.

Having your own pony at the age of eight in a field close to the middle of Milan was quite a novelty in those days, a bit like keeping a tiger in the centre of London. Until then I hadn't enjoyed my brief skirmishes at riding school. I was as scared as hell, and hated it, perhaps because I was so small. I'd been overshadowed by my sister in whatever I did. She was the posh one, but when she left there was nobody else to lean on, so I had to grow up fast. Having my own pony certainly helped.

On a rare day off at home my dad took me out to the stables, tied up Silvia and demonstrated how to groom her properly and muck the stable out until it was spotless. He said he would only show me once. He brushed her coat, mane and tail, used a pitchfork to remove the dung in the box and replace it with fresh straw, banked it up around the walls, cleaned out the manger, brought in hay for her to eat, and filled the water bucket with fresh water. It was an impressive lesson from a master, for this had once been his daily task as a stable lad in Rome and would eventually become mine when I became an apprentice. It was fun in the summer, but once winter arrived looking after Silvia became a horrible chore. Working in the dark in freezing weather didn't appeal to me then and doesn't appeal to me now.

There were consolations. I would rush home from school, put on my jodhpurs and racing silks in the colours of Carlo d'Alessio, run out to the stables, saddle up Silvia and set off on her at a million miles an hour around the field. There was no question of grooming her first or cleaning out her droppings. That lesson from Dad had already been forgotten! All I wanted to do was ride like the wind with my knees under my chin. I never had any doubt that I would be a jockey.

I was barely nine when I rode in my first Derby at the San Siro track in Milan. Never mind that it was only a pony race – to me it felt like the greatest race on earth. I trained and practised for weeks on Silvia in the field at home, but on the big day I was horrified to discover that all the others ponies were giants compared to Silvia and all the other jockeys giants compared to me. The course for this Derby was laid out on the jumping track between the last two fences and probably stretched to less than half a mile. It seemed like a marathon to me and I was a nervous wreck as we formed a ragged line at the start.

There was no fairytale start to my career as a jockey, quite the opposite. It was a case of 'slowly away, then faded' for Silvia and her hapless rider. Once the starter's flag fell we were left behind and were tailed off throughout. To add insult to injury, when Silvia saw the crowd at the finishing line she dug in her toes and sent me sprawling into the water jump.

Despite that humbling setback, my days at school were largely spent dreaming of riding when lessons were over. I was quick at maths and liked geography. In those two subjects I was a furlong ahead of the rest of the class. But I was hopeless at history and my stumbling attempts at English were embarrassing. If only I'd paid more attention to my English teacher.

Silvia and I were inseparable for about a year but the novelty quickly wore off when she began to get the better of me. She was strong and increasingly wilful and there were too many times when I couldn't control her. She was taking advantage of me, knew every trick in the book, and soon there were days when I was too frightened to ride her. Our partnership came to a painfully abrupt end one afternoon when she ran off with me under a metal paddock rail. I grabbed the pole in an attempt to save myself, but it broke off in my hands and fell onto my chest as I hit the ground. I was in so much pain I could hardly breathe. I thought my ribs were broken, and by the time I was on the way to hospital I'd decided riding was definitely not for me. My plans as a jockey were in tatters. Luckily Dad took the hint and promptly sold Silvia. After that I didn't go near a horse for a year.

As the smallest boy at school I was the obvious target for

bullying, but I became quite adept at avoiding nasty incidents. Christine, who used to work in a bank, offered some sound advice when she suggested thinking my way out of tricky situations. I was dead sharp even then and much cleverer than the bullies, so I usually managed to work my way out of trouble when danger threatened. Somehow I could fiddle my way around confrontations. I didn't have that many scraps because I usually managed to sidestep when danger threatened. Nothing much has changed since then!

Despite my size, I played a mean game of football at school during the long lunch break which stretched to an hour and a half in the hot Italian sun most days. I was small, light and nippy on my feet and spent most of the time as a goal-hanger lurking near the penalty spot, trying to convert any chances that came my way – and was disappointed if I hadn't scored a hatful by the end of the game. If the final score was 23–17 then I'd sometimes be responsible for eight or ten of them. I saw myself as Roberto Bettega, who was a famous centre-forward for Juventus in the seventies.

Although we lived in Milan, I supported 'Juve' – based in Turin – from the moment an uncle gave me one of their shirts for Christmas. I wore it all the time, which was quite a brave thing to do if you lived in Milan. Naturally my first heroes were all giants of Juventus. Initially Roberto Bettega was my inspiration, but I switched my allegiance to Liam Brady when he moved from Arsenal in June 1980. Liam was outstanding in Italy and won two Italian championships with Juve.

A few years later, when I was working for Luca Cumani in

Newmarket, I finally met Liam when he came to an open day at the yard. For once in my life I was speechless, hopelessly star-struck, yet he was keen to talk to me because I'd ridden a few winners by then. It was very strange. Liam loves his racing, and whenever I can get to an Arsenal game at Highbury – where he is now head of youth development – I give him a call and meet up with him. Michel Platini, who followed Liam to Juventus, was another of my early heroes.

In those days my pals and I used to climb over the gates into the San Siro stadium at around eleven in the morning, a good three hours before kick-off. We'd hide in the grandstand until people started coming through the turnstiles. That way we could watch the Milan games for free and the money we saved would be spent on tickets for the basketball. Alas, my dream of a football career moved rapidly downhill after a long summer's holiday when I was about twelve. By the time I returned to school everyone else had grown a foot and I seemed to have shrunk, so I used to get a right pasting when the big boys tackled me. Even so, the manager of the boys' team I played for at the weekends felt I deserved my turn as captain.

On the big day, the parents of all the other boys turned up to support them but as usual my father was off riding somewhere – and as Christine always accompanied him I was the only one there without family. It hurt at the time and, you know, I can already see the same thing happening with my son Leo when he starts to play competitively in a few years' time. Every Saturday and Sunday I have to work, too, so he will be missing his dad if he plays football at weekends.

A source of endless fun for me and my friends came at the races on the days we all pretended to be horses and staged our own sprints. Each racehorse carried a plastic number on its bridle in the paddock. These were often discarded before the competitors cantered to the start. We'd collect the numbers, attach them to the belts of our trousers and have our own series of races using branches torn from trees in the park as makeshift whips to whack our own legs.

After a year's break from ponies I started to get the old hunger back for riding once more. The spark for my renewed interest came from writing reports for the school magazine on the racing at Milan, which my dad tended to dominate. For a while at school I was like a racing reporter. I would go with him to the races at the weekend, have a flutter with my friends, then on the Monday morning I'd cut out the pictures of the finishes from the local paper and write my articles around them. Sometimes I filled as many as six pages with photographs and reports. That was the limit of my endeavour in the classroom. Usually I let two fingers of dust grow on my school books while I sat at my desk dreaming about horses.

Those early trips to the races opened my eyes to the riches that racing offered. Once in a while my dad would take me with him to Rome on a long weekend. The drive from Milan could take up to five hours on the Saturday and we would then walk the track on Sunday morning. One day he pointed out Lester Piggott, who was already a legend with nine Derby winners. 'Look at him', said Dad. 'You could be just as successful if you work hard enough.' It was a lofty ambition and it made a big impression on me.

We were out on the course at Rome on the morning of the 1981 Italian Derby when we ran into a group of English jockeys, including a baby-faced teenager called Walter Swinburn. I was wearing a tee-shirt and short trousers and here was this young jockey who was all the rage looking hardly any older than me. Glint of Gold, trained by Ian Balding, won the Italian Derby that year, and just over three weeks later he finished a distant second in the Derby at Epsom to Shergar ridden by the same Walter Swinburn.

While Dad was busy riding through the afternoon my mates and I were betting on every race. The pocket money he gave me was usually spent on bets at the Tote window. Most of my pals then were sons of jockeys, too, but we never seemed to benefit from inside information and thought we'd done well if we were left with a few lire after the last race.

Soon I was back at riding school for more lessons. Although I felt a bit stronger and more confident than before, I was hardly prepared for the next step when I started riding out in the school holidays with Carlo d'Alessio's string of horses, which by then was trained by the two brothers Alduino and Giuseppe Botti following the death of Sergio Cumani. Most of the time, I was restricted to walking and trotting on the roads. If the horse I was on was due to canter or gallop, I'd be replaced by a professional work rider.

I already knew this was the life for me and was further encouraged by two memorable experiences at Milan races in 1983 when I was twelve. The first came on one of those special days when my dad took me into the jockeys' changing room with him and I found myself sitting next to Steve Cauthen – who was known as the Six Million Dollar Kid for his exploits in America before he moved to England in 1979.

Steve had flown over to ride the English raider Drumalis. I was still so short that when I sat beside him on the bench my feet didn't reach the floor, but I watched spellbound as this world-famous jockey proceeded to put on all sorts of fancy riding equipment. You name it, he wore it. He had leggings and ankle protectors inside his riding boots, specially designed socks, and a whip with feathers on the end. My eyes never left him as he changed into his silks. I was fascinated by every little detail and it was only when he walked out to the paddock that I spotted a pair of red sponge ankle pads.

The temptation was irresistible. One minute they were there on the ground beside his bag, the next they were in my pocket. My dad, riding Bold Run for Alduino Botti, then inflicted further pain on Steve by beating him on Drumalis by a nose, but by the time he came back to 'weigh in' I'd left the scene of the crime. Four years later I'd just begun riding in England when Steve spotted me wearing his distinctive red ankle pads. 'Those are mine, you thieving little Italian bastard. Give them back', he demanded in menacing tones. I tried to bluster my way out of trouble but was eventually forced to plead guilty as charged. It was typical of Steve that he forgave me pretty quickly and soon became a great friend by giving me lifts to numerous race meetings in his chauffeur-driven Jaguar.

Four months after nicking Steve's precious ankle pads I was back at Milan with my dad, walking the course as usual, when a big helicopter flew over us and landed close by. Nobody had ever seen a helicopter at a race meeting in Italy before then. For me at such an impressionable age, it was like witnessing a spaceship drop out of the skies. Moments after the door opened the pale figure of Lester Piggott appeared at the top of the steps, followed by the trainer John Dunlop and others associated with Sheikh Mohammed, a member of the Royal family in Dubai who were just beginning to expand their already considerable racing interests. Dad explained that the Sheikh owned the filly Awaasif who'd been sent from England to run in the Gran Premio Del Jockey Club. She won it easily, too, by six lengths. How strange to think that within a few short years I'd often be travelling in a similar helicopter to the four corners of the world to ride for Sheikh Mohammed.

By now I was totally addicted to racing, mad keen to become a jockey and was finding my last year at school increasingly tedious. I became totally obsessed with the idea of following in my dad's hoofbeats and couldn't see any point in remaining in the classroom a second longer. It helped that my dad shared my ambition and finally allowed me to leave school in the summer of 1984 at the age of thirteen and a half.

In a rare heart-to-heart, he had the sense to tell me that the years ahead would test my resolve to the limit. He explained that for every small boy who sets out to become a jockey only one in a thousand succeeds in making the grade. In the back of his mind, and that of Christine – who by then had become my stepmother – was the suspicion that I lacked the necessary motivation and aggression to make the breakthrough.

It is fair to say that in their presence I tended to be quiet, almost meek. That was because I felt intimidated by them. Away from home there were plenty of people to testify that I was almost too exuberant, and at school I was known as the naughtiest boy in the class.

Despite Dad's well-intentioned warning, I had no doubt that I would become a jockey, too, as I set off to work full-time in a racing yard for Alduino and Giuseppe Botti at the princely wage of around £10 a week. It quickly proved to be a disheartening experience, basically because at well under five stone I wasn't strong enough or experienced enough to ride big, hard-pulling thoroughbreds.

I hope I didn't behave too much like a spoiled brat, but that was probably the impression I gave as I turned up on the first morning in my immaculate jodhpurs and flashy jacket. My father was stable jockey and sometimes rode out there, so everyone was scared of treating me badly or giving me any worthwhile challenges. Nor, because I was Franco Dettori's son, were they prepared to take any risks with me or make me do the dirty or dangerous jobs normally reserved for newcomers. You need someone pushing you constantly to help you improve but I wasn't given the opportunity, probably because I wasn't ready.

It was also a major disadvantage that Carlo d'Alessio's team of forty racehorses was the classiest in Italy. The last thing he needed was one of his expensive stars running away with a new lad who should have been wearing L-plates. So I ended up riding the slowest, quietest horses in the yard which, looking back, was just as well. I continued to live at home and cycled to work earlier than everyone else each morning because initially it took me longer to tie up the three horses I looked after and to muck them out properly.

I enjoyed the routine of caring for the same three horses and brushed their coats until they shone like a mirror, but I was by far the slowest lad in the yard at my work. At least I was doing what I wanted after the restrictions of school, but it was pretty clear after only a few weeks that I wasn't making any progress. Dad would turn up every few days to check up on me and immediately start shouting: 'Let your leathers down, you're riding too short, keep your bum down, try to look tidy – do this, do that, do the other.' I tried to take it all in, but most of his advice was forgotten by the time I climbed onto another horse and I would be back to riding with my stirrups too short again. The truth is that whatever I did he was never satisfied, and the next time he appeared at the yard he would start shouting at me all over again. This went on week after week until I had the firm impression that he felt I was useless. I began to go into my shell whenever he drove into the yard and kept quiet because whatever I said didn't please him.

I was frightened of upsetting my father and the trainer. I was also frightened by all the shouting because I didn't know how to do the job properly and was terrified I'd make a disastrous mistake on a valuable horse. Some of the lads tried to help with useful hints, but no-one had any confidence in my ability and often I ended up on the same horse twice in the morning because it was the only safe one available. She was so lazy and fat she needed to go out twice to lose a little bit of weight.

Things weren't much better at home in the evenings. That summer my dad fixed a long set of leather reins onto the metal frame of a well in our garden which was covered in ivy. Night after night he'd show how to hold the reins, the right way to make an arch with them, and then encourage me to change my hands on the reins while holding a whip as though I was riding a finish.

At this stage I could trot and canter – but in racing terms I could hardly read or write, and I couldn't understand why he was taking such pains to teach me the basics. Why the hell did it matter so much? The lessons continued for half an hour or more on most evenings whenever Dad was home. He would start me off, then mow the lawn or sit down and read a newspaper, keeping an eye on me all the while, shouting instructions and occasional encouragement as I wrestled energetically with the reins.

Within a few months I was changing my reins and passing my whip through from one side to the other without thinking about it, all because of those endless lessons beside our garden well. Once I started race riding it came as second nature to me, and even now I don't think about switching my whip or changing my hands. I just do it. Sometimes after a race the stewards will ask how many times I used my whip in a finish, and I don't know the answer until I see the video. That's because I do these things automatically, without a moment's thought. Although I'm right-handed, all those sessions beside the well helped me become equally effective with the whip in either hand – which is a big advantage for a jockey. Strangely, though, if you ask any of my rivals, they will probably say I am more vicious with the whip in my left hand.

When you are twelve or thirteen and your dad tells you what to do you don't have any choice. Everything he said I took as gospel. We had our differences, but to me he will always be a genius for clawing his way to the top of the tree by meeting every challenge with the whole of his being until he dominated flat racing in Italy like no jockey had ever done before or since. When I started in racing I was lost in his shadow, but I was hugely proud that he ended 1983 with a record of 229 winners in Italy – a score that is unlikely ever to be matched.

By the time the summer season was drawing to a close I'd reached an important crossroads in my life. In the late autumn everything closes down in Milan, which can be as cold as New York in the winter. My dad didn't want me wasting my time trotting around an indoor school for three or four months, learning nothing but bad habits. He then had a flash of inspiration by sending me to work for Tonino Verdicchio at his winter training quarters in Pisa, a three hour drive further south. At the age of thirteen it seemed so far away from home that I felt he was sending me to the moon, but it proved to be the making of me.

four

Growing Up Fast

Tonino Verdicchio was one of my dad's oldest friends. They got up to all sorts of mischief as apprentices in Rome and kept in close touch when Tonino later became a trainer. He was the man chosen to further my education in and out of the saddle. He and his wife Antonietta had three daughters and throughout that winter they treated me as their own son. I slept on the sofa because they didn't have a spare bedroom, and worked harder than ever before in my life.

Dad's instructions to Tonino were short and precise: make sure Lanfranco works hard and pay him peanuts. Tonino fulfilled both to the letter. He met me at Pisa station a few weeks before my fourteenth birthday in December 1984, greeted me warmly, and showed me nothing but kindness during the four months I spent with him. He took me home for a quick change, then immediately put me to work that afternoon at his stables beside the local racecourse.

The yard was built in an L shape. Once he'd armed me with a pitchfork and huge wheelbarrow, Tonino gave me my orders.

'You start at that end, I'll start at the other and we'll meet in the middle', he suggested. This was an alarming development because I could see at least two dozen horses' heads peering out at us over the doors, and this madman, who I'd just met, obviously thought I was going to muck out half of them. I started to protest. 'But Tonino, in other stables where I've been you only have to do three horses.'

I'll never forget his reply: 'Well, there is no-one else here for the moment so just get on with it.' I did, too, though I'd finished only two boxes after he'd completed ten. I was doing the job properly just as I had been taught by Sergio Cumani and Aldo Botti. Each of the two boxes was immaculate by the time I closed the doors. When Tonino came to inspect my efforts he was clearly unhappy at what he discovered. 'Don't waste so much straw. Just chuck out the worst, put the rest back and freshen it all up', he explained. It was an early education into the harsh economics of racing for most trainers who have to balance the books. Tonino then helped me finish the remaining boxes before taking me back home for supper with his family.

The next morning I was up early as usual dressed in my smart jodhpurs and shiny boots – which proved to be a bit over the top since all the lads at the others yards in Pisa wore jeans and trainers. On the drive to the stables Tonino stopped to collect a double espresso, poured it into an empty bottle, then knocked on the window of the lads' hostel beside the yard. A large hand emerged from the window and grasped the coffee. Moments later a dishevelled, unshaven, fat guy came stumbling out of the hostel to join us, the life-restoring coffee clutched in his hand. This turned out to be Tonino's head lad Chippolo.

So now we had three to share the workload – and what a workload! We mucked out 25 horses between us and each rode eight of them at exercise. Naturally I fell off a couple of times that first morning and by the time we'd finished I was close to collapsing. The place seemed more like a circus than a well-run racing stable. How on earth was I going to survive?

My early attempts in the saddle on Tonino's horses were embarrassing. Because I still had the puppy fat of a schoolboy my body wasn't prepared for the shock of riding so many horses each morning. Some ran off with me, others dropped me, and one or two could barely be bothered to put one leg in front of the other as they hacked half-heartedly down to the start of the area where they used to work round a six furlong sand track. Then when we turned round ready to canter back they were off like Spitfires.

Being run away with by a big, hard-pulling racehorse is not for faint hearts and it happened to me most mornings. The harder I tried to hold them by pulling on the reins the faster they galloped. Tonino bollocked me all the time, but always with a smile on his face.

One day I completed seven laps of the circuit on a horrible old gelding which always took liberties with me. The further we went the weaker I became until my arms gave out. I was screaming at Tonino to help me, and eventually he did by placing the horse that he was riding firmly in our path just as we were in danger of setting out on our eighth lap. The old thief stopped in two strides and sent me flying over his head.

Another time at the end of the morning I was on a difficult horse which launched me into orbit as he prepared to charge up the gallop. I managed to cling onto the reins but I was still so short at that stage that I couldn't jump back into the saddle without help. So Tonino stepped off the sprinter he was riding, came to my assistance and, in trying to give me a leg up, sent me tumbling straight over the other side onto the ground again. In the mayhem that followed both horses broke loose and we were left to walk home.

However many times I hit the ground I always bounced back for more. As my strength developed and my muscles firmed up I began to grow in confidence – to such an extent that within six weeks I was riding work on his better horses alongside decent jockeys. In the beginning I was so exhausted after riding eight horses each morning that I'd fall asleep all afternoon back at Tonino's house before returning with him later for evening stables. After a few weeks he decided he didn't need me back at the yard at the end of the day. Then I had much more time to myself and would play video games and wander around the town with his girls and their friends once they had finished at school. On Sundays we never missed the local disco.

Suddenly I was growing up fast. I was a typical young teenager, desperate to be cool and trendy, though that's not so easy when you are exceptionally small. Tonino's girls did their best to keep me in my place by giving me a hard time. Life was beautiful without the strict regime of discipline I had grown up with at home. How I welcomed my new freedom! I loved every minute of my stay with Tonino, Antonietta and the girls.

They introduced me to the sort of normal family life I had never experienced before. That was the point where I began to come out of my shell.

It helped that I was starting to believe for the first time: I *could* become a jockey. I felt by then that, if necessary, I could ride a horse the wrong way round standing on its quarters. Looking back now, I realise I was pretty advanced for my age after sitting on so many horses every day all through the winter. When work was over I'd be arguing and fighting with Tonino's girls, enjoying ourselves in the way that youngsters do.

I wished my stay would never end but, late in March, after four months my dad returned from a riding tour of Australia and South Africa and soon I was on the move again. He drove down to collect me from Pisa, then on the return journey to Milan started to outline his grand plan for my future. It was not so much a discussion, more a lecture. First he wanted to send me away to England for six months. Then it was on to France for a further six months. After that he would let me come home to Italy in midsummer. It was a crucial timescale because in those days apprentices in Italy could starting riding in races once they were fifteen and a half and I would reach that milestone in mid June, 1986.

When I had the chance to speak I made it clear that the last place I wanted to be was England. I pointed out that I'd been hopeless at English at school and much preferred to continue my racing education in my own country. But as usual in these matters my thoughts didn't count. My dad's mind was made up and he was keener than ever to send me to England once

41

he took me to ride out with him the next morning at Aldo
Botti's yard in Milan.

Before he went away at the start of the winter, my riding
had been a disappointment to him. Now he was visibly shocked
at how swiftly I had progressed. Within days Aldo was happy
to let me lead important work on top-class horses due to run
in the Italian Classics. It was fast work too, upsides some of
the best jockeys in Italy. I was riding with my stirrups as short
as ever, too short really. I listened to the instructions and carried
them out to the letter. I could see for the first time that my
dad was proud of his son, and that heightened his ambition
for me. So England it would be, to join Luca Cumani, the son
of Sergio – but not before a setback that could have ended my
career before it ever started.

Once I was back at home in Milan I swapped my bicycle for
a little moped to speed up my daily journey from home to
Aldo Botti's yard where I was working until my departure for
England. To beat the boredom of my daily run of just over a
mile I used to clock myself, then try to beat my own record by
missing out a junction or a couple of traffic lights.

I was made to buy a large crash helmet, but appearances
already mattered to me and I didn't feel very cool with my
head encased in something that resembled a big mushroom.
Nor was it compulsory to wear one, so it used to hang idly
from a hook on the scooter. Only grown-ups wore helmets then
– all the kids I knew rode their scooters bare-headed.

So off I raced to work one morning early in April, intent on
setting a new personal speed record. I was making good time

too, as I approached a junction leading to the stables. One fork was for cars, the other was for horses and had sand on top of the tarmac. To shorten the route I turned onto the road reserved for horses, skidded on the sand, lost control and found myself hurtling along the ground towards a large lamppost. I put out my right arm to save myself but careered with sickening force into the post.

As I lay in a heap, groaning with pain, I knew I'd hurt myself badly. My right elbow was in bits and my head hurt like hell. Soon an ambulance arrived and I was carted off to hospital. X-rays confirmed that I had shattered my elbow into over twenty pieces. My dad then arrived and was immediately furious with me for what I had done. Instead of giving sympathy when I needed it most, he and Christine tore into me so heavily that the people sitting next door were shocked.

Despite outward appearances, I knew that my parents were really concerned for me. Dad swiftly arranged for me to be moved to a private hospital where surgeons operated using screws and pins to repair the damage. A few days later, while I was still in hospital, Dad – riding a horse called Wild Dancer – was just pipped by Irish jockey Michael Kinane on Again Tomorrow in a tight finish to the Italian 2,000 Guineas. He blamed himself for riding a bad race because he was still so upset about my injuries – which, at that stage, he feared could prevent me fulfilling his dreams for me to become a jockey.

The damage took time to heal, and when the plaster was taken off I promptly fainted! I then discovered to my horror that I could barely extend my elbow 45 degrees. We were all concerned at first, even though we were told that it would eventually be as good as before with the help of regular physiotherapy. So my routine for the next month was to catch a bus to the nearest swimming pool, where I swam for an hour before returning home to carry out all the chores I'd always avoided in the past. In the afternoons it was back to the pool for more swimming.

Each day I could extend my arm a little further but progress was painfully slow. My dad became increasingly impatient as the days passed and I was still no nearer leaving for England. Eventually he put his foot down and decided on a novel way of sorting out the elbow once and for all. He took me with him to Aldo Botti's yard and loaded me aboard an old sprinter called Fire Thatch who had once been trained by Henry Cecil in England.

By this stage of his career Fire Thatch was the quietest animal in Botti's stable, a saint of a horse but one who still had his moments. As I hadn't ridden for almost three months I was a bit apprehensive, mostly because I knew my arm still wasn't right. I betrayed my nerves by gripping the reins much tighter than usual as we turned to set off on what should have been a routine canter. Fire Thatch immediately grabbed hold of the bit and set off like a rocket.

A second earlier my arm wouldn't extend fully. Now, in one moment of extreme pain, both my arms were straight out in front of me as I tried in vain to prevent Fire Thatch from running away with me. We covered five furlongs flat out and every stride was agony for me before he eased to a halt at the end of the gallop. In little more than a minute the horse had accomplished what the doctors and physios couldn't achieve in eleven weeks. The pain continued for a while as I returned to riding out full-time again for Botti, though luckily there was no lasting damage after this unconventional comeback. My elbow has been fine for years, but still I can't stretch my right arm quite as far as it is supposed to go.

Once he knew my recovery was complete, Dad was anxious to send me on my way to England. He'd already introduced me briefly at the races to Luca Cumani – who had been an outstanding amateur rider before becoming Henry Cecil's assistant. Later Luca had set up on his own as a trainer at Newmarket.

I flew from Milan on 10 July 1985 with a bucketful of dreams, one million lira (£366) in my pocket, and an identification tag around my neck so that someone could collect me after we landed at Luton. As the plane clawed its way into the sky I felt as if I was on Mission Apollo, heading for the stars. My life was changing forever and I had no control over it. I was met at Luton by Luca's chauffeur David, who did his best to make me welcome even though he couldn't speak a word of Italian.

As we listened on the car radio to the July race meeting at Newmarket, I heard the name of a horse named Lanfranco being called in commentary in the big race of the day. Suddenly I didn't feel quite so far from home.

five

I Used to Cry Myself to Sleep

Our first stop in Newmarket was the house in the Bury Road which was to be my home for a few short, increasingly unhappy weeks. When we knocked on the front door at around four in the afternoon there was no reply. Since David was keen to take me to Luca Cumani's yard, I left my big bag outside the back door, at his suggestion, convinced that I'd never see it again. At home in Milan I was used to kids trying to rob you as you walked along the street. Leaving all my precious possessions outside the house seemed to be asking for trouble.

Then we headed for the office at Luca's yard nearby. He was not around, but his secretary took me to the bottom yard where I met his veteran head lad Arthur Taylor – who could speak some Italian because he fought there in the war as a sergeant in the Cavalry regiment and (I learned much later) had been involved in the battle for Montecassino at the same time as my grandfather Mario.

Arthur handed me a dandy brush and towel, led me to the fillies' barn and put me to work. I was still wearing my suit, so

I took off my jacket, hung it up, unbuttoned my shirt and started dressing the filly over as best I could. Half an hour later Luca appeared at the door of the box, said a brief *buona sera!*, told me to be in the yard by six the next morning, then went on his way round the yard at evening stables.

It had been a long day and I was already beginning to feel homesick as I was delivered back to my digs – and found to my surprise that my bag was still there. The whole family was there to meet me, including the father who was so massive he resembled the famous old wrestler 'Big Daddy'. I was shown to my room upstairs under the corner of the roof next to the main road. In the weeks that followed it felt more like a prison than a refuge.

It was little bigger than a broom cupboard with just enough space for a small bed, a sink and a cupboard. Beside the basin was a jug of orange squash. I poured myself a glass, drank deeply then spat it out in disgust. I'd never encountered neat orange squash before and couldn't imagine how anyone would want to drink it. In Italy I was used to fresh orange juice. It was one of many culture shocks I experienced in the next few days.

My first evening meal in England was another disaster. In an attempt to make me feel at home they laid on a plate of ravioli, but this was far from the delicious treat which I was used to enjoying back in Italy. This ravioli came instead from a Heinz tin! Everyone else tucked in but I thought it smelled awful – and when I tried a spoonful it *was* awful. The landlord was obviously irritated by my reaction so I struggled through a few more mouthfuls to keep the peace.

The family's three children sitting round the table were a bit younger than me and we were also joined by several other lads who lived in the back of the house. Conversation was impossible because I didn't speak any English. The only word I understood was Swinburn. Apparently my new landlord was a fanatical fan of trainer Michael Stoute who employed Walter Swinburn as his stable jockey. Aware that I was working for Luca Cumani he banged on endlessly about Stoute, Swinburn and Shergar, but most of it went straight over my head. I was utterly miserable as I trooped upstairs to bed.

Riding out with the Cumani team the next morning made me feel a little better, though I was overwhelmed by the size of the place and the sheer number of horses we could see on Newmarket heath. After the delights of Milan and Pisa, Newmarket truly did seem like the headquarters of racing, with almost sixty trainers squeezed into the town. Luca trained a string of just over one hundred horses that season, a total that would almost double in the years ahead. Half of them were in the main yard beside the house, with the rest in the bottom yard which was where I started. I'd never been involved with such a huge racing set-up before, and it was quickly made clear to me that the guv'nor, as everyone called him, expected things to be done properly. All the lads seemed in awe of him as he moved around the yard like a Roman emperor.

At lunchtime that first day I used some of the cash my dad had given me to buy a bicycle for £80. That evening I rode it proudly to work, but as the week went on I felt more and more isolated. At fourteen I was several years younger than any of the other lads and nobody much seemed to want to talk to me – except a nice old boy called George Dunwoody who'd trained and ridden horses in Northern Ireland for many years. More recently he'd looked after a Classic horse – the previous year's St Leger winner Commanche Run.

In a way we were the 'odd couple' thrown together by fate, the young Italian nuisance at the start of his career and the veteran stableman who was helping out around the yard at the other end of the rainbow. George always had time for me and tried to explain things as best he could. Later, as my English improved, he told me that his son Richard was making his name as a jockey over fences. George rather took me under his wing and we would sit outside on a couple of bales of straw most mornings that summer, eating breakfast together.

Others weren't too friendly at first. Some picked on me, mimicking my voice, generally giving me a tough time and giving me a clip around the ear whenever they felt I deserved it. No wonder I was homesick! If there were dirty jobs to be done you can be sure that L. Dettori was the one told to do them. That's the way it has always been in racing: the youngest and weakest learn the hard way. It's the law of the jungle. As they grow stronger they in turn make life difficult for the latest newcomers.

Luca is on record as saying I was pretty wild when I arrived from Italy, badly in need of a firm hand to straighten me out, but that isn't how I remember it. Far from it. It might have been the case four years later, but until I found my feet I was naive and so quiet you wouldn't believe it. For the first six months I was probably the best apprentice in the yard, keen as mustard. I was up so early I arrived at the yard before the head lad so I was usually the one who opened up the tack room. Realising that I was a slow worker, I wanted to make sure my horses looked immaculate.

I was also incredibly lonely in those early days and often used to cry myself to sleep. At the beginning it was almost a game with Luca Cumani. I had agreed to go to him without supposing for a minute that I'd stay very long. I felt I only ended up in England because football dominates every other sport in Italy.

For the first six months it was work, to bed, work, to bed again . . . nothing else. The worst nights were Mondays. Then my dad would ring from Italy on the dot of seven, ask how I was getting on, and encourage me as best he could by saying that, if I stayed at Luca's, I too could one day have a big car and fly in private planes like famous jockeys such as Lester Piggott and Pat Eddery. It was his way of brainwashing me. He also made it clear that it was a hard and tiring job, and at times a thankless one. I would need to make enormous sacrifices if I wanted to be a jockey.

When I was talking to him I usually managed to hold back the tears, but when I put the phone down I was utterly miserable. It was all part of growing up but I've no doubt that my dad was far tougher than me. He had such a hard upbringing and didn't hesitate to send me away to another country to further my future. I question him about it all the time. How would he have felt if I'd failed? He says he can't answer that one because

I became so successful. I know I am a thousand times weaker than him because I couldn't do the same to my own son Leo. I am as soft as butter with my own children and could never send them away like that.

I soldiered on as best I could, concentrating on my work, carefully looking after my three horses, and riding out every morning. Initially my social life was non-existent. I was quiet, withdrawn even, but as I began to find my feet I started to come out of my shell and be my more natural cheeky self. Initially I owed much to the friendship of Valfredo Valiani, another Italian apprentice with Luca. He was my saviour. Years later he returned to England in triumph as a trainer, winning the valuable 2001 Yorkshire Oaks with the filly Super Tassa.

Things picked up further when I joined forces with two apprentices, both five years older than me, who also worked in the bottom yard. Initially I fought with Colin Rate and Andy Keates. It was madness to argue with them really because the age gap between us should have made me more cautious. To me they were the hierachy. They forced me to do all their chores, but after a few light-hearted skirmishes we teamed up against the rest of the lads.

Colin had come late to racing at seventeen after training as a carpenter. He rode three winners for Newmarket trainer Ben Hanbury and would go on to achieve a fair bit of success for Luca Cumani. As he is from Sunderland, the biggest hurdle to our friendship in the early days was that we couldn't understand a single word we said to each other. Colin quickly became my best friend. There is not a day when we do not speak and he always tells me exactly what he thinks.

Colin's mate Andy had more of a racing background. One of his uncles, Joe Mercer, had been champion jockey in 1979 towards the end of a great career, and another uncle, Manny Mercer, was killed tragically young in a fall at Ascot. Andy had a few race rides once he joined Luca shortly before me in 1985, but he was never going to make a jockey. For the past fourteen years he has worked for me as my driver and Man Friday.

This duo were soon leading me astray, though I didn't need much encouragement. We shared a genuine love of horses, a well-developed sense of the ridiculous, and a hunger for adventure that frequently left us broke. Part of our daily ritual was a 20p each-way accumulator on the afternoon's racing because that was all we could afford. I'd been a mad keen punter in Italy on my visits to the races. Now Colin and Andy introduced me to the habit of spending the afternoon in a betting shop – and when we had collected the place money on our first accumulator I was hooked.

When you are that young you cannot go to pubs or drinking clubs so I ended up as a typical betting shop punter, 'doing my brains' every week. Colin and Andy were just as bad. We were all addicted to betting. We'd take lunch together in the New Astley Club, a base for so many stable lads, play snooker and pool, then rush across the road to place bets and listen to the commentaries in a betting shop owned by a character called Cuthie Suttle.

Cuthie soon became a useful source of funds when I was

hard up. Sometimes he'd lend me the price of a haircut in the barber's shop nearby when I needed one, or maybe £5 to keep me afloat at the weekend. When I backed a winner – which was not very often – I repaid his kindness by sharing bags of fruit and sweets with his customers.

However, my new friends couldn't save me from the ritual embarrassment of having my private parts greased, the fate of all newcomers to racing. It happened without warning at the end of work one morning. A gang of them held me down near the dung heap, removed my jodhpurs and pants, then encouraged one of the girls to cover my pride and joy with hoof oil. They finished off their handiwork by stuffing a carrot up my backside to loud applause, before leaving me writhing with embarrassment on the dung heap. Removing the carrot took only a moment but cleaning up all the grease and oil from my skin took several days of energetic scrubbing.

Around the same time, I finally had the sense to change my lodgings which had become more and more like Fawlty Towers. The children there were driving me mad, my room upstairs was like a cell, and it was too expensive, even though I had to take my washing down to the launderette every Sunday. I also had to feed myself on Sundays and ended up having a large Wimpy while my clothes were drying. The parents of one of our stable lads, David Sykes, had a spare room at their council house five minutes from the yard. He took me to meet them and I moved in on the spot. It was one of the best decisions I've ever made.

Although Val and Dennis Sykes struggled to make ends meet

they treated me like their own son from day one. For all of my two years with them I ate like a pig – which was probably not the most sensible habit for someone who wanted to become a jockey. Every evening, when I returned from work, a roast meal complete with Yorkshire pudding and all the trimmings would be waiting for me on the table. Val was superb at cooking cream cakes and egg custards, which I couldn't resist the moment they came out of the oven. She and Dennis spoiled me too much and let me do what I wanted in the evenings.

Twice in the early days Val even took me to her weekly bingo sessions in the town with her mother. This didn't appeal to me so I invented an excuse when they invited me again. Val and Dennis were generous to a fault and made me feel great, though Val had her moments when I came back from work and deposited straw and mud on the stairs on my way up. She dug out the vacuum cleaner and stood over me as I cleared up the mess. I used to call Val 'mum' and she called me Pinocchio! She and Dennis had a smashing black labrador called Jamie which I often rode like a horse on the carpet in the evenings. When I heard a few years later that he'd died I took them an instant replacement in the shape a boisterous yellow labrador – which they immediately christened Frankie.

After the tight discipline of home it was a relief that Val didn't mind when I stayed out late with Colin and Andy as we trawled the pubs on Friday, Saturday and occasionally Sunday nights, if our funds lasted that long. We had the time of our lives, a right laugh. The boys were into drinking pints of vodka but I restricted myself to grapefruit juice. As I was only fourteen the hardest part was smuggling myself into a pub. Sometimes I borrowed a leather jacket with padded shoulders, and then I hit on the idea of smearing print from newspapers on my face to make myself look a bit older. It usually worked, too, though I was turned away once or twice until people got to know me.

Luca Cumani treated me like the little kid I was in those early days. Most of the time he spoke to me in English, but when he was angry with me – which was frequently! – he tended to shout in Italian. It was not that he didn't care, more that he had bigger fish to fry. At times he could be just like a dictator, very cold and professional. At evening stables he would run his finger along the top of my horse's back, showing up the dirt on its coat I hadn't touched, and then give me a bollocking. When I protested that I was too small to reach its back he told me to stand on a bucket. Then he'd come round the next night to check I'd done what he said. I used to call him all sorts of names out of his hearing, but he was a master of his trade and I wasn't living up to his standards.

One of my early jobs was to groom any horse turned out in the paddock in a metal pen, but as usual I couldn't reach their backs to brush them. I got round this by using an upturned water bucket to climb on to the horse's back. Sometimes, just for fun, I'd perch back to front facing its tail. That way I could brush its quarters properly while the horse grazed peacefully under me. I was really pleased with myself at this piece of enterprise – until Luca caught me one day and called me every name under the sun for taking unnecessary risks.

My initial enthusiasm for looking after my horses properly

began to wane as Christmas drew near. Instead I developed into a Jack the Lad, a right little rascal. I'd got wise to the way things were done and started to cut corners by ducking out of as much work as possible. I did all the things that apprentices were not allowed to do. Single-handedly I changed the system. Luca would get to hear about it and encourage his senior lads to control me. I was a rebel then and used to upset everbody in the yard. No wonder they picked on me and gave me plenty of whacks, but I still got away with murder.

The job I hated most was having to spend hours on the chaff machine, a huge contraption used for chopping up hay into small bits for the horses. I cut chaff for five years, from fourteen to eighteen, and loathed absolutely every minute of it. When you are small and have already done a day's work you are usually too knackered to force the handle round, so it used to take me half an hour to fill one bucket full of chaff. And if you loaded the hay too thickly into the machine you couldn't move the handle.

Eventually I hit on a brilliant plan which saved me hours of toil. I'd climb onto the handle, then jump up and down until it snapped. Each time it broke the kids in the main yard had to cut the chaff for us, too, on their machine. Unfortunately Luca's handyman usually repaired the damage within a few days. Then it was back to the grindstone for me until I damaged it once more.

If one of the bigger lads picked on me I used to get my own back when he wasn't looking by flooding one of the boxes he was working in. Two barrels of water in a box of straw or paper takes a lot of clearing up. Flooding boxes was one of my specialities, but because no-one else was daft enough to do something like that, they always identified the culprit and then I'd get another whacking.

Colin and I were lighter than the other apprentices, so we had the task of riding away the youngsters bought by Luca and his owners at the yearling sales late that year, as part of the process of breaking them in and getting them used to a saddle on their back. It was an amusing sideline which almost led to my being placed on the transfer list. It happened when we were caught racing Luca's yearlings round the paddock at breakneck speed like jockeys in a head to head finish. That was the year that Steve Cauthen and Pat Eddery dominated the jockeys' championship, so as we rode away the yearlings I played the role of Steve while Colin fancied himself as Pat. First we'd have a trotting race, then another one going a fair bit faster. Of course one thing led to another because our rivalry was so intense. We snatched two branches from the hedge and used them as whips as we tried to imitate our heroes by driving the yearlings ever faster in an imaginary finish.

This carried on for day after day. Sometimes we'd have seven races round the paddock on the same pair, even though we knew that forcing unfurnished youngsters to run faster than was good for them was madness. These were expensive young babies with a big future, and we were treating them as recklessly as dodgem cars at the fairground. By the time we finished they were often covered in sweat with their eyes popping and their flanks heaving. We were asking for trouble and it was only a matter of time before we were spotted by the stud's head lad. He immediately reported us to Luca – though luckily he didn't realise that we had been up to the same tricks for days on end.

Luca went ballistic. He was incandescent with rage as he read the riot act to us in his office. I thought he was going to sack us both on the spot, and if he had known the full story he probably would have sent us packing. Instead he threatened me with all sorts of dire punishment if we ever did it again – including a move to the Midlands trainer Reg Hollinshead, who had a reputation for being an even sterner disciplinarian.

After six months at Newmarket, I headed home to Italy for a Christmas break just after my fifteenth birthday. I wasn't sure I wanted to go. By then my English was picking up quite well, I'd found a family who treated me as one of their own, I had a few pals, and I was starting to have a bit of a life in Newmarket. We'd play snooker in the New Astley Club for pennies, eat a few pancakes and share our accumulators. There was always plenty of laughter – particularly on Saturday nights when we'd all go to the disco, where the rest of the lads would get legless while I stayed on soft drinks, so I often ended up looking after the worst cases. I loved all this nonsense. Life was definitely looking up now that I was coming out of my shell.

Scratching together the air fare to Milan was a bit of a struggle, but Cuthie Suttle came to my aid with a loan of £20 – which I repaid by post since I was half expecting to be sent to work for the trainer Patrick Biancone in France in the New Year as the next stage of my dad's Grand Plan for Lanfranco.

But Luca must have seen enough to want to keep me, so soon I was on my way back in January to the coldest winter I have ever endured. It was so bleak, particularly in February, that Newmarket felt like Siberia. Jump racing came to a halt for a month because of the state of the tracks, and most of the time we were restricted to trotting endlessly round Luca's indoor riding school.

Working in those conditions was horrible. However many layers of clothes we wore we were still frozen to the bone as soon as we stepped outside. Because every penny counted for Val at my digs, she frequently complained about the cost of electricity in her house. Maybe she didn't realise that I had an electric blanket and a heater going full blast in my room all the time. Ever since then I've managed to slip away to the sunshine for part of the winter at least. It's the only way I can stay sane.

To help keep warm in the sub-zero temperatures, my mates and I used to spend all afternoon in the betting shop. Horses, greyhounds, boxing and soccer – I gambled on them all. The horseracing was cancelled in February and early March, so then I became quite an expert on the dogs. I always went for trap 1 or trap 6 and – against all the rules – I tried to delay handing over my betting slip until I'd seen if my selection had jumped well out of the traps. If it missed the break I walked away without having a bet.

The weather improved enough for horseracing to restart later in March, and I'll never forget the day I backed the great mare Dawn Run to win jump racing's top chase, the Cheltenham Gold Cup. Small patches of snow still lay infield and the grass at Cheltenham was scorched brown by the frost. The odds about Dawn Run were just under 2–1 and I had £50 on her nose – which was a decent bet for me. We all watched the race on a big screen at the New Astley Club near the betting shop, and the style of her victory moved me in a way that no other jumping race has ever done. She just refused to give in when all hope seemed gone and fought back like a tigress on the final testing hill to take the prize. It was beautiful to watch.

That was the first time I cried over a horse race and I haven't seen one like it since. I rushed out of the club into the cold outside with tears pouring down my face, jumped on my bike to return to work, and was still crying when I got there five minutes later.

Some time before Christmas, George Dunwoody confided during one of our many chats that his son Richard was convinced he would win the Grand National the following spring on West Tip. The horse had been tanking along disputing the lead when falling at Becher's Brook on the second circuit in the race the previous April. You could hardly ask for better inside information, so at lunchtime I rushed down to Cuthie Suttle's shop and invested my last £5 at the time on West Tip at 33–1, and topped it up a week or two later with another £5 at 28–1. All winter the messages from Richard, via his father, were upbeat. The horse was well and, barring accidents, would definitely gain compensation for his previous bad luck at Aintree.

So every week that winter I would put on another £5 or £10

at the best price I could negotiate with Cuthie, and by the time the great day arrived I worked out that I stood to win almost £2,000. By then West Tip was favourite at 15–2. Watching spellbound from the arm of the sofa with Val and Dennis, a cup of tea in my hand, I never had an anxious moment. The horse jumped those mighty fences to the manner born, and Richard Dunwoody – who was barely out of his teens – showed incredible coolness by waiting until well after the last fence before allowing him to stride clear.

I shouted West Tip home every step of the way. When he landed safely over the final fence I threw everything up in the air and rushed out of the house to collect my winnings. I felt like a millionaire! Normally I was left with less than £20 a week in my pocket after various deductions from my paltry wages, and suddenly I had upwards of £1900 burning a hole in my wallet. The first thing I did with the money was to buy a new washing machine for Val who'd been struggling with a worn-out model for years. It was the least I could do for someone who would share her last penny with me. I also bought her a new iron. Then, on the Monday, I splashed out on a decent Vespa scooter for myself.

Over the next few weeks I blew a lot of the money away, but this time I still had something to show for it, and I even managed to save a little bit in the metal box I used as a secret safe hidden away in the chimney of my bedroom. I don't think I am talking through my pocket when I say that West Tip is the one horse I would love to have ridden in the National. You could jump a house on him with your eyes shut. He was the living best at Aintree and I was in ecstasy for six months at the memory of his performance.

I was soon in trouble with the law for riding my new scooter illegally on pavements. Once again Val came to my rescue when two burly policemen turned up on the door intent on booking me. By the time I appeared timidly from my room she had convinced them that the reason for my error was that I couldn't speak or read a word of English.

Cuthie Suttle's betting shop had become my second home by then. I was punting just about every day. If necessary I'd gamble on two flies crawling up a wall. When things got really bad, and I did all my cash – which was most of the time – I helped out as the chalk boy. Cuthie paid me £5 for an afternoon's shift, scribbling down the latest prices on the wall in the last minutes of trading, then filling in the results. There were two problems with this arrangement. First of all I couldn't reach the top of the board to complete the early results. Secondly my spelling was hopeless. No-one seemed to mind, though I sometimes had to skip the last race or two to rush back to work at evening stables.

Val, bless her, became so concerned at the amount of money I was gambling away that she marched down for a confrontation with Cuthie, demanding that he stop taking my bets. Cuthie tried to explain that if he barred me from his betting office I'd merely move to another one in the town where I'd probably fare even worse. Once I was in the habit of losing every week I started to work for other lads in the yard on my weekends off to get the money back. I'd also borrow £5 here, or £2 there.

When I look back now I was silly. Legally I was too young to bet, but punting is a way of life for most stable lads and I was no exception.

It was a costly habit which left Luca Cumani close to throttling me on one memorable occasion in May 1986. It happened after just about everyone in the yard had done their brains on a horse called Saker at the York races. Saker was what we call a morning glory. At home he always worked like a serious horse and had shown great promise when he finished an eye-catching sixth on his debut a fortnight earlier in a decent maiden race won by another of our horses.

Saker started joint favourite at York but ran like an old man in tight boots as he trailed in a distant fourth. That evening at work I told anyone who'd listen – including the second head lad Stuart Jackson – that Luca couldn't train a bicycle, let alone a racehorse. When Luca was looking round a little later you can imagine my feelings as Stuart Jackson asked him the Italian word for bicycle.

'Why do you want to know?' asked the trainer. Stuart then dropped me right in the cart by repeating my view that he couldn't train a bicycle. The look on Luca's face told me I was in serious trouble. There were no preliminaries for what followed. He asked Stuart to take over the horse I was holding, seized me forcibly by my collar with both hands, lifted all five stone of me into the air and rammed me against the wall a foot off the ground. I'll never forget the words that followed. As usual when he was angry with me, they were delivered in Italian.

'Maybe I can't train a bicycle Frankie, but while you work for me I will always be the greatest trainer in the world. Do you understand?' he roared, shaking me like a dog. By the time he dropped me onto the floor of the box I was in no condition to speak, let alone answer back, but obviously I didn't learn my lesson because I was back at Cuthie's betting shop the next day trying to recoup my losses.

An interesting bunch used to meet there most afternoons. Some days the place seemed more like a private members' club. One of the regulars, Shippy Ellis, is now agent for several jockeys, including George Duffield and Philip Robinson. I also met Peter Burrell there. He was always looking for new challenges and was helping Julie Cecil run a few syndicates at the time. Within days of meeting me, Pete offered to look after my business affairs even before I'd had a ride in public. I was flattered that he had such faith in me.

Another member of our circle was Mattie Cowing, a smashing guy who was a walking form book. He was just like Frank in Eastenders (played by the comedian Mike Reid), with a deep voice and a great sense of humour. Mattie used to be employed full-time in a factory making boxes until a stroke prevented him working and allowed him to indulge his passion for racing. He seemed to live in the betting shop and was a mine of information.

We hit if off from the start, but he clearly thought I was a rascal, an Italian idiot who gambled away everything and was going nowhere. A year later he turned me down when I first asked him to book my rides. Luckily I persisted and he eventually became the most loyal of allies as my agent. A few years later one of the biggest punters of modern times, Barney Curley, joined the group gathered round the screen – but by then I was no longer a member of the club because I was pretty much riding full-time.

six

Riding Like an Italian

As summer approached in 1986 I was getting uptight at the knowledge that I wouldn't be able to race in England for almost another year. Every morning I was going through the motions, partnering nice horses in their work, often upsides decent jockeys. But in the afternoons I was forced to be a spectator, normally in the betting shop. Years ago apprentices were allowed to start at an incredibly early age in this country. Lester Piggott, for instance, was only twelve when he rode his first winner at Haydock in 1948. Times change, and almost forty years on you had to be at least sixteen before you could ride in public here. The rules are a bit more relaxed in Italy where apprentices can be licensed at fifteen and a half, so I began to count down the days to 15 June when I would reach that landmark. My dad swiftly organised three rides in a week for me at home towards the end of the month. I flew to Milan, met the local stewards and was immediately granted a licence.

I prefer not to dwell on my first ride on a filly called My Charlotte at Milan, on Wednesday, 25 June. The best I can

say is that at least I didn't get in the way of the others. I'd
been dreaming of this day for years and then it was over in a
flash, so quickly that I cannot recall too much about it except
that I was hopelessly nervous. I couldn't believe how quickly
things happened around me. My Charlotte made a poor start,
we trailed the field into the straight, the race finished and
we were stone last.

It seemed to flash past at a hundred miles an hour and as
far as I can tell I learned nothing from it. I barely knew my
own name, let alone how to push along a racehorse to improve
its position. Emotion and excitement took over. We jumped
out of the stalls, the rest was a blur and at first I wasn't even
sure where we'd finished.

After a stern talk from my dad, I was back at Milan racecourse
three days later to ride a big, chestnut filly called Maria di
Scozia, trained by Alduino Botti, in a nine furlong race. Now
I am not saying that the Dettoris had a monopoly on Italian
racing at the time, but the family was responsible for four of
the eight jockeys. Lined up against me was my uncle Sergio,
my cousin Robert and my dad on Nina Hagen, a stable companion of Maria di Scozia.

This time, primed by my father, I jumped out alongside the
others and somehow managed to make the running. As we
came to the bend we were still in front and I thought I was doing
well as we raced round it into the straight. In my innocence I
hadn't realised that by taking such a wide route I could have
let the entire field up my inside. The next thing I began to hear
a screaming sound close behind me. It was my dad ordering

me to move over to the rail. By then I was pushing so hard I was already close to exhaustion. The harder I tried the more uncoordinated I was. Head down, arms flailing, I almost fell off when I tried to hit my filly in a pitiful attempt to make her go faster.

To my amazement, we still led the race with less than two furlongs left and now my father was shouting even louder. 'Hit her, hit her again, push her, whatever you do keep her going", he cried. He could have saved his breath. Poor Maria di Scozia was weary, totally confused by the little dervish on her back. As we weakened, Maurice Depalmas came past on the inside to take the lead on Perzechella before, with less than a hundred yards left, Nina Hagen swept by on the outside with my dad sitting as quietly on her back as a church mouse. By some miracle my filly held on for third prize, which would barely have bought a round of drinks.

Then the fun started. Although I was knackered I felt a sense of pride that we'd finished in the first three. That was definitely progress after my feeble attempts on Wednesday. My feeling of elation didn't last long. As I headed back to the unsaddling enclosure people began laughing and making gestures at me. The closer we got to the stands, the louder the comments grew. I started a panic attack, wondering what I had done wrong. It was one of those moments in your life when you are so embarrassed you just want to run away and hide. But first I sheepishly removed the saddle, before disappearing to the sanctuary of the weighing room.

Soon a stewards inquiry was called. I trooped anxiously

behind my dad into the stewards' room and watched in bewilderment as the film of the race was replayed. At last I knew why everyone was so amused and, to my intense relief, I wasn't the guilty party. That was my father who, in his desire to help me ride a winner, could clearly be seen on the film whacking the backside of my horse with his own whip all the way round the bend. What made it far worse was that, since our two horses were in the same ownership, they were coupled together for betting purposes. That meant that punters could pick up their cash if either of our horses won. If my filly had held on and won, we would probably have been lined up before a firing squad, but as my dad's horse did eventually prevail, we escaped with a sharp lecture.

Things didn't improve much on the final ride of my brief trip to Italy. This time I made the mistake of believing I knew all about being a jockey. The chief sufferer was the grey horse I rode in the race, which was a minor event at Turin. I finished third again, despite hitting my mount at least fifty five times in the finishing straight. Nor am I exaggerating. I remember thinking if I whip it all the time it must win. My dad, who was very tidy and effective in a finish, used a floppy whip with big flaps on the end. In trying to copy him in Turin I was so loose and out of rhythm that I struck myself almost as often as I hit my mount.

I did ride a winner soon after I returned to England. It came in the annual donkey Derby held at the Recreation Fields at Newmarket not far from my digs. Several well known riders took part and some of them failed to finish because donkeys are notoriously unpredictable and delight in dumping their jockeys. I managed to win my heat on one donkey, then sat tight on mine in the final and was so pleased at winning that I gave an extravagant salute as I passed the post. You would have thought I'd just won the Derby at Epsom.

Another event that left a big impression on me was a night out with Paul Eddery and his family in Newmarket. Paul was in the top flight of jockeys and lived with his wife Sally in a superb flat with white carpets, vast white sofas and beautiful pictures. While everyone else drank pink champagne I remained on fruit juice. To me Paul's home was straight out of Dallas. We all ended up that night with two of Paul's brothers, Robert and David, at the Onassis restaurant in town. The Eddery family made me so welcome, treated me to dinner and left me wanting more of this way of life. I thought it was brilliant.

Nineteen eighty-six was the year I started to lead up a few horses at the races. One of the first was a two-year-old called Vevila who was just beaten in a decent fillies maiden, ridden by Pat Eddery, at Sandown in May. The way she was working before her next race at Lingfield's evening meeting two months later convinced me that she was a certainty. I conjured up £200 from somewhere and put the lot on her pretty nose. But as so often in racing there was a snag. Pat was due to ride her again, but first he had a more important engagement at Ascot that afternoon on the brilliant Dancing Brave. He had two more rides before flying to Lingfield for our race due off at 5.50. It was always going to be tight and unfortunately for me he failed to arrive in time. Rae Guest, our stable stalwart, took over on Vevila and was beaten a short head.

At the time I blamed the jockey because, like most losing punters, I was always talking through my pocket. Maybe Pat would have made a difference, but anyway the result left me skint. Since we were staying overnight at Lingfield the rest of the lads in the hostel headed for the local pub at the end of racing. Without the funds to join them I settled for an early night. My black mood wasn't improved by the shocking state of the hostel. It was filthy in those days, and as my bed didn't have any sheets on it I had to make do with a rug. Perhaps that's why I was up at the crack of dawn.

Wide awake and with hours to kill before we set off for Newmarket, I returned to the racecourse, climbed over the security gate and made my way to the weighing room where I sat on the scales, pretending to be a jockey. Then I wandered past the deserted grandstands to a big marquee beside the paddock. To my surprise some tables were still set as if waiting for customers to arrive.

The temptation was too much. Almost without thinking I removed a large, clean tablecloth, converted it into a sack and began filling it with six glasses, six large plates, six smaller plates, six soup bowls, six cups and saucers, and matching cutlery. It seemed the ideal present for Val who certainly couldn't afford such a smart set of china. On top of my booty I placed an empty champagne bucket. Then, after checking that no-one was in sight, I carefully placed the swag on my back, and began to make my way towards the stable lads' hostel.

With every step I took I could hear the crunch of the china moving in the homemade rucksack. As I approached the security gate I was horrified to hear the sound of dogs barking ferociously, and when I looked over my shoulder my blood turned to ice as I saw two dobermans galloping towards me. There was barely time to escape. The moment I dropped my booty the sound of smashing crockery could be heard all over the racecourse. Just about the only thing that survived undamaged was the champagne bucket. I paused to snatch it up, then gave a passable impression of Linford Christie as I sprinted for the gate with the hounds of hell on my heels. I reached it with seconds to spare, clawed my way desperately up the fencing out of their range, clambered over the top, jumped down on the other side and disappeared back to the hostel as fast as my legs could carry me. When I reached my room I hid under the bed and was too frightened to emerge until the rest of the lads were ready to leave for Newmarket.

I spent a lot of time falling off horses during my first year in England because I rode with my knees under my chin. The more I was told to drop my stirrups to a sensible height, the more I resisted. It was a case of being too flash. The horse that gave me the most trouble was a lively grey three-year-old colt called Dallas who was being aimed at the Cambridgeshire in October, one of the biggest betting races of the year. Talented but quirky, Dallas was one of those cunning horses who could whip round and drop you without a second's warning. He used to dump me regularly to the delight of everyone else riding out. One moment we'd be trotting along quietly, the next he'd be standing over me, as I lay cursing on the ground, as if to say what are you doing down there? He did it out of high spirits, rather than malice, and even when I couldn't cling on to the reins he didn't run away. All the bruises and embarrassment seemed worthwhile when he won the Cambridgeshire ridden by Ray Cochrane.

By then I was preparing to resume my riding career in Italy. Luca Cumani wasn't keen on the idea because he preferred to have me working in the yard over the winter. Also he was anxious to make use of the weight allowance inexperienced apprentices like myself can claim until they have ridden a certain number of winners. He saw no point in wasting that allowance in Mickey Mouse races in Italy, but my dad was determined that I should further my racing education. So, early in November 1986 I flew to Milan once more.

I had a couple of rides straight away, then set off on 16 November to Turin for a race where I was to partner a horse called Rif, which had been bought by my father to give me some much-needed experience. Rif was no great shakes. I remember that he had big floppy ears and was one of those horses that went best in bottomless ground. It was a typically miserable winter's race day in Turin, horribly cold and wet with heavy going – ideal for Rif. The place had the atmosphere of a graveyard with a massive, deserted grandstand and a handful of frozen punters – but for a few unforgettable minutes it felt like Royal Ascot in June as I squelched home on Rif to record my first win as a jockey.

We started well, sat handy, pulled out in the straight and

won tidily without my needing to attempt too much with the whip. I have the photograph to this day in the snooker room at home. Afterwards I was exhausted and ecstatic. When I caught up with my dad I wanted to rush up, hug him and shout about my great achievement. But I'd been brought up so strictly that I was almost subdued as I described my precious first triumph to him. People always say winners breed confidence and I tend to agree. The next day I doubled my score with another success in an apprentice race at Livorno for the young trainer Andrea Picorarro, who'd spent a bit of time with Luca at Newmarket. I made the running on this one and thought I gave it a decent ride.

When I was a small boy my father once took me with him to a church in the mountains near Livorno to pray to the Madonna di Montenaro. It was something he tried to do every year to ask for a safe passage through the season, and it left a lasting impression on me. My trip to Italy as an apprentice gave me the opportunity to visit the church again and collect a medallion to protect me while I was racing. I tried to follow my dad's example because I believe in God but, as I became busier in England, it became harder to find the time. Since Italy is a very superstitious nation it seemed natural to put my faith in positive omens, but eventually I was carrying so many bits and pieces round my neck and in my boots it was getting silly. So I took them all off and now I rely on one normal crucifix.

Soon I moved to Naples for the rest of the winter to work in a satellite yard run for Aldo Botti by his wily assistant trainer Peo Perlante. It was to prove quite an education in more senses than one. Naples is only a few miles along the coast from the brooding monster of Mount Vesuvius, which erupted in AD 79 sealing Pompeii in a ten-foot blanket of ash, lava and mud.

Naples racecourse at Henano is in the bowl of another, much smaller volcano, long extinct. The public sauna baths we used almost daily to lose unwanted pounds were pretty basic. It was little more than a cave in the mountain rock with hot tubs of water. The centre of the sauna was so hot you could only last a minute there at a time. It contained a small, round hole, covered with wood. If you were brave enough to lift the cover you found yourself staring down hundreds of feet into infinity. The whole place stank of sulphur, a bit like rotten eggs.

It was during hours spent in that sauna that I first became friendly with Bruce Raymond, a vastly experienced jockey who was on his way home from a riding stint in Hong Kong. He is a gentleman and I respect him because he had to work extremely hard to make it as a jockey. He was always immaculate, on or off a horse, never swore, and conducted himself in an old-fashioned way. I came to respect his judgement and have often turned to him for advice.

Another fine jockey in Naples that winter was Marco Paganini, the shining new star of Italian racing. I was average, at best, in those days and tried to learn from him and Bruce by watching them in their races. I stayed at the home of Tonino Cantante, one of the yard men, on a small council estate. Most of the lads working alongside me were apprentices, too, and since they were more established they tended to get the rides when racing took place once or twice a week. I wasn't flavour of the month with Peo Perlante, who always left me last in the queue when it came to riding for the stable. He did me no favours at all. Maybe it was to do with an old feud with my father. Whatever the reason, I had to rely on other stables for spare rides.

Obviously it helped that I was light and that my claimer's allowance would reduce a horse's weight even further. The racing was as low-key as you could find, but I was gaining valuable experience away from the glare of publicity and over the course of four months I managed fifteen more winners. I was doing all right, though deep down I was aware that I rode like an Italian. I badly needed to add some polish.

People often ask whether I would have been as successful spending my entire apprenticeship in Italy. I've no doubt about that one. Staying in my own country would not have been a great idea. Because of my dad, life would have been too easy for me, and that's the last thing you need if you want to fight your way to the top. Perhaps my dad sensed this. Yes, I'd have ridden plenty of winners because doors would have been opened for me, but how much further would I have gone?

If you are faced with a harsh challenge, self-pride takes over. By sending me away to England, Dad was dropping me in the ocean with a lot of sharks circling. When they first let me loose I was nothing because I was too young to know my limits. Just to prove that I could survive, I eventually became bigger than all the other fish. If I'd stayed in Italy I'd have lacked the motivation that being in England provided. Most of all I forced myself to be successful for my father. He was the one I wanted to please above all others, although it was unbelievably difficult in the first few months in Newmarket. Once I moved to Naples that winter I began to flourish. There were other delights, too.

After racing on Sunday a gang of us would go for a meal together, then end up watching blue movies in a seedy, back-street cinema. Some of them would then set off for a liaison with the local call girls. At this stage of my teens I'd had a few girlfriends but was still pretty innocent and several furlongs behind the others. One night they all decided it was time for my sexual initiation. All the boys were eager to take me to their favourite prostitute who plied her trade in the back of a big car parked at the top of the hill in the red-light district.

They decided that I should take my turn first, issued their instructions, then bundled me into the back with the waiting girl. She removed her skirt and skilfully helped me wriggle out of my trousers, before producing a giant pink condom that looked more like a balloon or a Michelin tyre, slipped it on and asked me if I was ready. As if I would have known! What followed was a blur, a bit like my first ride in a race. Again I was hopelessly nervous and everything happened much too rapidly. I was definitely not in charge and I remember wondering what all the fuss was about.

Aware that it was my first time, she tried to help me as best she could but for me the earth didn't move – though the car certainly did. The boys were all standing on the pavement, peering through the back window, cheering me on, and when they saw me moving they immediately began rocking the car violently up and down. When it was all over, or I thought it was all over, I grabbed my trousers and opened the back door, ready to escape. I was immediately seized by several pairs of arms and propelled into the middle of the road as three of my pals fought for the right to be next to continue the contract with the hooker who'd just got rid of me. I thought it was hilarious.

Another encounter was not so funny. Each night on my way into work on my moped I passed through the area where most prostitutes touted for business. Every lamp-post at night had a call girl underneath it, and one of their pimps used to deliver bundles of wood to them from a three-wheeled cycle to fuel the bonfires that kept them warm. As I sped past, my eye was caught by a gorgeous, tall blonde wrapped in a fur coat. She wore fishnet tights and stiletto heels and was just like one of those girls from Charlie's Angels. The first few days I just looked at her then, gaining in confidence, I'd wave and beep at her every evening as I rode by. Sometimes she turned round and gave me the eye. At night I used to dream that soon she'd be mine.

My fantasies were cruelly shattered. As I approached her on my moped I began to beep as usual in friendly greeting. She turned to see who was coming, spotted me, gave me a look of pure venom and lifted her skirts. Even at 30 mph I couldn't fail to notice that she, or rather he, was an extremely well-endowed man. I was so horrified I almost crashed in my haste to escape. I rushed home, locked myself in, and climbed into bed terrified that he would chase me and assault me. I was traumatised for days afterwards and changed my regular route to avoid any chance of further contact.

While I was enjoying myself in Naples, Luca Cumani was monitoring my progress, increasingly unhappy that I was wasting my valuable claiming allowance in what he considered to be races of no consequence in the middle of winter in Italy. In England, apprentices start off claiming 7 pounds until they have ridden fifteen winners. Luca was furious that I'd already passed that point. He made urgent contact with my father and soon I was on my way back to Newmarket once more.

seven

Priceless Lessons in California

I quickly came back down to earth at Newmarket. All those winners in Naples didn't seem to count for much once I was back in the old routine mucking out on freezing cold mornings and bitter spring evenings. When I returned to my digs after evening stables I'd sit on top of the fire. No-one else could get near it.

Colin and I spent our spare time at the yard practising our whip actions. Once everyone else headed off for lunch we were left to sweep the yard and tidy up the feed-house. After that was done we rushed to the warmth of the tack room, armed ourselves with the nearest available whips, dipped the flaps in a bucket of disinfectant, then stood crouching at a jockey's height on a small bench, and whacked the side of the ancient coal fire burning behind us for ages until our arms ached. The first mark left by the wet flap on the fire was our target for the day. Then we tried to hit the same spot over and over again. We wrecked the stitching on the flaps of lots of whips, none of them ours. After six months there wasn't a whip in the place with the flap intact.

As I was sixteen, I was ready to start my career in England but had to wait so long for my first ride I thought it would never come. Opportunities were scarce and winners were a distant mirage. The new flat-racing season was well over a month old before I was booked for a 33–1 shot, Mustakbil, late in April. This was at Kempton's bank holiday meeting, and the man who booked me was the Derby winning trainer Peter Walwyn – who is affectionately know in racing as Basil for his resemblance to the character played so memorably by John Cleese in Fawlty Towers. My claim should have reduced Mustakbil's weight by 5 pounds, so Walwyn's mood was probably not helped when instead I put up 4 pounds *overweight*. Even so we looked like winning until my horse tired in the final furlong through lack of fitness. My conversation with the trainer afterwards might have come straight from a scene in that TV comedy.

Perhaps he expected a polite thank you. Instead I managed to leave him almost as apoplectic as Basil Fawlty after a row with his head waiter Manuel. When Walwyn asked me what had happened in the race I pointed to the horse's tummy and replied 'Not fit'. It wasn't the most diplomatic answer to a man who had been champion trainer, and I was hardly qualified to speak on the subject since at that stage I could scarcely tell the difference between a racehorse and an aeroplane.

At first Walwyn didn't seem to understand what I'd said. Then the penny dropped. 'What! Not fit! You cheeky little bugger. Not fit!', he spluttered. It could have been Fawlty speaking.

'That's right', I agreed, too stupid to realise I was moving into dangerous territory. 'Not fit, too fat', I added before heading for the safety of the jockey's room to protect me from further explosions. The next morning Walwyn rang Luca to tell him he wouldn't be using me for a year. When he finally relented more than twelve months later and gave me a chance at Folkestone, there was a further disaster. His horse played up so badly in the stalls that I was forced to take my feet out of the irons and rest them on the bars. At that very moment the starter let the field go and Splintering, my mount, shot out of the stalls without me and reached the winning post riderless well ahead of the field. This time I could hardly blame the trainer for being speechless.

My first winner in England finally arrived at Goodwood on 9 June, three days after my father broke his left leg in two places when his horse crashed into a concrete post in Milan. The filly who made the breakthrough for me was Lizzy Hare, named after Luca's secretary who drove me to the course. She was led up that day by Colin Rate in a lurid new black suit, with pink seams, pink shirt, tie and socks. You could hardly call him shy and retiring then or now.

Lizzy Hare was a promising filly who would go on to much better things in America, but that day she was dismissed as a 12–1 shot in a hot little handicap featuring three champion jockeys – Steve Cauthen, Pat Eddery and Willie Carson. We travelled well behind the leader Betty Jane, partnered by Willie, and then Steve took over with a strong run on Interlacing. For a brief moment there were five fillies spread across the course, but Lizzy Hare was finding plenty for me and squeezed through a gap on the far rail to take the prize by one and a half lengths from Interlacing. I was thrilled to win and ever more pleased to beat my great hero Steve Cauthen into second place. I knew Colin had backed Lizzy Hare and the way he rushed out to greet us suggested that he'd landed a nice little touch.

In the car on the way home, I wrote on a box of tissues *Frankie Goes to Hollywood*. At last I was on my way, but if I was expecting a rash of winners it didn't happen. The reality was that I was an Italian learning in a foreign country, so just to be getting a few rides was good. I didn't panic – far from it because I had this inner belief that I was going to make it. There was absolutely no doubt in my mind. My father had been brainwashing me for so long during our weekly phone conversations I had begun to believe him.

I already had so much experience on good horses on the gallops that by the time I was sixteen I knew I could ride in apprentice races with my arms tied and my eyes blindfolded. Compared to the other kids starting out that year I felt I was at least a couple of years ahead. Though I didn't know it at the time, Luca's head lad Arthur Taylor shared my belief that I'd make a name for myself. The stirrup irons that I wore on Lizzy Hare hold pride of place on the mantelpiece of his home. Apparently he removed them the same night because he wanted a memento of my first success!

At the time everyone was talking about Dale Gibson as the next superstar apprentice. I had my doubts when I met him. He is skinny now but then he was about 5 stone, and so much of a skeleton he looked as though he was always on a hunger strike. I thought, if he's my chief opposition, I can give him a run for his money. All I needed was the chance. You don't want to be waiting forever but the days seemed to go so quickly.

Increasing weight was already a worry, probably because I was eating too many cakes and ice-creams. My feeble attempts at sweating then were sporadic and lacked any discipline. Sometimes at the end of the day I'd take a dustbin liner from Val's kitchen, cut a hole for my head, put it on, then run round the streets of Newmarket to work up a sweat.

Although I'd had only one winner so far, I was riding at least twice a week, getting the odd 50–1 shot and a few for Luca in apprentice races. I felt my time would come. Another Newmarket trainer, Clive Brittain, had given my dad a few rides years before and now he booked me for Merle in the Royal Hunt Cup at Royal Ascot. To be riding on the greatest stage so soon was a big boost. I'd never experienced anything like it: the unique atmosphere, the dressing up, the tradition and four days of top-class racing in the presence of the Queen. Suddenly I was part of the best race meeting in the world. It was a bit like being at Wembley for the FA Cup Final.

Though Ascot would later turn out to be my luckiest course there was no fairytale start. The correct colours failed to turn up, so I wore a makeshift bib, which started to come open and flap around my shoulders as Merle moved into contention soon after half-way. I was tickled pink to finish a respectable sixth in the famous handicap race.

Chris Wall, one of Luca's former assistants, provided my

second winner, Crown Ridge, at Ripon on 24 June. Chris took me in his car and maintains to this day that I worked my way hungrily through a bag of sweets and Mars bars on the long drive to Yorkshire. The horse started long odds-on favourite and won easily. The next evening I was back at Goodwood for another success on Lizzy Hare. This time we made all the running.

Two winners in two days! Things were picking up at last. Early in July, Chris came up trumps again by booking me for another winner, Camallino Rose, who beat Rae Guest on Luca's colt Fill My Glass in a photo finish at Carlisle. Although the winning distance was only a head, I won quite cheekily, and on the way back to unsaddle I made the mistake of giving Rae a bit of stick. Chris told me later that Ivan Allan, the owner of Camallino Rose, was furious with me for being so cocky in the finish. Ivan is a huge gambler, and when his money is down he likes them to win by twenty-five lengths. Apparently watching me playing jockeys had almost given him a heart attack.

Next time I really made a mess of things on Camallino Rose at Hamilton, and it was all down to the lip I'd given Rae Guest at Carlisle. I didn't know that some of the other jockeys had taken exception to the way I spoke to Rae. They got their revenge at Hamilton where they managed to box me in on Camallino Rose in a four-horse race. I just had to sit and suffer, trapped in on the rails, and though she flew once we escaped it was all too late. That taught me a valuable lesson because we should have won by five minutes.

I was in trouble again two days later at Ascot after winning an apprentice race for Luca on Local Hero by a length and a half from Red River Boy. The rider of the second, Stephen Quane, who was also apprenticed to Luca, immediately objected to the stewards, claiming we had crossed in front of him. It was my first experience of an inquiry in England and I was immensely relieved when we kept the race, but that was not the end of the matter.

Ron Hodges, the trainer of Red River Boy, then appealed against the Ascot stewards' decision, so we all had to go to the Jockey Club's headquarters at Portman Square in London. Ron's solicitor believed their case was watertight, but Ron wasn't so confident when he arrived at the hearing to discover Luca having a cup of tea with the JC stewards! Luckily for me Luca and our solicitor did most of the talking during the hearing and the appeal was thrown out.

My sixth victory that year came at Brighton early in August. I travelled to the meeting with Steve Cauthen in his chauffeur-driven Jaguar. Steve was very good to me when I was young. Of all the senior jockeys he was the one who took time to speak to me. He quickly became a good friend, but in those days I used to irritate him like mad on long journeys. He would be trying to doze sprawled across the back seat, clutching a can of diet Coke, and listening to tapes of Fleetwood Mac, while I sat in the front next to his driver asking him a zillion questions, always trying to pick his brains. Steve was a cool dude, who seemed to have life well organised since his move from America in 1979. He was one of my first heroes in racing, a lovely guy who knew how to treat people properly – and he was the jockey

Early days in Italy. With my dad
Gianfranco and stepmother
Christine (above) and with my
sister Sandra (right).

Days on the beach and
fooling around at home
were my ideas of a good
time as a youngster.

A tiny nine-year-old on my pony Silvia, in my first Derby in Milan. We finished last.

On holiday (right) and with my cousin Eric (above).

Top: In Sardinia with Nadine, Christine, Dad and cousin Eric.

Above (left and right): Relaxing with Dad in my favourite position on the floor. And a demon on the slopes.

Right: A badly broken elbow delayed my departure to England in 1985 when I was fourteen.

My old friend Raffaeli
Lai enjoys a day at
Wolverhampton races.

I'm Champion
Apprentice in 1989.

Pirate Army, twice a
winner for me in 1990.

Clean cut – and ready for the off.

With Willie Carson, as we try out Britain's largest and smallest breeds of horse for size. Talk about a pea on a drum!

My first Group 1 success on Markofdistinction in the Queen Elizabeth II Stakes at Ascot in 1990, ahead of Distant Relative and Green Line Express.

An unexpected bonus. Winning the French Derby on Polytain in 1992.

All in a day's work.

Triumph in Rome.
With my stepmother
Christine and
Luca Cumani after
Legal Case lands the
Premio Roma in
November 1990.

Lochsong wings home
in the Prix de l'Abbaye
at Longchamp in 1994.

My great ally Peter Burrell holds court at Ascot.

Another Classic in the bag as Island Sands (right) pips Enrique in the 2,000 Guineas in 1999.

Poetry in motion. Dubai Millennium out on his own in the Queen Elizabeth II Stakes at Ascot in 1999.

Our wedding day. When I first met her all those years ago, I said to Catherine: 'Allo darling, where have you been hiding?'

Our home in Stetchworth, near Newmarket, where we started married life.

Watch out Steve Redgrave. Hard at work in my gym at home.

Luca suggested I watch more than any other. I didn't need a second invitation. He'd already been champion jockey twice, was a wonderful judge of pace, and the day he took me to Brighton he needed only two victories to reach the 1,000 mark in this country.

Voracity swiftly took Steve on to 999 early in the afternoon. Then, riding Know All for Luca, I ruined the script by pipping his mount In The Habit in a tight finish. It looked like being a long walk home from Sussex for me, but luckily Steve had one more ride in the last race on Picnicing, which won easily. The racecourse executive presented him with a bottle of champagne but he was more interested in devouring a huge ice-cream as we left the track. I was swiftly forgiven and we drove back to Newmarket in style.

When I could I always tried to ride John Francome's horses in the hope that his gorgeous wife Miriam would be in charge at the races. The first time we met was at Salisbury. As I weighed out there she was, an absolute stunner. Still is. Anything in a skirt would excite me in those days, but Miriam was the real thing, a beautiful model with a lovely nature to go with it. I was overcome standing beside her in the paddock, letting my mind run wild. I was heartbroken when John gave up training shortly afterwards to concentrate on his TV career and his golf.

By now I was well into the swing of an English season which often involved long journeys to distant racecourses for one ride without any obvious chance. At least Our Krystle finished third for me at Newcastle on August bank holiday Monday, but she had hung so badly left in the closing stages that a stewards' inquiry was a formality. She was disqualified and I picked up a three-day suspension for careless riding.

I was looking forward to a night in the pubs of Newcastle but managed only a couple of drinks before I was forced to change my plans. A drunk Geordie punter decided that he wanted to kill me because he'd backed my horse each-way and had done his money when it was disqualified. He was so aggressive that I rushed straight back to the lads' hostel and, as usual in times of danger, locked myself in my room.

The next morning I caught the train to Chepstow. This involved a marathon trek across country involving several changes, and then a long walk on a boiling hot afternoon from Chepstow station to the racecourse with my bag on my shoulder, because I couldn't afford a taxi. I was melting by the time I staggered into the weighing-room. I'd come for the one ride, a 20–1 chance, and you can imagine how I felt when the trainer told me the horse wasn't fancied. Sure enough we finished in the rear before I managed to hitch a lift back to Newmarket.

I had much better fortune when I returned to Chepstow ten days later. William Haggas, in his first season as a trainer, booked me for a horse called Far Top in the second leg of the apprentice race, while Colin Rate was down to ride Girotondo in the first leg. Colin and I persuaded a friend to drive us down to Chepstow, but none of us was very experienced at finding our way to Wales and we became so lost that we arrived at Chepstow just in time to see Girotondo romp home ridden by a late substitute jockey. Far Top, who started hot favourite at 4–9, then scrambled home with me by a neck.

So far I had managed only seven more winners in seven months in England. For someone who badly wanted to set the world on fire I was having trouble igniting the spark. Despite having plenty of confidence in my ability, I began to wonder if I would ever make the big breakthrough. My doubts grew in September during a lean spell at the same time that I was forced to move my digs after two happy years with Dennis and Val. The local council, it appeared, objected to tenants taking in paying guests. I didn't want to be the cause of them losing the house and felt the only course was for me to pack my bags. Several years later I was delighted to hear that their daughter had bought the house for them from the council, so now they have a home for life. Finding somewhere to match the comfort of the last two years was always going to be an impossible task, but a friend, Bernice Emanuel, who was Ben Hanbury's secretary at the time, had a room in her house and was prepared to put me up for a month until I sorted out something more permanent. I ended up staying two and a half years.

I'd been to her home before for supper with parties of Italians she hosted from time to time. Bernice made me more than welcome and proved to be a loyal friend, but straight away she made it clear she wouldn't be cooking for me very much nor was she planning to wash and iron my shirts. Instead, she taught me how to use an iron.

Soon after moving in I spoke to my father about my lack of success in England. The next morning I told Bernice that I was determined to try my luck in France, which had been part of my dad's original plan. Luca was having none of it. He rang my father and persuaded him that I should persevere in this country. A few days later I rode my final winner of the season on Luca's filly Sumara in a maiden race at Haydock. She was owned by Sheikh Mohammed who would later play such a key role in my success as a jockey.

Most mornings I was allergic to climbing out of bed. I was working long hours and trying to keep my weight down, so I often slept straight through my alarm. I was late at least once a week, and many times Luca would ring Bernice to ask if I had shown any sign of life. Then I would make a mad dash to the yard, be given the inevitable lecture and try to catch the others up. To teach me a lesson when I was seriously late, Luca would take me off the horses that were working or galloping and put me instead on ones that were on the easy list, walking and trotting.

I had no difficulty waking up on the morning of the famous storm on 16 October 1987 which left a huge path of destruction as it swept through the town. The noise in the early hours would have woken the dead. The tempest was at its peak shortly before dawn and brought down power lines and even large trees. I set off for work on my scooter more in hope than expectation. The wind was so strong that several times I was nearly lifted bodily from the saddle. Eventually, I battled my way through without mishap but a huge tree had come down onto Luca's covered ride, and others had fallen in the yard and paddocks, so there was little we could do except feed and muck out the horses.

As far as I am aware only one person in Newmarket slept

through all the mayhem. That was my father who was over with Christine in his large camper van. They had come to dinner at Bernice's house the night before and then returned to the van in a car park nearby. The wind was rocketing past his window, roofs were disappearing, slates were flying in all directions, rows of trees were falling over like skittles, and their van shook as if it was at sea in a force 9 gale – but Dad slept soundly through it all, before emerging later that morning to ask what all the fuss was about.

As the season drew towards its close I expected to be heading home for another winter in Naples, but this time Luca put his foot down and insisted that I shouldn't be allowed to fritter away my claiming allowance in Italy. He and my dad debated long and hard before coming up with a plan to send me to California, where I would continue my education as a work rider at Santa Anita racecourse under the guidance of Richard Cross, one of Luca's first assistants. It was a decision that had a profound effect on my career.

Santa Anita in December – against the stunning backdrop of the San Gabriel mountains – was a vast improvement on Newmarket but it was hardly a picnic. I stayed with Richard and his family that first year at their home in Pasadena, fifteen minutes from the racecourse. We started work at dawn and then rode up to ten horses each morning round the tight left-hand track.

With the rest of the day to myself I'd play cards in the track kitchen before watching racing in the afternoons and having a few little bets to keep myself entertained. Luca had told Richard to be tough on me and keep me under control, but I managed to escape his watchful eye most of the time – though there is a limit to the damage you can inflict on $100 a week.

This was the golden era of jockeys in California, with Bill Shoemaker, Chris McCarron, Eddie Delahoussaye, Angel Cordero, Fernando Toro, Laffit Pincay and the young star Gary Stevens in action most days. Shoemaker – who died in October 2003 – was tiny but wonderfully effective, a legend who, by then at the age of 55, was as cute as an old fox and still difficult to beat in a finish. 'The Shoe', as he was knicknamed, retired three years later with a record of 8833 wins. Laffit Pincay eventually passed that total and had reached 9530 winners by the time he retired in 2003. Some day someone will overtake that record, but it is still an amazing total when you think I was still just short of 2,000 winners in England at the start of 2004.

Angel Cordero quickly became my favourite jockey in America, perhaps because we are quite similar. He was a crowd-pleasing showman whose trademark was to produce a flying dismount after his big race victories. It was stunning to watch. Soon, in the privacy of Richard Cross's barn in a quiet corner of Santa Anita, I was indulging my fantasies by practising my own flying dismounts in front of a baffled audience of a few Mexican horsewalkers and grooms.

Often my last task of the morning was to ride the tack horses, the ones that had just come back into training after injury or for some other reason were not ready for anything more strenuous than gentle exercise walking round and round Richard's barn. Completing endless laps at such a slow pace for up to an hour was mind-numbing, so to keep myself awake I listened to tapes on my earphones and amused myself by trying to mimic the mannerisms and styles of the great riders of the day. Then I would invite Richard's grooms to identify which jockey I was imitating.

I managed a passable Shoe, and a decent Chris McCarron, but the impression I enjoyed the most was always my Cordero flying dismount. Not that I would have a chance to unveil it in public for another nine years. When the hour was finished I used to launch myself as high as I could like Angel. That's how it started. I just copied him. The trick is to use the irons as a springboard. Angel was an inspiration and had a massive influence on me. He was so strong he could lift a horse in a finish. Most of all I loved his personality, perhaps because I am naturally outgoing, too. Years later I heard that one of his flying dismounts had gone spectacularly wrong. As he jumped off, one of his feet remained trapped in the irons with the result that he fell head first under the horse. Luckily only his pride was hurt.

Somehow, probably without realising it, I was taking the best from each of these riders as I tried to improve my own style. The last thing I wanted was to stand out like Ned the Coachman among these great jockeys! So I worked hard to improve my riding and streamline my position in the saddle – though I wasn't yet tempted to try the toe-in-the-iron style that is now the fashion on both sides of the Atlantic. That came a few years later.

All American jockeys ride with their right leg a fair bit shorter in the stirrups than the left one. It is a method known as 'acey-deucey' and gives them better balance on their tracks which are all left-handed (anticlockwise). Naturally I tried this by altering the length of my irons in the mornings, though long before I visited California for the first time I was already in the habit of riding with the leathers on my right leg a hole shorter than on my left. I've just done it from day one. Don't ask me why.

There was a further bonus from my daily card sessions among our regular school in the track kitchen. It came from contact with a tiny little character who was one of the heroes of American racing. By the time I met Johnny Longden he was already in his eighties but he had a sparkle in his eyes to match the diamonds on the horseshoe rings he wore on his chubby fingers as he played cards each morning. He had short grey hair, wore glasses and remains the only man to have won the Kentucky Derby as a jockey and as a trainer.

Johnny's story was a fascinating one. He was born in Yorkshire but emigrated to Canada with his family at the age of five. Later he worked in coalmines in Alberta. He rode in unofficial bareback races before moving on to seek fame and fortune in America. He retired in 1966 with a record 6032 wins, but was still drawn to the racecourse each morning. I regret that we never talked much about riding. More than anything I wish I could go back and chat to him again now.

I was lucky that I could play cards with people like Johnny, although they probably looked on me as another sucker to provide them with easy money. It was a strange time for me because there I was, just seventeen, living in a grown-up world which I found quite scary. One thing I did learn on that first visit to California was to ride against the clock until it became second nature. American horsemen rely heavily on the stop-watch to measure track work, and within a few months I could complete a gallop to order to within fractions of a second. It is a gift shared by every American jockey and explains why they are such brilliant judges of pace and so comfortable at making the running in races.

The hardest part of the job that winter was gaining entry to Santa Anita racecourse. The Americans have always been pretty strict about issuing track permits for visiting riders, and for some reason all I had was a tourist visa. So each morning I had to smuggle myself into the racecourse, either behind the back seat of a car or hidden in the boot. It helped that there were two entrance gates to the stable area.

On the occasions I was caught I usually managed to slip through unnoticed at the second gate. But eventually they became wise to me at both entrances, so then I had to slog all the way to another racecourse, Hollywood Park, which was at least a forty-five minutes drive from Santa Anita. That meant getting out of bed at the unearthly hour of 4 a.m! Without a track licence I was not insured to ride work at Santa Anita. In effect I was an illegal immigrant, but I enjoyed the challenge of trying to beat the system each morning. It made life more exciting.

eight

Give the Kid a Chance

My first task in the spring of 1988 was to find myself an agent to help book my rides. The obvious choice was Mattie Cowing who had shared so many entertaining days with me in Cuthie Suttle's betting shop. Mattie was already handling Bruce Raymond's rides, but he turned me down because he was not convinced that I took my job seriously enough. Next I turned to Simon Crisford, the Newmarket correspondent of the *Racing Post*, but he – sensible fellow – said he had to look after his own career and was not going to let me drag him down! Years later we would become the best of buddies working together for Godolphin. Eventually I signed up with Cliff Woof who'd just opened a jockey's agency with Willie Ryan as his first client.

After a winter tightening up my style in the warmer climate of California, I felt stronger and more confident than before and was determined to make a quick start in my second season. Once again rides were scarce in the opening weeks, until I was given a crucial opportunity on Heroes Sash for Luca Cumani in a valuable race at Haydock at the end of April. Ray

Cochrane, by then our stable jockey, was at Newmarket for the 2,000 Guineas that day. When he heard Luca was struggling to find a suitable rider for Heroes Sash, he suggested 'Give the kid a chance.' Heroes Sash didn't win but I did nothing wrong and from that point I started to pick up some decent spare rides.

Nineteen eighty-eight was the year of Kahyasi who gave Luca his first Derby success. The horse was owned by the Aga Khan and looked after by my pal Andy Keates, who'd been telling us all winter that his charge was Derby material. Most of the lads were on at nice prices. I remember watching on TV in my tracksuit as Ray brought him through to win at Epsom, before setting off for a run to try to lose some weight as I had a light ride at Carlisle the next day. I put it all back on and more at a mother and a father of a Derby victory party that night which carried on until the early hours.

There was a price to pay the following morning as, with thumping heads, Colin and I set off on the four-hour journey to Carlisle, wearing tracksuits, with the heating turned full up on a boiling hot summer day. We both felt terrible – which probably explains why, between us, we failed to tack up his mount Expound securely for the opening race. As a result his saddle began to slip after a furlong and Expound was beaten in a photo finish with Colin perched precariously on his back.

Five minutes later, his work completed for the afternoon, Colin came swanning into the weighing room clutching a large ice-cream. It was too much for me as I struggled to boil away excess pounds for my single, lightweight ride which I knew had little chance. I seized the ice-cream, spread it all over Colin's face and fled into the sauna before he could retaliate.

Things began to pick up later in June with my first double win on Norman Invader and Mischievous Miss at Redcar, swiftly followed by the success of Follow The Drum at Folkestone. Andy was unable to lead up Norman Invader as he was recovering at home from serious injuries sustained when the horse kicked him in the face. He was found unconscious in Norman Invader's box with his face in bits, and countless broken bones in his jaw and cheek which caused him to be off work for almost three months.

Early in July I won on a nice horse of Luca's called Casey at Catterick. We were hacking up until I complicated matters by easing him so heavily in the closing stages that we only just scraped home by a neck from the fast-finishing runner-up Kirsheda. Some of the Yorkshire punters shouted abuse at me as I returned to unsaddle, but I was certain that we'd held on. I was smiling when I came back, but only with relief, and the stewards gave me a telling-off for being too confident. If I'd been caught on Casey, they warned, I would have been suspended and heavily fined. The next morning I stole the headlines for all the wrong reasons. The *Racing Post* declared 'Frankie Lives Dangerously'.

Worse followed when Luca called me in and watched the video with me before delivering an almighty rocket. A few days later Casey's owner, Gerald Leigh, sent me a photograph of the win with a cryptic note which read 'Too much attention to the camera and not enough to the finish!'

I'd been waiting for the chance to gain my revenge on Norman Invader for almost killing Andy and finally got the chance when I was booked to ride him in the Magnet Cup at York. I taped a piece of lead into the flap of my whip, then started to hit Norman Invader with it as soon as we moved into contention about three furlongs from home. I am ashamed to admit that I really wanted to hurt the horse, to punish him for what he had done to Andy. I gave him a good hiding. It was madness, of course, a horrible thing to do. The chief sufferer, apart from the horse, was my greatest friend Colin Rate who was making a move up my inner on Chartino. In a sense I killed two birds with one stone. As Norman Invader hung left-handed away from the whip he almost put Colin over the rails. I heard a lot of cursing and shouting just behind me in a familiar Geordie accent, but by then the damage had been done and both of us finished towards the rear. Somehow the stewards missed what happened – but Luca didn't and we were both on the carpet in his office once more. If he'd known about my whip I suspect I would have been looking for alternative employment.

A stormy July reached its climax ten days later when I returned to Catterick to ride Torkabar, owned by the Aga Khan. The horse was a red-hot favourite to win an uncompetitive maiden, but he was a monkey and had thrown away victory in our previous race at York by veering violently in the closing stages. Once again he was determined not to put his best foot forward. The more I asked, the more he resisted.

Just after we passed the line a well beaten third I lashed out with my whip in temper and struck him over the head. It was done out of frustration after losing my rag, and I knew immediately I was in the wrong because hitting horses on the head is unacceptable. It was a childish thing to do. Once again I was marched before the Catterick stewards and this time they weren't so lenient. I made up some story about giving him a tap to prevent him ducking through a gate towards the paddock. The panel listened in stony silence before banning me for three days for improper riding. That wasn't the end of the matter.

The following morning I was standing in the doorway of a stable in the bottom yard, facing inwards, half-heartedly scratching around in the straw with a pitchfork when I received a painful kick up the backside which sent me sprawling head first in the far corner of the box. I almost ended up in the feed manger. The next moment Ray Cochrane was leaning over me, going absolutely mad, shouting and screaming that I'd let the side down by my treatment of Torkabar. It was bad enough, he suggested, to strike any horse over the head. But to do it to one belonging to the stable's principal owner, the Aga Khan, was idiotic. I quickly got the message and started mucking out the stable with new vigour, then slowed down again as soon as Ray disappeared out of sight.

Luca was away in America at the sales, but when he returned he let me have it with both barrels and promptly suspended me from riding for a further two weeks. A fortnight on the sidelines at that stage seemed like a lifetime, but I knew I was in the wrong so I had to take it on the chin.

The second head lad Stuart Jackson was also keen to keep my

feet firmly on the floor. He always seemed to be waiting for me when I bounced into the yard after a good day at the races. Some days he'd hide behind a door, then kick me in the backside for the hell of it. On other occasions he'd ask how the race had gone, listen to my description of how clever I'd been, then wait until my back had turned before kicking me. When I protested he'd reply mysteriously 'You know what that's for.' It was all part of Luca's strategy to keep my head from swelling.

I picked up the winning thread again on Burnt Fingers at Haydock on 5 August and completed my second double at Yarmouth later in the month. I also collected a fine of £200 on the same afternoon for giving one of Luca's a 'quiet run'. Since Allez Au Bon wasn't fit enough to do himself justice in the race, Luca was keen that I looked after him and didn't finish too close to the red-hot favourite, Pure Genius, who won easily. Unfortunately I overdid the waiting tactics.

August ended with a significant breakthrough with my first winners for the multiple champion trainer Henry Cecil – who was still the King and had shared two victories in the 2,000 Guineas with my father. I was thrilled that Henry turned to me when Steve Cauthen was injured. My first success for him came in a maiden race at Newmarket on Opening Verse, who eventually won the Breeders' Cup mile in America. Two days later I rode my second winner for Henry as part of another double at Wolverhampton.

It had been an eventful season and the best was yet to come. Late in September Luca called me into his office to say that the Aga Khan would be running two pacemakers for our Derby winner Kahyasi in the Prix de l'Arc de Triomphe, the highlight of the season in Paris, and I would be on one of them – Roushayd. It was a fantastic opportunity for someone with such limited experience. The Aga must have forgiven me for my behaviour on Torkabar.

The weekend went like a dream. At the age of seventeen I found myself climbing aboard a private jet at Cambridge late on Saturday with a group of trainers, jockeys and racing managers all heading for Paris. Anthony Stroud was in charge of the party, who all seemed to be staying at the Ritz. As I hadn't booked a room, I had to bed down on a couch in a massive sitting room in Anthony's suite. I was still living in digs at the time and had never seen anything like it. When everyone else headed off for a night out, I was left on my own with the newspapers, a vast television, a bowl of fruit and a big cocktail bar which I didn't dare touch. Within minutes I was on the phone to mother saying guess where I am? I can still remember my excitement at such luxury.

The plan the next day was for Rae Guest to tow the field along for the first mile on Taboushkan before I took over on Roushayd, with Kahyasi waiting to pounce late. But just as I made my move Tony Ives arrived alongside on Emmson, said 'Where are you going, son' and squashed me on to the rails. Tony killed me, the rascal, and that was the end of my pacemaking duties. Every time I tried to get out someone else would come and hold me in.

At least it didn't make any difference because Kahyasi ran well below his form, finishing sixth to the Italian winner Tony

Bin, ridden by John Reid. Two weeks later my dad managed to get beaten on Tony Bin in a five-horse race in Milan!

That first ride in the Arc was the highlight of my season which had produced twenty-two winners. I've ridden in the race every year since. I love the track and the special atmosphere that crackles with excitement on Arc day. For me it is one of the great races in the world.

Once the season was over early in November I headed for California again to continue my racing education at Santa Anita. This time I had the correct documents so was able to move around the course without looking over my shoulder like a criminal. At home in England I was beginning to build a bit of a profile, with the occasional interview and report on my winners, but in America I remained an anonymous figure, just one of the legions of foreign workers drawn together by a shared love of racing. That way, at least, nobody noticed my mistakes.

I even picked up a couple of race rides, but any danger of becoming over-confident was swiftly ended during a brief discussion with the record-breaking trainer Wayne Lukas. After completing four lots for Richard, I sought out Lukas one morning, introduced myself, and offered to ride out for him at any time. I was trying to drum up some business and he was the best trainer in America.

He looked me up and down, then replied with a devastating put-down: 'We're in good shape right now', the short interview clearly at an end. Since then I've ridden in the mornings for all the biggest trainers in the game in America, including the legendary Charlie Whittingham and Bobby Frankel. But you can be sure I will not be offering my services to Wayne Lukas again.

Soon it was time to return to England for the 1989 flat season for which I'd been installed as 3–1 favourite to be champion apprentice, but when I caught up with Cliff Woof he hinted that I should look for a new agent. This suited me because now he had several more jockeys on his books and was developing other business interests in racing. I wanted someone who could work full-time trying to get me rides. Once again I turned to Mattie Cowing. This time, with a bit of encouragement from Bruce Raymond, he agreed to take me on. Mattie still suspected that I was a scallywag but he'd seen me ride enough winners in 1988 to know that I could do the business and Bruce wasn't quite as busy as before. It was the start of a brilliant partnership. What began as a commercial arrangement soon developed into a close friendship. Mattie was a star and treated me a bit like an uncle looking after his favourite nephew.

Shortly after I joined him Mattie converted the small spare bedroom of his flat into an office. Once we were up and running I bought him a computer to make his job easier. He spent the mornings on the phone, ringing trainers, putting me forward wherever possible, then headed for Cuthie Suttle's betting shop to watch the racing. He was one of life's punters and now, working with Bruce and myself, he was better informed than ever. But he still used to lose his cash most days.

Luca rarely has his horses ready for the early part of the season, so I had to look elsewhere for support in April and

May. The first Dettori to make a big impact that season was my father who won the Italian 2,000 Guineas on Sikeston for English trainer John Dunlop.

Things improved dramatically after I rode two winners at Newmarket on 13 May. The first of them came in a valuable sprint that was shown live on TV. My horse Didicoy was well backed and I produced him fast and late to catch Hafir on the line. That was a massive victory for me, the start of a fantastic season. Half an hour later I managed a second narrow triumph on Khaydara. I was on my way!

Another double at Catterick twelve days later set me up for a month of unrelenting success in June. Whatever I touched turned to gold. In the space of three weeks I achieved four trebles. The first of them came at Leicester, where I lost my 5 pounds claim by winning on Versailles Road, trained by Susan Piggott. She had taken over her husband's training licence in January 1988 while Lester was serving a prison sentence for tax evasion, and she kept it when he was released in October. It was my first ride for them.

One of my trebles that month illustrates the crazy routine that flat jockeys are forced to follow at the height of the season. The day before this treble I had ridden at Brighton's evening meeting and didn't reach home much before midnight. The next morning I left for work at dawn, rode one lot for Luca, then hitched a ride with Willie Ryan to Redcar, where I managed a double. Then it was off again on another long-distance trek to Warwick where I won the final race of the evening shortly after 9 p.m. on Tears Of Happiness. At least we could catch up with our sleep on Sundays in those days. Not any more. Now there is wall-to-wall racing seven days a week and all the boys are exhausted by high summer. It's reached the point where they almost welcome a suspension which forces them to step off the treadmill.

It was on one of those Sundays that I experienced my first and last game of cricket. I foolishly allowed myself to be talked into turning out for the Cumani XI against a team representing fellow Newmarket trainer Michael Stoute who, as a native of Barbados, is a cricket fanatic. I spent the first half of the afternoon bored witless in the field, hoping desperately that the ball didn't come my way. Later, when it was my turn to bat, I wandered into the middle without a clue, stood there holding my bat awkwardly in front of me and was bowled first ball by Stoute. I hadn't realised how fast the ball comes at you! To this day the game is a complete mystery to me and I cannot understand why apparently sane people like Michael and Julian Wilson, the ex-BBC racing presenter, are obsessed with it.

There was another, much more pleasant interlude that summer when I took a rare Saturday off to attend my sister Sandra's wedding in Milan. She married a Scottish basketball player, but sadly the marriage didn't last long.

My push for the apprentice title got a boost in July when Ray broke his collar bone. By then Luca had recruited another promising newcomer, Jason Weaver, who soon became a close friend. Although his father was a professional footballer, Jason was so keen on riding that at the age of ten he flogged his mother's fridge freezer to a neighbour, added his life savings of £25, and bought his first pony which he called Volvo. When his mum came home from work the freezer had disappeared and Volvo was grazing among her flowers and plants in the garden of their home near Chepstow.

Jason lost some of his teeth and broke a few ribs in his days as a plucky schoolboy scrum-half. He was solidly built even then, but managed to shed almost a stone in two months on a diet of apples and boiled rice to convince the Newmarket racing school that he was small enough to be a jockey. Weight was always going to defeat him in the end, but he fought a valiant battle with the scales for years and it was obvious from the start that he could ride. So when Ray was injured Luca allowed Jason to take part in a serious bit of work for the first time on Legal Case. For him it felt like sitting in a Rolls Royce.

The plan was for Jason on Legal Case to lead me on Markof-distinction during a piece of work on Long Hill, just about the only training gallop in Newmarket where every string in the area can see what is going on. Towards the end I was supposed to draw alongside so that we finished together. Since both horses were due to run in the next few days Luca stressed that we shouldn't overcook them. Jason set off a bit quicker than I expected and then, just when I thought it was time to move up to join him, he kicked his horse in the belly, shook the reins, picked up his whip and shot five lengths clear. The louder I shouted at him to slow down the faster he went until he was almost out of earshot. I knew if I chased him I'd punish Markof-distinction, so I let Jason win the gallop with ease, then tore into him as we started to pull up.

'What the hell did you think you were doing? Are you —ing crazy? You ruined the work and could have killed both horses. You're —ing mad!' I screamed at him. By now he was looking totally ashamed. 'I'm sorry mate, the truth is that I heard the crowd, got excited and just had to win!'

For a moment I didn't understand what he was saying. Then he turned and pointed to the rest of Luca's string nearby who had enjoyed a grandstand view of our one-sided duel. There was no answer to that, particularly as I used to make the same mistake when I started riding work. The temptation to show off is hard to resist. Jason hadn't yet ridden a winner and saw the opportunity to put one over the stable's star apprentice.

Luca arrived on the scene with a face like thunder and seemed close to sacking Jason on the spot. It made a welcome change for someone else to be in the line of fire, but this was a mega bollocking and I suspect Jason wasn't forgiven for a long time. He certainly dropped back down the queue of hopeful apprentices waiting to be given a chance in races, but he was much too talented to be left on the sub's bench forever. He just needed to get his brain into gear. When it happened he became champion apprentice on his way to a glittering career.

With Ray Cochrane still on the sidelines I stepped into the gap on some of the stable's better horses. It was an important time for me because people take notice when top trainers give you a chance at the highest level. The first notable success came at Lingfield on 15 July on the talented Markofdistinction, having his first run since finishing fourth to the mighty Nashwan in the 2,000 Guineas that year. The task at Lingfield was simple and he won easily. Two days later I cruised to victory on Legal Case at Windsor. Luckily he showed no sign of exhaustion after that infamous workout with Jason.

The next afternoon I reached another career landmark when I lost my apprentice's right to claim a weight allowance with my victory on Versailles Road at Beverley. It was the eighty-fourth success. Soon after I arrived at the Beverley track I took a call in the secretary's office from Lester Piggott. I assumed he was trying to give me instructions on how to ride Versailles Road. It's well known that Lester tends to mutter, and sometimes on a good day you can't be sure what he's saying. Nor did it help that the line was crackling and that my English was still pretty poor. Frankly I didn't understand a word he said, but it didn't matter a hoot because Versailles Road won unchallenged.

By this stage I had extended my repertoire of mimicking other jockey's styles to include Steve Cauthen, with his toes barely in the irons, and Pat Eddery, bumping along in the saddle in a finish, but I missed the chance to copy Lester for the good reason that I'd never ridden against him. That would come later.

Now I would be taking on the big boys on level terms without the advantage of a weight allowance. It is a big leap for an apprentice, the acid test, and many have been found wanting – partly because trainers can have short memories once you have used up your claim. At the time I was flying, brimful of confidence. But there is a long list of star apprentices who later disappeared without trace, and in the next few weeks I began to wonder if I'd soon be joining them.

Things began to go wrong the day after Beverley when Sean Keightley gave me a lift to Catterick. First we ran into a traffic jam; then his car broke down just as we set off again. Stranded in the middle of nowhere 45 miles from the track, I managed to flag down a passing taxi and offered him a bonus if we made it to Catterick in time for me to ride the favourite Snow Glint in the opening race. We arrived to see the horse win snugly under late substitute jockey John Carroll.

This was the start of a depressing barren run for me that lasted for almost a month. I couldn't do anything right. If I had the choice of two meetings, I'd end up at the wrong one. If I did look like riding a winner, I'd be caught on the line or pipped in a photo finish. A jockey's confidence is, at best, fragile. When things are going well you ride on instinct and can win on horses that aren't entitled to be placed. But when the winners dry up and the gaps fail to come when you want them, you become so anxious you start to doubt your own ability. I began to realise it wouldn't be so easy without the advantage of my apprentice's claim. Luckily for me the drought ended as suddenly as it began and I extended my lead at the top of the apprentices' table.

Then, at the end of August, I was pitch-forked onto the front pages of the racing papers. It happened after Ray Cochrane revealed that he would be leaving Luca Cumani at the end of the season to ride for Guy Harwood in 1990. Ray had been a constant source of encouragement. He helped me whenever he could and wasn't slow to put me straight when I stepped out of line. Now his departure was nudging the door open for me. Within days I was appointed as his successor.

nine

A Job Made in Heaven

When I heard that Ray Cochrane was leaving Luca Cumani's yard I obviously hoped that Luca would offer me the job, but I wasn't counting my chickens. Several of the papers seemed to believe that my appointment was a formality. They even hinted that my rapid progress had influenced Ray's decision to 'jump ship'. I wasn't convinced because that conveniently ignored the truth that this chance had arrived much earlier than anyone had expected.

The fact that I was only eighteen and still so inexperienced was bound to count against me with some of the more prominent owners in the yard. It was a job made in heaven, the one I had wanted from the day I first stepped off the plane at Stansted just over four years earlier, but was it coming a bit too soon?

The whole thing was in the melting pot when I received an urgent message to ring my father at the end of August. I could tell by the tone of his voice that he was unusually excited. Apparently he'd been speaking to Luca over the past two days and the deal was done: I would be Luca's stable jockey the following year. I could sense that my father was doing double somersaults on the other end of the phone. He was so thrilled for me that I could almost reach down the line and touch the pride on his face.

I was so shocked it didn't sink in at first, but we talked for a long time and he gave me a lot of sound advice. He also shared my concern that the responsibility of riding for one of the country's best trainers might have come a year too soon. I would be in the spotlight as never before. Every move, every mistake would be made under the public's gaze. The time for fooling around was over.

For me it was such a startling turn-up I hardly slept a wink that night. I'd arrived in Newmarket without a word of English. Two years after that I was still scratching around for the odd spare ride, so depressed at one stage that I wanted to move to France. Now – as Arthur Daley used to say in *Minder* – the world was my lobster. I could hardly believe my good fortune.

The next morning I met Luca in his office to hammer out the details. I sat in the chair where I had been on the receiving end of so many lectures and listened almost in a trance as he spoke of retainers and the horses I could expect to ride in the future. His faith in me was touching, but inevitably, one or two important owners wanted further proof of my ability before allowing me to ride their best horses. At this stage, Luca explained, they reserved the right to choose a top jockey in major races. It was up to me to put an end to their doubts.

I left Luca's office on cloud nine, ran back to my digs, beside myself with delight and immediately rang my friends with the news. There were precedents which offered encouragement. Lester Piggott was eighteen when he signed up to ride for Sir Noel Murless. Walter Swinburn, too, was in his teens when he joined forces with Michael Stoute, and Pat Eddery was barely twenty when he was snapped up by Peter Walwyn. All three partnerships had been hugely successful. Could I maintain the sequence?

That week someone tipped off the papers about my weakness for chocolate mousse. Bernice tried to keep my appetite in check, but eventually she agreed to make a large mousse for every ten winners I rode. I loved sweet things, still do. *The Sun* ran a feature that contrasted my passion for chocolate mousse with Ray Cochrane's routine of running up to four miles a day on a diet of fresh air to control his weight at no more than 8st 4lb. No prizes, then, for guessing which of us was more dedicated in those days! I still can't resist an ice-cream or sometimes a bottle of cold beer at the end of the afternoon's racing. When you are sitting in the sauna for hours on end, boiling away unwanted pounds, your craving for these things dominates your thinking. Of course when you give in to temptation all your hard work is undone. That's why some jockeys who live in the sauna eventually become so miserable.

Once my deal with Luca became public I was bursting with impatience to begin my new role. I got the chance much earlier than expected when Ray broke his collar-bone in an horrific pile-up in the Portland Handicap at Doncaster – which ended the careers of two senior jockeys, Paul Cook and Ian Johnson.

Ray was out for more than a month and I immediately took his place on our runners at a time the stable was in sparkling form. Faulty track drainage at Doncaster was found to be cause of the falls in the Portland and another race, so the rest of the meeting was abandoned. The final Classic of the season, the St Leger, was switched from Doncaster to Ayr seven days later, so my first Classic ride was in Scotland. That's one for the racing anoraks! It came on NC Owen for Luca, but we struggled in the mud and finished far behind the winner, Michelozzo.

Shortly before that I rode a treble for Luca at Goodwood, which included my first Group race win on Legal Case in the Select Stakes. That was important for me because his owner, Sir Gordon White, was among those who had questioned my appointment as stable jockey. Luca had to work overtime to get me on that one. I was in rampant form, gone beyond recall in the battle for the apprentice title, and completed a memorable month with three more victories at the meeting at Ascot which is now known as the Festival of British Racing.

I kicked off with a double on Thursday on Tidemark and Alwathba. Two days later I recorded my one-hundredth success as a jockey on Chummy's Favourite in the Group 3 Krug Diadem Stakes. That was a huge success for me, one that I treasure to this day. I was so emotional afterwards that I couldn't speak. When you are trying to make your name in racing and spend most of the time toiling away at places like Folkestone, Chepstow and Carlisle, you crave the chance to perform on a bigger stage. Now that opportunity had finally arrived, I was loving it. I ended the season in a blaze of publicity by running away with the apprentice championship with 75 winners, a total which equalled the postwar record set by Edward Hide in 1956.

After a long, tiring year I was badly in need of a holiday, but first I had to face the problem of acquiring a driving licence. There is a limit to how far you can travel on a moped so, most of the time, I relied on other jockeys to ferry me to race meetings. When that wasn't possible I paid one of the lads to drive me. That summer I forked out £200 for an ancient silver Mazda. Since I rarely had time for lessons, Andy taught me the basic requirements in the car park at Newmarket racecourse, then he or someone else who had a licence would sit beside me as I drove around town.

On the days I was really stuck for transport I removed the L plates, took a chance and drove myself. Obviously this couldn't become a habit, so at the season's end I booked a day with a 'Jim'll Fix It' firm in Manchester that guaranteed you would pass your test after an intensive course of lessons. I drove up there in my battered old Mazda, strolled through four hours of lessons, took my test that afternoon and promptly failed for going too fast. So much for my guarantee. The next week I returned to Manchester for another test and this time I passed.

Only then was I free to set off on a riotous fortnight's holiday with Colin Rate. First we headed for his home town, Sunderland, where we seemed to spend most nights drinking endless pints of beer. One evening I was guest of honour at the Pennywell Working Men's Club, where his father was a member. The place was packed with upwards of seven hundred people as I presented a series of darts prizes.

Later that evening we headed for the nightclubs before stopping at a kebab house on the way home. Soon we were joined in the queue by a striking couple. He was massive, built like a prize fighter, tall, rippling with muscles and distinctly menacing. She was such a stunner I couldn't stop myself staring at her boobs which, conveniently for me, were at eye level.

When I said something in Italian to her the boyfriend immediately took offence. As Colin stepped in to sort him out, the pair of us were sent flying through the open door into the middle of the road. Colin is not one to turn the other cheek, so as we picked ourselves up he started shouting that he was going to kill our assailant. I've always preferred diplomacy at times like this. When I pointed out to Colin that he was giving away height, reach and the best part of eight stone, he was forced to agree with me. We slunk away with our tails between our legs, searching in vain for a cab.

Help arrived from an unlikely source in the shape of one of Colin's mates. He produced a screwdriver, wandered down the street, forced open the door of a car, fiddled with the wires under the bonnet, started the engine, invited us to jump in and drove us to Colin's home. After a long week's partying in Sunderland we headed for the calmer waters of Milan where we played football most evenings in the square. I even took Colin to see my old school just to prove that I *had* received an education.

Suitably refreshed, I then set off for another winter in

California. This time, with the backing of my agent Bob Meldahl for the US season, I started to pick up a few rides. The best Christmas present of all arrived two days early when I broke my duck in America on Smart Dollars in a $27,000 race late in the evening at Hollywood Park. I remember that it was the last race on the card. It was almost pitch black as we arrived at the start, and I beat the great Laffit Pincay into second place on Racing Rascal. Best of all, my dad was there with Christine.

Chris McCarron was one of the first to congratulate me in the jockeys' room. He shook my hand warmly and put his other arm around my shoulders. I was immediately ambushed by half a dozen more jockeys who tore off my breeches and pants before brushing my willy and balls with filthy hoof oil. They then dumped me on my tummy and scribbled some graffiti on my backside before tipping some buckets of cold water over me. We were all in stitches and I was laughing as much as anyone because I knew it was their way of welcoming me into their club.

Smart Dollars was trained by a noisy character, with a manic laugh, called Chris Speckert, known to everyone as Noddy because of his habit of falling asleep over dinner. He booked a table that night for a celebration meal for us all at his favourite restaurant in Sierra Madre, and I was so animated after my first success in the States that he didn't have a chance to nod off.

Having a few race rides helped the winter pass more quickly. America seemed like a different planet to me as a kid and I still adore my trips there but I've never been tempted to stay full-time. Their racing is all about speed round sharp bends and down short straights, with long-distance events a rarity. Most results are usually decided in the opening moments. Its jump out, get a position you can defend on the first turn, go as fast as you can and see who wins. If you happen to draw stall number twelve out wide in all your races you might as well stay at home.

When you've been in America for a while you learn to appreciate the wide variety that British racing provides for horses and jockeys. No two races are the same, and if it suddenly rains a track's bias can alter dramatically. I relish the different challenges that each course poses, and love the culture and tradition of British racing. These do matter. It's not just a numbers game because there is a passion for it.

The problem with America is that everyday racing is extremely boring, all left-handed on flat, sharp oval tracks. I love the big races there and want to win plenty more of them, but for the rest of the time you feel you are going round not for yourself but for the betting people. Then you *are* just a number. My mind is too active to do that day after day for up to three months at the same racecourse. It's so repetitive. I guess I'm not a nine-to-five person. I just can't do it.

I've made good friends with the jockeys in California down the years, most notably with Gary Stevens. He looked after me in the early days at Santa Anita when all the others were a fair bit older then me. So many of them have retired now. Gary has exceptional vision and is always looking to broaden his horizons, but some of the jockeys who ride in New York have got big chips on their shoulders. I find their attitude that 'Americans do it better' both arrogant and off-putting.

I returned from California earlier than usual determined to make the best of the opportunity given to me by Luca Cumani. I rode out every morning through the worst of the spring weather, worked hard on my weight, and was as fit as anyone could be for the start of the 1990 flat season. Luca offered me a retainer of £15,000 for first claim on my services. It wasn't a king's ransom, but then I would probably have taken the job without the bonus of a fee. The wheel had turned full circle because Luca had earned around £50,000 from his share of my riding fees and winning percentages in my days as an apprentice. I'm not complaining because that is the system in racing here. It's been that way for centuries. We all need someone to push us in the early days and he had certainly helped put me on the map. The trick now was to stay there.

Luca suggested that it was high time I bought myself a decent car. My ancient Mazda had to go. Flush with my new retainer, I added a further £4,000 from my savings and splashed out £19,000 on a metallic, grey Mercedes 190E with reasonably light mileage. I also hired Andy Keates to be my driver. It was an arrangement that suited both of us and he continues to work for me to this day in a wide variety of roles.

From that point, until ill-health slowed him up, my agent Mattie Cowing often joined us for a day at the races. Soon we were known as 'The Three Musketeers'. Mattie enjoyed meeting face-to-face the trainers that he spoke to almost daily on the phone. This way, he felt, he could drum up even more business for me. Other agents prefer to work away locked in their bunkers at home. Mattie was a gregarious character with many friends in the game. It suited us both for him to go racing. Armed with a red-hot agent, a fast car and a new driver I was ready to conquer the world.

Sure enough I started the campaign with a bang in April, but not in the way I'd intended. After a handful of early winners things began to go wrong at Epsom's spring meeting when I took a bad fall on Long Island approaching the final furlong. Falls are part of a jockey's life. We all know it is a question of when rather than if you are going to hit the ground hard, at upwards of 30 mph. When it happens it is pure luck whether you walk away or end up heading for the nearest hospital.

This time I escaped with a severe shaking as I was thrown clear, but poor Long Island was not so lucky after another horse ran into the back of her. She hit the rails, before somersaulting through them, breaking one of her hind legs and had to be put down. The stewards decided that Michael Hills, the rider of Flying Diva, the horse who ran into the back of us, was guilty of reckless riding. He was suspended for 14 days. Michael apologised to me straight away but looking back now I accept that it wasn't entirely his fault. I wasn't to blame, but maybe I should have sensed what was going to happen. My horse was weakening and if Michael had waited for a couple more strides he could have come through without a problem. His horse was cruising and he switched to make his run a split second too soon. Because I was still pushing away like an idiot, his horse clipped the heels of Long Island. It was the impetuosity of youth.

After a break of two days I bounced back in the best possible fashion by winning my first Group 2 race on Markofdistinction in the Trust House Forté Mile at Sandown. I felt he had speed to burn and could be the equal of any horse in the country. He was a machine. The Cumani team then hit top form at the Guineas meeting at Newmarket with further Group victories from Statoblest and Roseate Tern. May proved to be a highly productive month for me, until two further dramas in the space of three days took the wind out of my sails. The wear and tear of constant travelling is a jockey's greatest enemy in the summer when you are riding soon after dawn and don't return home from an evening meeting until after midnight. Obviously it helps to have a driver, but there are still delays, frustrations and accidents.

Late in May I was asleep on the back seat of my Mercedes as we headed north on the M6 towards Haydock. I was woken by the sound of a mighty explosion behind me which sent me hurtling to the floor behind the front seats. When I scrambled out onto the motorway I discovered that a large white van had ploughed so fast into the back of us that the boot no longer existed. The strength of the Mercedes definitely saved me from serious injury. If I had been in my trusty old Mazda I could have been killed.

Three days later I took another heavy fall on a horse called Muirfield Village at Sandown. This time it was definitely my fault. He clipped the heels of the horse in front of me, stumbled, and sent me flying. As I landed among a forest of hooves I was still clutching his bridle. Muirfield Village escaped without harm. I was carried on a stretcher into a waiting ambulance, but the greatest damage was to my pride when Luca started to give me a severe dressing down. I was already nursing a sore knee from the fall and by the time he'd finished I also had a sore head.

Luca didn't mind if I hurt myself, he said, but if I continued as I had done on Muirfield Village I would maim or hurt other horses by cutting through their hind legs – and that, in his eyes, was unforgivable. My mistake was to ride so cockily that I allowed my mount to gallop too close to the ones ahead of me. I can't say I appreciated the way Luca spoke, because he was really angry, but deep down I knew that he was right.

If you ride every day you know instinctively how far a horse's legs can extend at full gallop. In those days I was always going a stride too far, poking into places where I shouldn't have gone. Nine times out of ten I got away with it, but obviously on Muirfield Village I didn't and it taught me a valuable lesson. At that age you are too stupid, not experienced enough and fearless. I see the young kids making the same mistakes today, letting their horses get in too tight, risking life and limb. Like me they will learn the hard way, hopefully without hurting themselves. That's how it is.

When I wasn't riding for a fall I was enjoying a brilliant season. It continued at Royal Ascot where I won the opening race of the meeting, the Queen Anne Stakes, on Markofdistinction. One of the first to congratulate me was my dad who had ridden to victory in the same race at the featherweight of 7st 10 lb on Imperial March for the top Irish trainer Vincent O'Brien back in 1975.

I started the year with an optimistic target of 100 winners for the season but was amazed to reach that figure months ahead of schedule at Chepstow on Line Of Thunder on 27 August. The next day the newspapers were full of it, partly because I was the first teenager to ride a century of winners since Lester Piggott 35 years earlier. What's more, he took two months longer.

Shortly afterwards I was pleased to win a race on Henryk for my friend Barney Curley, one of the great eccentrics of the game. He is best known to the general public for selling his Georgian mansion near Mullingar in County Westmeath, Eire, for a fortune, through the novel method of a nationwide raffle. Some years earlier, before the days of mobile phones, he landed a massive gamble on his own horse Yellow Sam at Bellewstown with the help of a burly accomplice called Benny O'Hanlon who blocked the only telephone box on the course for the final twenty-five minutes before the race. At the same time, in an operation of military precision, a group of his friends were backing the horse in betting shops all round Ireland. The off-course bookies tried desperately to phone money back to the course to shorten the price but, thanks to Benny, they could not get through.

Barney was counting his winnings for months after Yellow Sam won at 20–1. It was one of the great coups of modern times. Later he moved to England to start training in a small way at Newmarket and we eventually swapped houses. I love listening to Barney talking about racing. He has an original mind and is one of the few people I know to make a serious living from backing horses.

Henryk hadn't won for ages and was hardly in the first flush of youth, but Barney decided to go for a touch in a low-grade staying handicap at Nottingham in September. My instructions were to drop Henryk out towards the rear, then wait until the last moment before popping him in front on the line. I carried out my orders to the letter, and came fast and late to snatch the lead in the final strides. Barney looked an even whiter shade of pale than usual on my return. I couldn't really blame him for thinking I'd left it too late. When he'd recovered from the shock he told the waiting pack of pressmen that I'd be champion jockey one day. I was forgiven for nearly giving him a heart attack.

When the winners are coming in a torrent, all photo finishes seem to go in your favour, every day seems like Christmas, and you start to believe that you are invincible. Events at Haydock on 8 September swiftly brought me back down to earth again – literally. I'd just started to relax after being beaten on Baylis in a tight finish with My Lord. As we began to pull up, Baylis caught the heels of My Lord, stumbled onto his nose and fired me head first into the ground. The medics who rushed to attend me were sufficiently concerned to fit me with a neck brace before I was taken by ambulance to the local hospital. X-rays failed to show any fractures.

Aware that I was in no state to go home, Donald McCain,

who used to work for Luca, came to collect me and drove me to his parents' home nearby in Southport. It was a God-given opportunity to meet the immortal Red Rum, the only horse in history to win the Grand National three times. Red Rum was a pensioner by then, but for years he was trained on the local beach with a rare sureness of touch by Donald's father 'Ginger' McCain in the most unlikely setting for a racing stable. Ginger also sold cars for a living, and his yard was located behind the showrooms in a side street at Southport with a Chinese takeaway a few yards down the road and close to a railway crossing. Although I was nursing a massive headache, I still treasure that meeting with the greatest Grand National winner of them all and was thrilled when Ginger added an amazing fourth National triumph this year with Amberleigh House.

That summer I survived three falls that could have ended my career, so you can imagine how I felt when I heard that my friend Marco Paganini, the young champion jockey of Italy, had been killed in a fall at Grosseto. Apparently the horse he was riding was tricky entering the stalls. Given one final chance he finally consented to start, but then clipped the heels of another runner, pitching Marco onto the grass. The fall was not a bad one, but as Marco was about to get up he was kicked in the head by a backmarker.

At first I couldn't believe Marco was dead. He had taken over the champion's mantle from my father, had a glittering career ahead of him and was always full of life. That's why he had been such an inspiration to me when I began race riding in Naples. Try as I might I never did manage to beat him in a finish. The more I persevered, the more he teased me. Now his life had been snuffed out in the most tragic manner.

It is terrifying to think of all the jockeys who have been killed since I started riding, including Kieren Kelly and Sean Cleary in the space of three months in Ireland in 2003.

The one that hit me hardest was the death of Philip Barnard in a fall over hurdles at Wincanton on Boxing Day, 1991. We'd been really close in the days when he was apprenticed to Lester and Susan Piggott in Newmarket. We travelled together, ran together in the evenings to lose weight, spent hours in the sauna, laughed together and used to chase the girls when time allowed. Philip was a lovely guy and a real talent who had just started to make a name for himself over jumps.

The popular lightweight jockey Steve Wood, known to everyone as Sampson because he was so strong, was killed in front of my eyes at Lingfield a couple of years later. It happened on a horse that had been led round the paddock by his girlfriend. It wasn't the fall that killed him. I can still remember the horror of seeing him bouncing along the ground when he was unseated. Then he was struck with shattering force by another runner. It was like watching someone you know being knocked down by a double-decker bus. Two others came down in the mêlée and we all knew instinctively that Steve was in a bad way. Tragically he died from internal injuries.

The hardest part was forcing ourselves to go through the motions in the final race of the day because we were all so upset that none of us was in any state to do our jobs properly. We just rode on autopilot but the meeting should have been abandoned. When you are a jockey you know that sometimes the risks are unacceptably high. One false step, one dangerous manouevre and it could be all over. That's the way it is but you never think it will happen to you. If you do you shouldn't be out there.

My rich summer harvest in 1990 stretched into a golden late autumn with an amazing double at the Ascot Festival towards the end of September. Perhaps it was an omen for what was to come six years later. For two seasons I had desperately been trying to win a Group 1 race. In the space of little more than forty minutes I ended up with two. That was massive for me, absolutely massive. After a treble at Ascot on the Thursday and another success there twenty-four hours later, I arrived at the course on Saturday confident of a big run from Markofdistinc- tion in the Queen Elizabeth II Stakes, one of the richest races of the season. Although he was only fifth favourite I felt that his searing turn of foot could be decisive if I dared wait long enough to deliver it.

I dropped him out last of all in the early stages as Steve Cauthen took us along smartly on Shavian. Then just as I started to close up ready to strike Pat Eddery stole first run on me on Distant Relative on my outside. Aware that my horse was the biggest danger, cunning Pat deliberately let Distant Relative edge right-handed across us at the very moment the leaders began to fall back towards us. Suddenly the door was about to slam in our face. In another few strides Markofdistinction would have lost vital impetus as he was pushed into the back of the tiring leaders.

At times like this you discover the difference between a very good horse and a champion. Once I woke up and reacted, Markofdistinction shot forward and squeezed through the gap a moment before it disappeared. He was the one who got us out of trouble. Distant Relative still held a slender lead with a furlong to run, but I knew nothing could match the blinding pace of Markofdistinction over two hundred yards and he bounded ahead to claim a famous victory by a length. The measure of our achievement could be seen in the eight lengths back to the third horse.

The moment I crossed the line will live with me forever. Suddenly, for a few startling seconds the world turned dark. Then all I could see was a mass of flames around me as if the place was on fire. Even stranger, it was happening in slow motion. I was the only one moving at normal speed. Everything else near me seemed to be stopping. Then someone turned on the lights again and I found myself overwhelmed at what I had just achieved. I remember riding back on a rising tide of emotion and hugging my dad who was waiting with Luca in the winner's enclosure. By now I was 'in the zone' and brimming with confidence as I walked out to ride Shamshir in the Brent Walker Mile. We cruised into the straight close behind the leaders, took up the running just over a furlong out and galloped home to a comfortable success. What a day! Come on me!

There was just time for some interviews and a quick shower before I rushed off to catch a flight to Canada to ride Shellac for Luca in a valuable race in Toronto the next day. I was still somewhere up on the ceiling and drove the poor man sitting next to me on the plane right round the bend as I chatted non-stop about my famous double earlier in the afternoon. If he'd been hoping to catch up on his sleep he was out of luck because I didn't stop talking for the entire journey. By the time we landed he must have been suffering from a serious case of earache. Shellac came agonizingly close to completing an unforgettable weekend for me but in the end we were beaten a nose.

Early in October stories began to circulate that the old master Lester Piggott was planning a remarkable comeback less than a month before his fifty-fifth birthday. It was a sensation at the time, though at first I didn't quite share the sense of euphoria that he was to ride again after an absence of five years. I knew from what my father had told me that Lester was a phenomenon, but while I had always dreamed of riding against him I felt it was a little sad that he returned to racing merely to combat boredom. I wasn't alone in feeling a little disappointed because he couldn't possibly look like the peerless Piggott of the sixties and seventies.

One thing is for sure, you won't catch me still working as a jockey in my fifties. But riding was like a drug to Lester and he couldn't shake it out of his system. You had to wonder if the magic was still there at his age. We didn't have to wait long for the first success of his second career, at Chepstow, on Nicholas trained by his wife Susan. Just to show it wasn't a fluke he completed a double in the next race on Shining Jewel.

Clearly my misgivings were unfounded. Shortly afterwards Lester flew to America on Concorde for the Breeders' Cup meeting at Belmont Park. Anxious that his prison sentence for tax evasion could prevent him entering the country, he told immigration officials in New York that the purpose of his visit was pleasure. It looked much more like business to me as the old gunslinger snatched a stunning late victory on Royal Academy in the Breeders' Cup mile on the twelfth day of his comeback.

In as dramatic finish as you will ever see, all his old qualities of strength, timing and determination were on display once more as he lifted Royal Academy over the line a head in front of Itsallgreektome. The magic was certainly there that night. It was a breathtaking performance, madness really. I had an arm-chair view of it all from the back of Markofdistinction who failed for some reason to deliver his usual blistering finish. Afterwards Lester barely spoke a word as he changed. He just had a big smile of satisfaction on his face, then every now and then he broke into a giggle. Oh yes, you could tell he was pleased and I was glad to be part of it even though at that stage I couldn't see how I could ever win a Breeders' Cup race.

As Luca had sent over a small raiding party with Markofdistinction, I stayed on for another week camped in the suite of a smart hotel in downtown New York. I felt it was a lifestyle to which I could easily become accustomed, until I received some timely advice from the trainer. It all started when I hired a limousine, painted the town red with some friends and then invited them all back to continue the party in my suite. We were way over the top and completely trashed the place.

When I woke up the next morning I had a massive love-bite

on my neck and the place looked like the pits of the world, so I wore the collar on my coat turned up to try to hide the tell-tale marks from my night of passion while I rode out. Luca gave me an old-fashioned look before warning me that the owner of a horse I was due to ride later that day would be changing in my suite before racing. That was fine with me because I assumed that room service would have tidied everything up by then.

It was a big mistake because the suite was untouched. Worse still, I rode a lousy race on the horse, got boxed in and finished fifth hard on the bridle without getting a run. So the owner had double cause for complaint. Afterwards Luca pulled me aside to deliver a short, sharp lecture. 'Frankie, one lesson you have to learn is that whenever you party you must always clean up properly afterwards.'

Despite the fiasco at the hotel it had been a lucrative week and the best was yet to come. Before I returned home for the dying embers of the flat season I received a priceless lesson in the art of race riding from a legendary craftsman.

ten

Too Big For My Boots

Angel Cordero was my idea of the perfect jockey from the moment I watched spellbound as he rode to victory on Luca's filly Embla in the Cheveley Park Stakes at Newmarket in October 1985. There was something about him in the saddle that demanded your attention. He was strong, streamlined, wonderfully effective and showed just what he could do on a rare visit to England by beating Pat Eddery on Kingscote into second place in a thrilling finish. Early on, Embla was outpaced. Angel sat quietly towards the rear, waiting with clinical patience, keeping her balanced and conserving energy before launching her with a blistering late run which took them into the lead just before the line.

Later, during my winters in California, I had a chance to study him at first hand. There were days at Santa Anita where he made his rivals look inadequate when in reality they were all very good. He was in his late forties by then, in the evening of his career, but I thought he was a genius. He seemed to have the aerodynamics of riding down to a fine art, crouching very low on a horse's back to reduce wind resistance to a minimum.

Angel was so powerful that he could lift a horse in a way few, if any, could match. I loved his sparkling personality, too. He had the charisma only great sportsmen possess and was a natural entertainer. Even then I could see a bit of myself mirrored in him. I definitely resemble him in some ways, so you imagine how I felt when Angel invited Luca and myself to dinner at his house in New York after the Breeders' Cup.

Just for once I tried to listen instead of doing all the talking. He spoke of the benefits of riding with just his toes in the stirrups in contrast to the traditional European method of putting both feet into the irons as far as they could go. His style, he suggested, gave you more feeling and balance and when I look back he was absolutely right. After dinner, with the minimum of prompting from me, Angel took us to his gym to give a practical demonstration on his own mechanical horse, which was the forerunner of the horse equisizer that dozens of riders use for practice in England today. He showed me what to do, looking smooth and sleek and so stylish, then jumped off and invited me to have a go.

It was a hell of an experience, a bit like going to David Beckham's house for private tuition on how to take free kicks. Of course I made a fool of myself. It felt so strange at first and immediately put a severe strain on the back of my calf muscles but he encouraged me to persevere. From that day I was so determined to copy him but the time wasn't quite right to experiment then.

On my return to England I immediately bought my own

equisizer, which I used for a number of years before passing it on to my young cousin Diego, Sergio's son, who is starting out as a jockey in Italy. Recently I paid for a much more modern version which helps keep my legs and thighs in shape during the quiet spell towards the end of the year when our season is over and I am racing abroad once a week.

By the end of the 1990 I surpassed all my expectations by finishing fourth in the jockey's table with 141 winners. It was the year that Pat Eddery became the first jockey since 1952 to ride a double century. He ended up out of sight over the horizon with a total of 209. Pat and the others in front of me, Willie Carson and Steve Cauthen, were acknowledged masters and seemed to me to be in a different league. I couldn't see how I could ever be champion jockey while they were still around. It was a sobering thought as I departed for the Californian sunshine for the fourth successive winter.

This time my US agent Bob Meldahl organised such a decent spread of rides in California that I ended up with six winners in a few short weeks, including Free At Last, trained by Neil Drysdale, in a $100,000 race at Bay Meadows. The next day I picked up a $50,000 contest at Arizona Park. I was also delighted to repay Richard Cross for all his support by winning a $60,000 event for him at Santa Anita. I remained in California until the end of the Hollywood Park season on 24 December, spent Christmas Day in America, then flew to Tuscany for a three-week holiday with my family.

Shortly before Christmas, news broke that the Aga Khan was removing all his horses from training in England in protest against the doping procedures which had led to his filly Aliysa, trained by Michael Stoute, being disqualified on a technicality months after winning the previous year's Oaks at Epsom. At a stroke the heart of the yard was torn out and Luca lost 45 of his best horses. It was a devastating blow that would have damaging consequences for everyone in the Cumani team, not least the stable jockey. It was a bit like losing half the players in your football team. Maybe you can find replacements over a period of time but they may not be so good.

The situation played on my mind over the winter, though there was a welcome diversion when I was invited to be a guest on the popular BBC TV programme Question of Sport. I teamed up with Ian Botham and snooker legend Steve Davis against Bill Beaumont, the England goalkeeper Chris Woods and Kay Morley, the Commonwealth hurdles champion. At first I was nervous of showing myself up but then I relaxed after a couple of drinks in the hospitality lounge with Ian, a larger than life character, who made me very welcome. It also helped that someone tipped me off that one of my picture questions would be footage of my dad winning the 1977 Irish Guineas on Pampapaul in a tight finish with Lester Piggott on The Minstrel. It was great fun working alongside Ian and the quizmaster David Coleman, but when the programme was shown a month later I was surprised to see how much of our banter was cut out.

That spring I was also hired to work in the Guinness hospitality area at the Cheltenham Festival, scene of that never to be forgotten triumph by Dawn Run back in 1986. It was my first visit to the Festival and I loved it – the atmosphere, the passion and the top-quality racing which has so much in common with Royal Ascot.

Once the new flat season was under way in March it was obvious that Luca didn't have the same ammunition as in previous years. I sensed it would be a struggle to match my score of the previous season and unfortunately I was right. By the end of June I'd mustered a modest score of 28 winners and we kept missing out in the races that mattered most. I couldn't even find a ride in the Derby that year. It was supposed to be the greatest race of all and I still hadn't taken part in it. Three days later I did finish second in the Oaks – the fillies' Classic – on Shamshir, but the winner Jet Ski Lady beat us by the best part of a hundred yards and was already on her way back to Ireland by the time we crossed the line.

Things began to improve the following month when Mattie took a call booking me for a horse that on all known form had no chance in the German Derby. Temporal was considered to be by far the worst of four horses fielded by the Cologne trainer Bruno Schutz. On the day I was warned that Temporal was not a straightforward ride. Nor, I was told, did anything else in the race have a prayer against the raging hot favourite Lomitas, the superstar of German racing and one of the best horses seen there for years. So much for the form book.

I had a decent run on Temporal until we were pushed a bit wide by Michael Roberts on Leone coming into the straight – but this worked to our advantage because the going was better there. Lomitas set sail for home two furlongs out, looking all over the winner until I came sweeping past on Temporal and beat him by half a length. The German crowd was stunned by the favourite's defeat and Temporal paid a huge dividend on the Tote. I was beside myself with delight at finally winning my first Derby.

My percentage of the first prize of £153,114 would pay for a few bills and there was an extra bonus when I discovered that the jockey's prize included a methuselah of champagne, the equivalent of eight bottles. The hardest task of the day was carrying it back to my hotel room. The horse's owner also pressed a bundle of notes into the hand of Bruno Schutz's son Andreas before pointing us in the direction of the nightclubs in Hamburg. We didn't need a second invitation.

We started off in the red-light district, where I remember jumping through an open window to take a closer look at what was on offer, and it was daylight when we finally staggered to bed back at the hotel. There was still time for a short nap before my flight to England but I was so tired I fell into a deep sleep. When I woke up the plane had gone and so, apparently, had my chance of riding for Luca at Leicester that day. In a state of panic I rang Neil Foreman, a pilot who used to fly us around from meeting to meeting, and explained my predicament. He immediately agreed to fly over from Newmarket to Hamburg, collect me and deposit me at Leicester in time to ride in the third race at 3.15. We made it, too, though in the frantic scramble to the airport I left behind my priceless bottle of bubbly. Temporal was never so good again but I will never forget him. When we met Lomitas once more at Baden-Baden he beat us easily by seven lengths.

Second Set was probably Luca's best horse that year. He won twice before just failing against Marju at Royal Ascot, but then excelled at Goodwood where we beat the 1,000 Guineas winner Shadayid decisively in the Group 1 Sussex Stakes. An hour later we also took the Tote Gold Trophy with the heavily backed favourite Tidemark. For the Cumani stable that afternoon was the highlight of the season.

At the end of August, with a little bit of subterfuge, I managed to win the race named after me at Chepstow to mark my century there twelve months earlier. Not many teenagers are honoured with their own race. There were six meetings that day but I twisted Luca's arm to send me there, and once the conditions of entry were known I started working on him to make sure he provided a suitable mount for me. The one he chose was an improving filly called Mata Cara who carried me to a comfortable success.

All season Mattie beavered away on my behalf, trying to find me a fresh source of winners but the entire year was a struggle. It was quite a shock because things had come easily up to then. Suddenly I was discovering that it is a tough world out there. For almost three years, while I was on my way up the ladder, it had been success all the way without a serious setback.

It was a bit like going from nought to 100 in the car without a pause. I did it without thinking, or any feeling. Things just seemed to happen for me. Now the dice had begun to roll against me and I woke up to the fact that I'd been spoiled. I was still a teenager and perhaps I was becoming too big for my boots. But once you become used to dining at the top table it's not much fun living on little more than scraps.

Late in October, Second Set was another big disappointment in the Breeders' Cup Mile at Churchill Downs which was dominated by Opening Verse, but we didn't leave empty-handed. I won a valuable handicap on Shaima for Luca at Belmont Park, and also finished second the following day on Tidemark. My week-long stay in America was a welcome diversion from the reality at home. When the British season came to a soggy end at Doncaster in November, I'd slipped down the pecking order to seventh in the jockeys' table with 94 winners. Luca, too, inevitably had dropped down the trainers' table from the lofty perch that he'd inhabited twelve months earlier. It hadn't been a good year for either of us, and I couldn't see much hope of things improving in the next twelve months.

That November I finally broke my duck in France. It came in deep mud at Saint-Cloud on Susurration, a four-year-old filly trained by John Gosden who was beginning to provide me with a few winners. In the taxi on the way back to the airport I couldn't sit still for a moment as I provided John with endless slow-motion replays of my brilliance. My spirits were further boosted when the late Robert Sangster came calling. He'd enjoyed a wonderful run of success as an owner in a golden association with the Irish master Vincent O'Brien and Lester Piggott. More recently he'd bought the historic training estate at Manton in Wiltshire. In the season that had just ended it was clear that Robert had unearthed another exceptional two-year-old colt in Rodrigo de Triano, who was in the hands of his new trainer Peter Chapple-Hyam at Manton. The horse was deservedly the winter favourite for the following year's Guineas after victories which included the Champagne Stakes at Doncaster and the Middle Park Stakes at Newmarket.

Robert was keen to take a second claim on me after Luca, but when we spoke it soon became clear that he wouldn't let me ride either Rodrigo de Triano or his unbeaten filly Musicale, trained by Henry Cecil. He explained that he wanted to remain faithful to Willie Carson who had partnered Rodrigo in his final two juvenile races. As for Musicale, the trainer preferred to use his own stable jockey.

Naturally I was keen to join forces with Robert who was always likely to produce further stars from the ranks of his homebred horses. But I couldn't see the point of signing up for him if his two stars were not included in the package. He then agreed that I *could* ride Rodrigo in the next year's 2,000 Guineas if, as seemed likely, Willie Carson was not available.

That still wasn't good enough for me. I wanted to ride them all without any reservations on his part or we did not have a deal, so we agreed to differ. For me it was a case of all or nothing. I was good friends with Robert, one of the nicest and most genuine men in racing. Before his recent death we were closer than ever, but he and Lester Piggott had been an item for so many years that I felt he might be tempted to jock me off Rodrigo at some point in favour of Lester. And of course it was Lester who won the Guineas on Rodrigo de Triano the following spring when Willie Carson was required for

Muhtarram by his owner Sheikh Hamdan, the man who retained him. But I have no regrets at turning Robert down even though in different circumstances Rodrigo de Triano might well have been my first Classic winner in England.

The knowledge that one of Europe's principal owners was interested in hiring me helped widen my horizons at the end of a difficult season. Nothing in racing lasts forever and for the first time since I came to Newmarket I began to believe that it might make sense to part company with Luca at some stage in the future. You never know what is around the corner in this game, but if you want to be the top gun you need the best horses to provide the ammunition.

Perhaps I was already searching restlessly for new challenges. Whatever the reason, I decided not to return that winter to California which had provided such a valuable education for me over the previous four years. Instead I accepted a one-month contract from the Hong Kong Jockey Club. My first visit there opened my eyes to the opportunities in the colony. I managed four wins from twenty-five rides, hardly a brilliant start. I also earned an early black mark with a $100 fine for chewing gum during a stewards' inquiry! The next day the story was splashed over a quarter of a page in the local paper – they must have been short of news. Even so, I loved the buzz of Hong Kong, the style of the racing and the frantic pace of the night life. I would definitely be back.

While I was there I also took the chance to experiment by riding with my toes in the irons in the way that Angel Cordero had shown me. I was much too shy to try it at home, but I assumed nobody would be watching me in the mornings in Hong Kong. So I eventually worked up to ten horses a day with my toes in the irons. That's how it started.

At first it was absolute agony with the pain sharpest in the backs of my calves. It was killing me. I knew I had to persevere through the worst of the pain, but more than once I was tempted to give it all up and go back to the method I knew and trusted. Soon I began to developed thicker muscles on my calves and an extra, unexpected lump of muscle on top of my feet. I have two there that shouldn't exist.

Next, I discovered that my new riding position led to a different rhythm through a race. When you ride with your feet fully in the irons your sense of balance is very much on the horse's mouth. In America where everyone rides with just their toes in the stirrup irons, and the saddles are well forward, they jump from the gate and go, so jockeys aren't pulling on their horse's mouths.

Over the next couple of years I tried to combine the best of both worlds and eventually came up with my own well-rehearsed technique. When I used to come back from America in the spring I'd find that every horse I sat on wanted to run away with me. They were all pulling like hell. That's when I realised I had to develop my style into something that was effective and streamlined. If you sit too low on a horse too early in a race all they want to do is take off with you. So I decided to ride the English way in the first half of a race to keep the horse relaxed, and then switch to a lower, tighter American crouch in the second half of the race. All the time

I had in the back of my mind my father's advice to make an effort to look good on horseback. Looks do count.

Aerodynamics come into it, too. It's simple really. If you stand up on a motorbike or scooter you obviously slow it down a fraction. When I started as an apprentice, American jockeys tended to look more neat and economical. In contrast English riders flapped around more in a finish and offered a lot more wind resistance. Now nearly all the jockeys in England have switched to riding with just their toes in the irons.

There was an unexpected bonus in March when I was invited to Japan for the young jockeys' world championship staged at Nakayama. Others invited included Corey Nakatani, Johnny Murtagh and the local hero Yutaka Take who have all gone on to make it at the very top. I took Colin Rate rate with me as my agent though he seemed to fancy the role of minder. After a series of races held on the Sunday I was delighted to emerge as the overall winner. Nothing happens too quickly in Japan. We remained at the track after racing, attended a buffet dinner, and listened politely over a few glasses of champagne to endless speeches before every rider involved was presented with a variety of presents such as cameras, watches, jackets and key rings. My reward as outright winner was £20,000 in cash.

By the time we clambered into the coach for the long trip back to our hotel we were ready to party all night. As the coach began to move off I jumped onto the back seat, dropped my trousers and gave the waving spectators at the course a well rehearsed Dettori moon through the rear window. Back at the hotel I was horrified to discover that I had lost the £20,000

I had been given in an envelope a few hours earlier. Our interpreter Yoko came to the rescue. She rushed back to the bus station, searched our coach and found my money lying on the back seat.

Twelve months later I returned to Japan with Colin to win the young jockeys' championship again from a group that included the whippet-thin Irishman Richard Hughes who was a right laugh. This time I held on securely to the money but, encouraged by Colin, I bared my backside once more as we left the track in the coach. My gesture clearly had more of an impact than I realized at the time. When I flew to Japan a few years later with my wife Catherine we attended a reception the night before the Japan Cup. As we were leaving a racing official came up to us, pulled me aside, and with a straight face begged me not to attempt the treble. At first I struggled to understand what he was suggesting. Then the penny dropped. I have rarely been so embarrassed.

eleven

Giving in to Temptation

Nineteen ninety-two would turn out to be my final year as stable jockey to Luca Cumani, though I didn't know that at the start of the season. It wasn't a happy partnership, partly because we were seriously short of decent horses and winners. Also, I was distracted more and more by the delights of night life that have been the undoing of so many gifted young sportsmen. When you have bundles of money in your pocket and enjoy partying it is hard to sit at home with a cup of carrot juice and a lettuce leaf, when all your friends seem to be out on the town until the early hours.

Often, too, I freely admit, I gave in to temptation and headed out for a few drinks and a bit of entertainment. It's not my style to lock myself away, on my own, like a monk. Life is not a dress-rehearsal. It would take me a couple more years before I came to a sensible balance between the self-denial that is a necessary part of a jockey's life and the need to let off a bit of steam.

By now I was living in a flat at the top of the town near the swimming pool. It was a natural move for someone who wanted a bit more independence. I'd outstayed my welcome by two and a half years with Bernice Emanuel, who had generously given me a room in her house at such short notice. I sensed there were times when I tested her patience to the limit. Nor could I expect to sneak a girlfriend up the stairs to my room late at night without her asking questions.

Having my own flat made life easier for both of us. It helped that my previous landlady, Val Sykes, came in most mornings to clean up and tidy behind me. Her greatest complaint was that the flat was always too hot – for the good reason that I kept the central heating going full blast. It was something she had to accept because I've never been able to deal with the cold in Newmarket, which can seem like one of the bleakest places in the world in the spring, let alone the depths of winter.

Colin Rate stayed at the flat from time to time and looked after it for me when I was abroad. He vetted all my girlfriends and was never slow to voice his opinion on their suitability. I remember falling for one particular girl in a big way. The next morning over breakfast I confided: 'This is the one. For the first time I am *definitely* in love.' He looked at me with pity in his eyes. 'Don't be so daft lad. She's not for you. I'll tell you when you are in love!'

I'd waited a long time for my chance to ride in the Epsom Derby. It finally came on a colt called Pollen Count, who looked the part when showing courage and tenacity in taking the Thresher Classic Trial at Sandown, partnered by Steve Cauthen. When Steve picked another horse for Epsom, John Gosden booked me for Pollen Count. It was strange to be there on the big day because, up to then, I usually watched the Derby on television from Yarmouth or some other distant meeting.

The build-up to my debut in the Derby seemed to last for hours, but the race itself proved to be a big let down with Pollen Count trailing in with only two behind him. It was not a great start and I'm sorry to say that I still haven't had many memorable rides in the Derby. Pollen Count pulled so hard in the early stages that we led for a couple of furlongs, but he was on the retreat by the time we got to the bottom of the hill and turned for home.

Once again my campaign was rescued by an unexpected Derby winner abroad from an unusual source. Robert Nataf, a French bloodstock agent whose father had been friendly with mine, rang to ask what I was doing on the Sunday after Epsom. When I explained that I was planning a rare day off he urged me to fly over to Paris to ride an outsider called Polytain in the French Derby at the beautiful Chantilly racecourse. The horse had been bought out of a claiming race in the spring (runners in a claiming race are available for anyone to buy for a few minutes after the race). He had then shown improved form in better company and was absolutely flying at home. There was a strong Italian connection which explained my booking. Polytain was trained in France by Antonio Spanu, originally from Sardinia, and was owned by the glamorous wife of a Paris-based Italian called Bruno Houillion. Since the horse was dismissed as a no-hoper and all the leading French riders were unavailable, they turned at the eleventh hour to me.

For a horse said to have no possible chance Polytain gave me a terrific feel on the way to the start. I was very impressed. After everything that had happened over the previous year or more I didn't really believe in anything, but I had a good feeling about this horse as we waited to enter the stalls and told Steve Cauthen so. He thought I was mad.

We jumped out handily and sat sixth on the rail as we galloped past the Chateau. Turning for home I encouraged him to edge closer to the leaders. When I pulled him out to challenge one and a half furlongs out he took off with me, swept to the front with his ears pricked – the sign of a keen horse – and despite edging right-handed easily held the late thrust of Marignan.

Immediately a right old Italian celebration began in the winner's enclosure. There was nothing polite or demure as we all hugged and kissed and shrieked our delight. It was all the better for being so unexpected. Freddie Head, the rider of the fourth, Johann Quatz, lodged an objection claiming that he had to check his mount for a few strides when we passed him and swerved towards the running rail. The stewards, sensible fellows, chose to take no action.

Polytain paid 37–1 on the French Tote but he travelled like a champion throughout and won without a semblance of a fluke. Bruno Houillion and his wife landed some decent bets. They also collected upwards of £250,000 in prize money, which was a superb return on the handful of francs they had paid for him out of the claiming race. Flushed with success, Bruno promised me his gold Rolex watch as a present. I pinched it anyway before he changed his mind. I was somewhere up on the ceiling by then. The party lasted long into the night in Paris, but I missed the fun as I had to return to England in a private plane with a group of English trainers, jockeys and racing managers. They weren't best pleased when I held them up for half an hour, nor that I kept jumping up in the coach shouting 'I've won the Derby. I've won the ————ing Derby'.

Until that weekend I had an empty feeling at the way my career was going. I was beginning to fear that I'd soon be forgotten. I filled the void with Polytain. That's why I will remember him forever, but just like Temporal a year earlier in Germany, Polytain's display in the Derby defied the evidence of the form book. In his subsequent races with me he ran like an old man walking uphill in tight boots.

So to Royal Ascot, where I survived an attempt to savage me on the way to winning the Gold Cup on one of my favourite horses Drum Taps. He was trained by William Huntingdon, a solid supporter in my early days as a jockey. Drum Taps was already six by the time he struck gold at the Royal meeting, a hardened campaigner who'd raced in England at two, then moved to America for eighteen months before returning to this country. That year he was at the peak of his powers as we scooped decent prizes in Milan and then Sandown on the way to Ascot, where our chief rival was an old adversary, Arcadian Heights.

Races like the Gold Cup make the Royal meeting unique, though two and a half miles is a hell of a long way on the flat. The key is to switch your horse off as soon as possible so that you can conserve his energy for the end of the race. Drum Taps settled nicely for me at first, but by the time we reached the straight he was becoming impatient to go so I let him run. The next moment I sensed another horse coming alongside me and heard a shout of warning from his jockey Walter Swinburn. At the time I assumed he was upset that I'd pulled out in front of him. Far from it.

His mount Arcadian Heights had a well-known appetite for human flesh. Once at Newmarket he bit off the top of David Loder's little finger in the days when he was working as assistant to Geoff Wragg. Now he tried to take a chunk out of my backside as he came to challenge. Luckily the moment of danger passed as Drum Taps quickened away from him in the final furlong to win by two lengths. Afterwards the stewards ordered that Arcadian Heights should wear a net muzzle in future races.

Shortly after Royal Ascot, Pat Eddery set the racing world buzzing with seven winners in one day. I thought it was an amazing feat – and but for me it would have been eight. He kicked off with a treble in the afternoon at Newmarket and looked like winning a fourth on Anne Bonny until I caught him in the final furlong with a late run on Barford Lad. Pat then took to the skies in his own plane and, though he missed the first three races at Newcastle's evening meeting, he swiftly made amends by winning the last four. Seven in one day! It had never been done before in this country and I doubted that it would ever be done again.

That summer my father decided to retire after a splendid career which yielded 3800 winners. It was forced on him by an old back injury. He has hardly sat on a horse since but is still incredibly fit for his age. When Dad nominated his final day in Milan in September, Luca entered into the spirit of things by sending over a team of four horses for him to ride. Two of them won. Luca's father Sergio had given my dad his big break in racing as an apprentice, and the pair eventually became the most dominant force in Italian racing. It was an emotional farewell for my dad. For thirty years he'd been going to the races almost every day. Then, suddenly, it was all over. He packed his bag for the final time and left San Siro with a heavy heart. I badly wanted to be there to support him but was needed by Luca at Longchamp.

Soon I made my debut over hurdles at Chepstow in an annual contest between the flat jockeys and the jumps boys. I can safely say it wasn't my finest hour. Once I heard that I was riding Gold Medal for Martin Pipe, the record-breaking trainer, I took the precaution of ringing up Richard Dunwoody for some much needed advice. 'Look Woody, to tell you the truth, I haven't a clue because I've never jumped a thing in my life. What do I do?' I asked him.

He sounded amused as he suggested that popping over a few flights of hurdles at Chepstow would be no more arduous than my experience of horses jumping the paths at Brighton and other courses. He stressed that all I had to do was make sure Gold Medal had a decent view of every hurdle. The rest, he suggested, would come naturally when I saw a stride. Anyway, he concluded, the horse must be an ideal schoolmaster because he'd won last time out, ridden by an unknown amateur.

George Duffield was also riding for Pipe, who gave the pair of us endless instructions before racing. George had been a hunting man for years and also schooled point-to-pointers for his wife. So when Pipe asked if we had experience of jumping I didn't have the courage to tell him that I should be wearing large, distinctive L plates. Instead I nodded cheerfully as though it was the most natural thing in the world. Inside, however, I was feeling anything but cheerful.

Just to be cool I rode to the start with my knees under the chin. The plan was to drop my leathers to a sensible length once I got there, but the joke was on me when I discovered that the stirrups I was using would only go down two holes. Nobody in their right mind rides as short over hurdles as I was forced to do on my debut, but it was too late to do anything about it. To compensate for our inexperience over jumps, all the flat jockeys were allowed to claim a 7 pound weight allowance. The way I felt at that moment, 27 pounds would not have been enough to close the gap.

The tapes rose and Gold Medal shot off at a million miles an hour. We had a clear lead as he approached the first flight like a runaway car. I had no control whatsoever and had never been so frightened. Talk about a white knuckle ride! I was a total passenger. We jumped the first hurdle flat out with my eyes closed. Then, before I knew it, the next flight was looming up at a rate of knots. We popped over that fine and then, for the first time, I foolishly began to relax.

Going to the third I entered into the spirit of things by giving Gold Medal a slap down the neck a few strides off the hurdle.

He took off much too soon, launched himself like a rocket, landed on his neck and almost shot me out of the side door. By now the others had closed up so I called out to Woody 'What am I doing wrong?'

He told me to sit further back and to try to keep my legs out in front of me. It seemed to work because we crossed the next two flights without mishap, but by now horse and rider were beginning to tire. Soon afterwards, flat jockey Michael Hills came sweeping past on Silver Age followed swiftly by jump jockeys Brendan Powell on Flashthecash and the champion Peter Scudamore on Chiasso Forte. Somehow Gold Medal clambered over the final hurdle without dislodging me, before struggling home a weary fourth. The horse was well named because I would give a gold medal without hesitation to every jump jockey in the country. They really do earn their money every time they go out to ride.

Later, as we changed, I asked Richard what stride he had been talking about because I'd been looking in vain for it throughout the race. He replied that I'd had my eyes shut most of the time and he was right. Chepstow tried to lure me back again the following year but the promise of the crown jewels wouldn't have tempted me to have another go over hurdles. I was definitely unavailable when they called.

I thought I was King Kong in those days. One night at a fund-raising evening at a club with girls swarming all over the place, I made sure I was noticed by bidding for a painting of the great Derby winner Nijinsky, signed by Lester Piggott. It was knocked down to me for £1700. This was just an ego trip really, to show that I was a big shot. The next day I collected the painting and saw to my dismay that the horse in it wasn't Nijinsky, a handsome bay, but a washy chestnut with a big white face. I'd been done!

Although Luca was badly short of stars that year, he unveiled a very exciting prospect called Barathea who impressed me greatly by the manner in which he won his maiden at Newmarket at the start of October. Luca seldom winds up his two-year-olds first time out, so plenty were preferred to him in the betting market. When I asked him, Barathea quickened up like a top-class horse and won without knowing he'd had a race. A fortnight later he confirmed the promise of that debut with a spirited victory in the Houghton Stakes, a traditional late-season trial at Newmarket that has thrown up a lot of outstanding horses down the years.

In time Barathea proved to be right up there with the best of them. He was a horse to take home and dream about. But someone else would be sharing the glory with him because I was about to enter the most turbulent year of my life.

twelve

Throwing it All Away

When the British 1992 flat racing season reached its muddy conclusion early in November, I was in Milan enjoying a welcome big race double for Luca at San Siro on Only Royale and Inner City. They were to be our last successes together for some time. Previously hidden cracks had begun to emerge in our relationship – and although nothing was said I knew instinctively that it was time for me to move on in search of a freedom I could never achieve if I remained working for Luca. Once again, without the considerable firepower previously provided by the Aga Khan, we hadn't had the greatest of seasons. In the circumstances my final score of 101 was a reasonable return which left me seventh in the jockey's list once more.

It wasn't simply that we were both missing out at the highest level, more perhaps that Luca was still very much the boss in our partnership. I'd worked for him for almost eight years. Once I'd been the naughty new kid, the one in the yard who was always in trouble. Eventually I became his stable jockey but somehow we both failed to adjust to my new status.

I wasn't sure what I was searching for, but I did know beyond any doubt that I had to try my luck elsewhere. Unless I raised my sights I would never cross the gulf which still separated me from the greatest riders in the world. Most other jockeys would probably have settled for what I was preparing to throw away. Even with a reduced team Luca Cumani was still one of the country's best trainers – astute, hard-working and ambitious. In a sense I'd achieved everything I ever wanted as his first jockey, but I didn't realise it at the time, wasn't happy with the way things were going, and wasn't enjoying the job. So I had to go.

Later in the year I flew to Hong Kong, where I had once again accepted a one-month contract with the HK Jockey Club. No sooner had I arrived than an outbreak of horse sickness forced the authorities to call off racing for the next four weeks! Suddenly I had time on my hands to savour the delights of one of the most vibrant cities in the world. I don't mind admitting I was well and truly seduced by the night life. I was like a runaway train heading downhill, out of control. I remained in Hong Kong for an extended holiday over Christmas and well into the New Year, partying relentlessly and increasingly tempted by the idea of riding there full-time.

Talk about sowing your wild oats! If I'd wanted I could have had more girls than a porn star. I was looked after like a king, with all expenses paid, having the time of my life. Being a playboy came easily to me, let me tell you. Aware that many jockeys had made a fortune in Hong Kong in a few short years, I began to see pound signs in every window. The money was

fantastic, the lifestyle better than anything I'd experienced before, and basing myself there would mean an end to countless long journeys on the A1 to Catterick and all points north.

I had a ball in Hong Kong that winter. I was like a small kid who wanted every toy in the shop. Soon I had an approach from Gary Ng Ting-Keung who'd been training there for a few years. He had some big owners behind him who were keen to sign me up to ride for them the following season, which started in August.

There were long lunches and dinners, I was given a couple of gold watches and the terms we discussed were beyond my wildest dreams – over a quarter of a million pounds over two years. When they began talking telephone numbers over my contract I was hooked. I thought 'Here we go, I'll have a bit of this. I'm not going to be a jockey all my life so I'll take the money.' I saw myself way up there with Michael Jordan, then the best-paid sportsman in the world. If it didn't work out then I'd be able to return to England for a second start two years later.

Stupidly, I couldn't see then that I'd had too much too soon, though it was hard to turn down the money being dangled in front of my eyes when I wasn't getting that much of a retainer from Luca. By the time I was eighteen I'd already done things that many jockeys never achieve, but it all came too quickly for my own good and I made the mistake of thinking I'd cracked it big time. I was seduced by the money, the bright lights and the excitement of it all. Really I was brainwashed into agreeing a contract in Hong Kong.

I talked it over with my dad before deciding anything, but

foolishly neglected to inform Luca of my plans. Basically I was too scared to tell him because I knew for sure how he'd react. I'm no different from anyone else in the way that I duck confrontation. I prefer to wriggle around a problem in the hope that it will go away – but this one wasn't going to disappear. Instead I made things worse by putting off the moment to ring Luca who, my dad warned me, was aware of the rumours and was trying to track me down to discover my intentions.

Then, to my dismay, news of my plans to join forces with Gary Ng leaked out in the papers at the start of February. At that stage I hadn't signed a contract – for the good reason that Gary hadn't yet been given the nod by the HK Jockey Club to retain a stable jockey. Nor had they approved my application to ride there full-time. But once it was out in the open there was no going back. I had nowhere to hide.

At the same time a game of musical chairs was taking place among the leading jockeys in Britain, set off by Steve Cauthen's decision to end his role as Sheikh Mohammed's jockey and return home to America. Michael Kinane was the obvious choice to succeed him, but he preferred to remain in Ireland. So the Sheikh's advisers turned to Michael Roberts who had just become champion for the first time in Britain.

Against this background of change and uncertainty, I finally returned to England in March for my showdown with Luca. It was every bit as difficult as I expected. I walked into his office, feeling a sense of guilt, and told him straight away that whatever he said wouldn't change my mind. I was set on a new life in Hong Kong starting in the late summer.

Luca went ballistic. I knew what was coming but was still surprised by the ferocity of his anger. He pointed out my shortcomings, told me exactly what he thought of me, and kept repeating that I was throwing my life away. For perhaps five minutes he tried to persuade me to reconsider. Hong Kong, he insisted, was for jockeys at the other end of the rainbow. I was much too young to be going there full-time. Once he realized he was wasting his breath he brought the interview to an abrupt halt.

'I never want to see you again', he told me as I left. I didn't doubt that he meant it. I'd been clinging to the hope that at least I could continue to ride for him in the next few months before I headed for Hong Kong. That was no longer an option. Within days I heard that Ray Cochrane would be rejoining Luca as first jockey. One door had been slammed in my face. Now I had to rely on my new challenge with Gary Ng being as rewarding as I'd been led to believe. But that wouldn't start until late summer and it still had to be passed by the HK Jockey Club.

My spirits lifted briefly when I won the young jockeys' world championship in Japan for the second year. Then it was back to the cold reality of life as a freelance once the new season flickered into life at Doncaster late in March. Most trainers had finalised their riding arrangements months before, so it was a case of my agent Mattie ringing round looking for spares while I tried to establish new contacts.

The next few weeks were a nightmare. I started to hear on the grapevine that my deal with Gary Ng wouldn't be given the seal of approval by the HK Jockey Club. Theirs has always been one of the strictest regimes in racing. One slight mistake in a race and you can be put on the sidelines for weeks. What's more, they didn't have to justify their reasons for turning down applications to ride there. Nothing was official yet – but if the rumours were right my shining new career in Hong Kong was over before it had begun!

I began to feel like one of those crazy rowers crossing the Atlantic, except that I was marooned in mid ocean without the benefit of oars. My confidence was shattered and I have never felt so alone. I was up s*** creek: there was just me, myself, and I.

My early-season drought extended well into May. Rides were scarce, winners as rare as snow in the Sahara. Good friends like Ray Cochrane and Bruce Raymond could see that I was miserable and did their best to pump me up. But a patient needs to take his medicine to help him turn the corner, and I wasn't helping myself. Where once I wore a suit to the races, I was turning up at the last minute in trainers and tracksuit, showing all the signs of not giving a damn. Then, as often as not, I would be out clubbing at night, mixing with people who wouldn't worry one jot if I was late for work the next day. I was on a dangerous downward spiral, confused, unhappy and uncertain where it would lead. First I lost my job. Then I lost my direction.

If I ran into Luca at the races we passed by like strangers, heads down, not speaking. He, too, was enduring a shocking start to the season. David Loder, fiercely ambitious, was the newest trainer in town. I started riding out for him and he provided me with a handful of winners. Clive Brittain, William Huntingdon and his brother-in-law Ian Balding were other loyal allies at this difficult time. Reg Hollinshead was another supporter. Even so my confidence was at an all-time low.

The season was already more than a month old and all I had to show for it was three winners, two of them on the all-weather track at Southwell. Then matters improved at Newbury in mid April. I kicked off by landing the Group 3 John Porter Stakes on the 25–1 shot Linpac West. I also took the following race, the Greenham, on Inchinor for Roger Charlton. Then in the Queen's colours I completed a rapid treble on Tissisat, trained by Ian Balding, in the Ladbrokes Spring Cup. A second Royal runner, Talent, ridden by Alan Munro, finished out of the money in the same race. Afterwards Alan and I posed in our silks with Her Majesty with Ladbrokes PR man Mike Dillon beaming alongside looking for all the world as if he was the Royal racing manager.

It is amazing what a few winners can do for you. Half an hour later I jumped on Clouded Elegance's back in the paddock before the next race fully expecting to triumph on him, too! He finished second, but I ended the day with a fourth success on Winged Victory. As I headed home to Newmarket that night I dared to believe that my fortunes had finally taken a turn for the better. Then the sky fell in.

thirteen

Arrested with Cocaine in My Pocket

Ever since I became an Arsenal fan I'd dreamed of supporting them at Wembley in a Cup Final. My chance arrived the day after my much needed four-timer at Newbury. Arsenal were playing Sheffield Wednesday in the final of the Coca-Cola Cup. A party of us from Newmarket had managed to get some tickets and we set off in a minibus piled high with cases of beer. Colin and I painted our faces red and white in the colours of Arsenal and had already worked our way through several cans of beer by the time we were dropped off near Wembley.

Then it was into the nearest pub for a few more drinks, so I was absolutely on fire by the time the players ran onto the pitch. Watching a Cup Final is one of the great treats of sport, especially when your team is winning. Arsenal slammed Wednesday 3–1 in a style which gave me a buzz that lasted for several hours.

We found our driver and set off back towards Newmarket in high spirits. Then two of the lads decided they wanted to celebrate in style in London, I didn't need much persuading to join them. It was a decision that would have grave consequences for me. We jumped out at a set of traffic lights, found a taxi to take us to the centre of London, and set about painting the town red and white. Drinking beer has never been my style. Towards the end of the evening I was well over the top, totally out of it, as we lived it up in a disco near Oxford Street.

I was in the mood for anything. So when someone came along selling cocaine I was persuaded to buy a tiny amount. Drugs have never been my scene and never will be, but – like a lot of young guys – I experimented without thinking of the consequences. I put the rest of the stuff in my pocket and forgot all about it.

We were fooling around in an alleyway outside the club in Falconberg Mews when a torch was flashed in my face and I found myself looking up at two policemen. Since it was all too obvious that we'd been drinking heavily they began to question us. Then, without warning, we were asked to turn out our pockets. My two pals were clean but I wasn't so lucky.

The moment the search unearthed the wrap of cocaine in my pocket I sobered up pronto. My pals were free to go but I was arrested, loaded into a van and taken to the nearest police station. Already I could see my world crumbling about me. If news of my arrest became public I could be finished. A day earlier I'd ridden a winner for the Queen. Now I feared I was about to become a guest at one of her prisons. I pleaded with the police to let me off but was wasting my breath. They searched me again, took my fingerprints, pressed me to tell them where I had bought the cocaine, and then left me sitting miserably on my own for ages in an interview room.

I was confused and worried to death about what was going to happen next. Would I be carted off to prison? Had I blown my career? Most of all, what would my dad say when he heard how stupid I'd been? Eventually, to my relief, they bailed me, kicked me out, told me to return in three weeks, and left me to find my way home. It was long past midnight, but I managed to find a taxi to take me to Newmarket.

In the morning Colin was shocked, and he wasn't the only one. I *was* totally in the wrong, but I also felt a bit unlucky to be arrested. If only Colin had been there to keep an eye on me! If only I could turn the clock back. But there was hardly time for self-pity as I set off for Nottingham races, where my black mood wasn't improved by a blank day in the saddle. I was tired from lack of sleep, depressed, uncertain what to do next, and not in any state to do my best. More recently the Jockey Club has brought in random dope testing of jockeys at race meetings. I often wonder if I would have passed a test that day. Somehow I doubt it.

I was still hoping against hope that I could keep my indiscretion a secret. That shows how naive I must have been in those days. On Tuesday morning the red-top tabloids had a field day at my expense. 'Queen's jockey in LSD quiz' was one of the more lurid headlines on the front pages. Believe me it's not fun having your face splashed across the tabloids for the wrong reasons. I felt shame and embarrassment, and even wondered how I could continue. I was waiting like a lame duck for the Jockey Club to become involved. What would they have to say, particularly if I was charged with possessing a class A drug?

My agony continued as I stumbled from one disaster to another. My arrest had certainly put an end to any thoughts of being allowed to kick start my career in Hong Kong in August. I already knew that the authorities there weren't keen to allow me to take up my contract with Gary Ng.

Nor were things much better in England. I slept badly, fearing what might happen on my return to Marylebone police station. Some days I rode in a trance because I was unable to concentrate. Exactly a week after my four-timer at Newbury, I picked up a seven-day ban for careless riding at Leicester. Then I received another suspension of four days, this time for improper use of the whip on the filly Dayflower at Newmarket in the 1,000 Guineas. Everything I touched turned to dust that fortnight. The world was against me. I collected two suspensions, got caught with drugs, lost a job and looked like losing my career. What else could go wrong?

I might have been more cheerful if I'd realised the significance of Dayflower's appearance in England. She was my first mount for what was the forerunner of today's mighty Godolphin operation. The previous year she'd been trained by Henry Cecil for Sheikh Mohammed. Then, in a brave new experiment, Dayflower had been sent home to Dubai to join a new trainer, Sateesh Seemar. Now she was back in England to take on the best three-year-old fillies in the 1,000 Guineas. Since the benefits of wintering horses in the warmth of Dubai weren't yet apparent, Dayflower was allowed to start at 33–1. She stayed on stoutly into fifth place behind Sayyedati in a style which offered promise of better to come over longer trips.

The moment I was dreading – the day when I had to face the music – was rapidly approaching. It helped that my dad flew over from Italy in my time of need. I felt ashamed at letting him down. When he arrived he gave me a good going over and told me I must learn a lesson from what had happened. He also persuaded me to hire a solicitor. Having my dad's support at this time meant everything to me.

After three weeks of torment, I arrived at Marylebone police station with my solicitor on 10 May to answer bail. It was a bit of a shock to discover several of the papparazi already there, waiting to pick over my carcass later in the day. My lawyer's plan of action was to try to limit the damage to a police caution for being in possession of a controlled drug. That way I wouldn't have to go through the anguish of a further court appearance at a later date.

It was a long shot, and for once I did little talking. We gathered in a room where the police read the riot act and explained that if I was charged with an offence which reached court it would seriously affect my chances of getting a visa for working abroad. At times I couldn't be sure which way it would go. I sat there, shaking throughout, like a naughty boy up before the headmaster, knowing that my future as a jockey was being decided.

Then, to my relief, I heard my lawyer agree that I would accept a police caution. The case was closed. I shook hands with my solicitor and thanked him profusely. I also thanked the police as they let me leave through a rear entrance to avoid the waiting photographers. My mood began to lift on the journey back to Newmarket. A police caution was serious enough but it was a slap on the wrist compared to the punishment I'd been expecting over the previous weeks. I hadn't won the fight but at least I'd beaten the count.

Even so, I now knew for sure that my dream of riding in Hong Kong was over, although it was another fortnight before my worst fears were confirmed in a press statement. The HK Jockey Club declared that is wasn't in their interests or mine to have me riding there that season. The door was well and truly closed to me for the moment, though they did hint that they would be prepared to 'entertain a further application from me at a later date'.

For the past few weeks I'd been stalled at the crossroads, wondering which road would be blocked ahead. I was too proud to let my career continue downhill, but turning it round proved incredibly difficult at first. I'd been sowing my wild oats for so long that riding had become something that I just happened to do for a living. The last thing on my mind each day was racing. All I thought about was partying and chasing the girls. That's why I ended up lost, on my own. I must have been crazy to let myself slip so far.

The presence of my parents, in support, at Newmarket certainly helped me turn the corner. They brought some much needed discipline to my life as I got stuck in, started to ride out for as many trainers as wanted me, and buckled down to the business of being a full-time jockey. We lit the fuse on my new career as a freelance jockey but it took an age to ignite.

Two suspensions had left me on the sidelines for eleven consecutive days early in May at the height of the crisis and I didn't know what to expect when I returned to action at Newbury on Friday, 14 May, four days after my police caution. Once again my parents came along with me to the races to support me. I felt embarrassed as I walked into the course, and awkward, too, uncertain what people were going to say to me. I needn't have worried. The boys in the weighing room teased me all afternoon, which was no more than I deserved, but there was also sympathy from the owners and trainers I rode for that day. Perhaps I wasn't such a criminal after all.

There was another shock in store as I set about retrieving my reputation. The following week I should have won on Mt Templeman at Goodwood. He was handily enough placed behind the leaders as the race came to the boil, but while I hesitated Pat Eddery surged past on Ajalan and stole a decisive advantage. Mt Templeman responded gamely enough but the damage was done and we had to settle for second place.

Things happen in a split second during a race. We all ride on instinct. When you see something happen in front of you there isn't time to think what you are going to do. You just react or the moment is lost and probably the race with it. The human brain works very quickly, but if you take time to work out your move it will be too late. The gap will have disappeared. Everything you do is automatic. You just do it. Things develop so suddenly that you have to be sharp, razor sharp. While you are thinking of making a move someone else has done it. That's what happened that day. I was sloppy. Indecision cost me the race. If I had been at the top of my game Mt Templeman would have won.

I'd flown from Newmarket to Goodwood aerodrome with a party including Barney Curley. He didn't say much on the way back after we were diverted to Cambridge, but as we drove away from the landing strip he asked me if I was serious about being a jockey or just playing at it. It was a loaded question if ever I've heard one and it immediately set me on edge. I assured him I was very serious about being a jockey. 'In that case', he suggested, 'come round to see me tonight and we'll have a chat over a game of snooker.'

It was a meeting that altered the course of my life. I listened in shock as Barney laid bare the shortcomings of my lifestyle over the past two years. He had lost his money on Mt Templeman that afternoon but wasn't simply talking through his pocket. He explained that after watching me in action over a period of time, he was convinced that I was riding badly and not concentrating, as though my heart wasn't in it. He added that I was playing around like Jack the Lad, not thinking straight and drifting so aimlessly that I was on the brink of ruining my career.

'You have a great talent but you are throwing it all away', he warned. The late nights and misbehaviour would have to end. I took it all in, admitted my failings, and then over the next hour or two tried to persuade him that I was still as hungry as ever and was prepared to mend my ways. There would be no more late nights. Frankly it was a relief to have a wise old bird like Barney to share my burden. He said that it was up to me to prove to him that I was deadly serious about being a jockey. If I did so, he would do everything in his power to help me. Knowing that I admired his house in Stetchworth, he threw in the added bait that he would sell it to me if I ever became champion jockey. Three years later we completed a deal to swop our houses.

Back in May 1993 my prospects looked bleak until Barney intervened. My heart-to-heart with him set me thinking. It sounded very much as if I was on probation. He'd laid down the law, now it was up to me. Later in the year I learned the vital role he played behind the scenes in persuading John Gosden to give me a chance. John, in turn, would open the door to Sheikh Mohammed's extraordinary Godolphin operation.

First, though, I received a welcome boost when Ian Balding asked if I would be able to ride his speedy mare Lochsong for the rest of the season. Willie Carson had often won on her in the past, but his retainer for Sheikh Hamdan meant that he wasn't always available. Balding and Lochsong's owner-breeder, Jeff Smith, were looking for a jockey who would commit to her long term. Was I interested? It was the start of a raging love affair.

Our first race together at Sandown at the end of May was a bit like the first moves in an old-fashioned courtship. We were just getting to know each other. Lochsong hadn't sparkled in her two races so far that season so I didn't really know what to expect from her in the Temple Stakes. Ian suggested I speak to some of the jockeys who had ridden her before, like Willie and Lester Piggott. I also took advice from Ian, Jeff and his racing manager, Ron Sheather. They all told me something different. Go to the front, save a bit, don't let her go too fast and so on. No wonder I was confused! That's probably why my first ride on Lochsong wasn't my best one. Lochsong took them along for two furlongs before finishing fourth to Paris House. It was a fair run but hardly earth shattering. The evidence, so far, suggested she was no more than a handicapper. I thought maybe that was as good as she was.

I arrived at Epsom on Derby day with only sixteen winners to my name all season. Things needed to improve fast. On the advice of my parents I'd stopped talking to the press to concentrate one-hundred percent on my riding. It certainly paid off that day as I took the opening race on the card on Moccasin Run and then completed a rapid double on the Royal colt Enharmonic in the Diomed Stakes. It doesn't get much better than winning a race for the Queen on Derby day, particularly on the fortieth anniversary of her coronation. She was clearly delighted by the success of her hardy old campaigner, but try as I might I couldn't see myself completing the treble in the Derby on Wolf Prince, a 40–1 outsider trained in America by Michael Dickinson. If it hadn't been for the past reputation of Michael in this country, Wolf Prince would probably have been a 100–1 shot. We finished in the pack way behind Commander in Chief.

Drum Taps then did his bit for my revival by landing the Ascot Gold Cup for the second year in succession. There was a highly embarrassing postscript to the meeting for me on the Saturday. As I was riding quite a lot for the Queen, her racing manager Lord Carnavon came to see me at the start of the week and gave me a long lecture on how I should approach her in the paddock. He added a stylish demonstration of how to bow and touch my cap and insisted that I addressed her as 'Your Majesty'. All week it worked like clockwork.

Saturday was different. The racecourse seemed empty after the huge crowds of the previous days and it never occurred to me that the Queen would be there to watch her disappointing filly Zenith who I was riding in the opening race. There wasn't a soul around as I wandered into the paddock, chatting away to jockeys on each side of me. We were sharing a joke when suddenly they went quiet. I looked round and there was the Queen two paces in front of me. I froze, didn't know what to say. I frantically touched my cap, gave a comical bow and blurted out 'Ow are you?' She responded with a warm smile, opened her arms and replied 'I'm still here.' Then she started laughing, but next to her Lord Carnavon was looking daggers at me. He would have sent me straight to the Tower of London.

I took another crucial step back up the ladder at Sandown's Eclipse meeting early in July. It began with my first victory on Lochsong. She'd appreciated a short break at Jeff's stud and felt stronger at Sandown. After talking at length with Ian Balding I decided to let her go as fast as she could from the start to take full advantage of her explosive early speed. She shot out of the stalls, was in command after a hundred yards and swept home unchallenged. Now we knew how to ride her!

After the breathless excitement of Lochsong, I was just pleased to be involved forty-five minutes later in the Group 1 Coral Eclipse on an Italian raider, Misil, who belied his odds of 25–1 as he failed by the shortest of short heads to overhaul Opera House. Some way back, in fifth place, my old friend Barathea was beginning to become frustrating – after initially justifying my faith in him by winning the Irish 2,000 Guineas in May ridden by Michael Roberts.

After my early-season drought, the rides were coming thick and fast with the help of Mattie Cowing. At last the tide had turned. My parents stayed over for two months in support in their large camper van, parked at the racecourse. We met up most days when my hectic schedule allowed. Although I was still not talking to the press they found nice things to write about me at Goodwood after Lochsong just gained the day in a mighty duel with the speedy grey Paris House in the Group 3 King George Stakes. Perhaps they wouldn't have been so complimentary if they knew that I had disobeyed Ian's orders to avoid getting into a battle with Paris House at all costs.

I thought 'Sod Ian's instructions. I'll do my own thing. I'm not going to give Paris House an uncontested lead.' So I just threw the reins at her and let her go from the front. We raced upsides with Paris House, going hammer and tongs for the entire race, locked together throughout – but it was Lochsong who found a bit more to gain the verdict by a head.

She was such an exciting mare to ride and by then we had begun to establish a rapport. I realised that the key to her was to let her bowl along without any interference from the man on top.

She was so fast I knew she would kill the others off. As the season progressed I felt there were times when five furlongs was a little bit too far for her, but she'd usually built up such an enormous lead in the early stages that it didn't matter.

That's what happened when she gained her first Group 1 success in the Nunthorpe Stakes at York in August. Once again Paris House finished second, but this time Lochsong was totally in charge from gun to tape and readily held his challenge by one and a half lengths. She was different to any other sprinter I'd ridden. She seemed to understand that she couldn't run flat out for five furlongs and had begun to relax at half-way, and prick her ears, before quickening again at the finish. It was as if she realised that she would benefit from a breather. So she developed a technique for dealing with it.

After that triumph I suggested that Lochsong was like Linford Christie without the lunchbox. When the racing press seized on this description I was left feeling a bit of a fraud, because it was Jason Weaver, not me, who thought of it first. It was a brilliant description and Jason alone was the author. Really Lochsong was a freak. Physical problems made it impossible for her to be trained seriously in Newmarket at two, and when Jeff Smith sent her to Ian Balding the following season she was still so big, gawky and unsound that the best he was hoping for was a minor victory, anywhere, before she retired to stud. That came over six furlongs at Redcar before she added a further success over seven furlongs at Newbury. How on earth she found the stamina to win over those distances remains one of the great mysteries of the turf.

The following weekend on a day trip to Deauville, the picturesque seaside town in Normandy, I had a glimpse of what it must be like to win the lottery. In the space of little more than an hour I won two races that carried vast amounts of prize money for the quality of horses that took part. My victory on Prince Babar netted £179,211 for the happy owner. The second, Dana Springs, collected a similar amount. My percentage from the pair came to far more than lots of people earn in a year.

That summer my rift with Luca Cumani remained as deep as ever. I felt uneasy when I saw him at the races, but couldn't bring myself to make the first move to heal the wounds between us and he was certainly not looking to seek me out. Then Barney Curley intervened. It was high time, he suggested, that I apologised to Luca for letting him down.

The first time Barney brought up the subject Luca told him not to bother. But Barney persisted until one evening at the end of August I found myself sheltering from the rain outside Luca's front door. When he finally answered I gave him a sheepish grin and asked if I could come in. Luca's reply summed up his attitude to life. He told me to wait there, then shut the door in my face. It was his idea of a joke but he was also making sure that I suffered for a little longer. A year or two earlier I would probably have walked away but this time I was ready to take my medicine. After a few minutes he opened the door again and invited me in.

We shook hands, then moved through to his office where I apologised straight away for the shabby way I had left him. I admitted my mistake and blamed it on the rashness of youth. Then I had felt invincible. Now after some hard knocks I knew better. As we chatted I felt a flood of relief that I was accepted again by the man who had done so much to put me on the map. We didn't have a long chat because it was only the first step, but at least we were talking again.

I said my piece, but as I left there was a sting in the tail which again was typical of the man. Luca told me that he hoped that I would ride for him in due course but because of what had happened over the winter he didn't intend to put me up on any of his horses for at least another year. I was forgiven . . . but not for another twelve months. Until then I was on probation!

fourteen

Sheikh Mohammed Offers a Lifeline

Shortly before I kissed and made up with Luca, I began riding out regularly in Newmarket for John Gosden, Sheikh Mohammed's principal trainer in this country following his return from a highly successful spell in California. Apparently Barney Curley had been promoting my cause with John. Aware that Michael Roberts' deal to ride the Sheikh's horses spread among dozens of trainers was not working as well as hoped, Barney suggested John should take a look at me.

When we first met at his stables I sensed that I was on trial. John knew all about my well chronicled problems in the spring and needed to be convinced that I was no longer a playboy. It helped that the dark days were already over. I was in form, riding winners almost every day, working hard on my weight – and the deeds of Lochsong were keeping me in the shop window.

Since John has never been a soft touch, he wanted assurances that I was prepared to toe the line. He promised that if I gave him one-hundred percent every day he would match that commitment. What he couldn't be sure about at that stage was whether I had the strength of will to pull myself together, so he made it clear that if I messed up I would be shown the door. Within a few weeks I'd established a warm friendship with him that has grown closer with the years. He is incredibly bright, understands the rhythms of racing and would make a first-class politician. At the same time he is down-to-earth, good fun and an outstanding trainer. I was lucky to find him at a time in my life when I was looking for guidance. I didn't know then that Michael Roberts was already coming towards the end of his contract with Sheikh Mohammed. His job was impossible, really, because often several of the Sheikh's trainers wanted a piece of him at the same time. That inevitably led to frustration for both him and the trainers.

Early in September, Ian Balding took a gamble in stepping Lochsong back up to six furlongs in the Group 1 Sprint Cup at Haydock, but as we both feared it proved too far for her. She was soon out in front as usual but John Gosden's duo Wolfhound and Catrail came steaming past in the final two hundred yards.

Consolation was at hand for me in the shape of an attractive young filly leading round my last mount of the day, for David Löder. Although I'd been riding out for David in the mornings I'd seen her only once before, briefly, in the stable yard. I immediately launched into my well-practised chat-up line – 'Allo darling, where have you been hiding?' – before asking her name, which turned out to be Catherine Allen. As we left the paddock I pressed her for a date.

At first Catherine, sensible girl, more or less blanked me and wasn't keen to give me her phone number. What's more, she declared, if she did tell me I'd forget it straight away. When I persisted she rattled off the number a moment before I cantered to the start. It had been a long day without any food and not much liquid because I was doing a light weight, but after meeting Catherine I was feeling on top of the world.

My mount Azola was beaten into third place, but as Catherine came out onto the course to lead her back I blurted out her telephone number. By the time I reached the enclosure reserved for the placed horses we had a date. The difficulty was finding a suitable evening that didn't conflict with my hectic diary. We couldn't go out that weekend because I was off to ride in Florence the following day, and the next weekend I was back in Italy once more.

Eventually I ended up taking Catherine to the cinema in Cambridge, then on to a Pizza Express afterwards. I did pretty much all the talking but discovered that she was only nineteen and in the middle of a degree course in Classical Studies at Surrey University. Since her parents lived in Cambridge, she often popped back from university mid-week to ride out for David Loder. The day we met at Haydock she was standing in for one of the girls on holiday.

On that first date I casually mentioned that I didn't appreciate girls wearing make-up. Catherine must have been paying attention because from that day to this she has never used any make up, not even lipstick. She didn't know too much about racing at the time but is very bright and picked things up quickly. Her dad William, known to one and all as Twink, came to this country from New Zealand as a young vet with his wife Diana on a scholarship to Cambridge and has never returned home. He is best known as the professor of equine reproduction at Cambridge University and is a leading authority on equine fertility. I call him the mad professor. All three of the children were brought up with ponies and Catherine soon developed into a tidy competitor at eventing.

There were times in our early courtship when I must have driven her mad. We'd arrange to meet up for a meal, then I'd ring at the last minute to call if off, explaining that I was too tired, or had to waste hard for a ride the next day. On other occasions I'd drop her off at her parents' house early in the evening then head home to bed because I had to be up so early in the morning.

My racing schedule made it difficult to plan things on a regular basis, and when I was tired I tended to be a bit short with Catherine. That would have put off a lot of girls but she seemed to take it all in her stride and things became a little easier as the year progressed. The romance blossomed so swiftly that we were soon an item, though Catherine sensibly completed her course at Surrey University and has a degree to prove it.

In the early days Catherine came to one or two Arsenal games with me at Highbury, but that stopped after we had the fright of our lives while queuing to collect our tickets for the derby game against Tottenham. A massive brawl broke out near us between rival supporters. As mounted police and dog handlers moved in we were trapped in the middle of the fight, pinned against a wall of the stadium by a screaming mob. It was terrifying.

At about the same time that I met Catherine, an agent approached me on behalf of the leading French owner, Daniel Wildenstein. I still hadn't mastered the art of riding the French tracks at that point so there was never any chance of my riding there permanently for him. At best we might have done a deal for me to ride in Paris on Sundays, but nothing came of that particular offer, mainly because I was on the point of agreeing a contract to ride Sheikh Mohammed's horses in training with John Gosden. Apparently John had met the Sheikh in an attempt to iron out the difficulties facing several of his trainers who all wanted to use Michael Roberts at the same time. Although Michael was the reigning champion, even he couldn't ride two horses in the same race, nor could he possibly ride work on all of them. It was simply not possible for him to keep all the Sheikh's trainers happy. Also, it hadn't helped that a series of suspensions had left Michael on the sidelines at critical stages of the season.

For John, at least, the solution was to retain a jockey solely to ride the Sheikh's horses in his care. The man he nominated for that role was me. I didn't think twice about accepting. I'd ridden enough for Sheikh Mohammed in the past to know that he was a dynamic figure intent on winning races at the highest level. With John's support, this was a job that could lead to the Classic winners I had craved for so long. Six months earlier I'd been heading out of control towards the buffers. Now I'd managed to scramble aboard a fast train going in the right direction.

The news of my appointment broke in mid-September. At the same time the Sheikh's racing manager, Anthony Stroud, revealed that Michael Roberts' one-year contract wouldn't be renewed. The press had been on the scent of both stories for some time, their suspicions fuelled by Michael losing the ride on Barathea in France at the start of the month, and me partnering the Sheikh's filly Anna of Saxony to victory in the Park Hill Stakes at Doncaster while Michael was on another one of his runners which finished sixth.

John offered a very individual explanation for our new liaison. 'I'm not an old man yet, only 42, and it is logical that I should prefer a young jockey on the way up. I've known Frankie since he spent a few winters in California. I think he has star quality and a great attitude to life', he declared. John added a tribute to Michael Roberts. 'I've never had a cross word with him. Michael is a good jockey and a nice man and will continue to ride horses for me. But how could one jockey sort his way through something like 600 horses and twenty something trainers. Logistically it was impossible', he concluded.

We sealed our new partnership the day that it was announced with the timely triumph of the Sheikh's filly Arvola at Nottingham. From that day to this neither of us has had cause to regret joining forces. We think along the same lines, are both positive in our outlook, and John is still the first one I turn to if I have a problem.

The horrors of the spring were fading as the winners came fast and furious through the autumn. Easily top of the list was my runaway success on Lochsong in the Prix de l'Abbaye at

Moonshell in charge
in the 1995 Oaks.

My dad and uncle Sergio
(right) join in the fun after
my victory on Shantou in the
Gran Premio del Jockey Club
in Milan in 1996.

It's a fair cop, guv.

Precious moments with my godmother Teresa Colangeli (left) and dad (below).

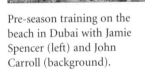

Pre-season training on the beach in Dubai with Jamie Spencer (left) and John Carroll (background).

More beachwear, this time in Sardinia, with Barney Curley (right) and Giovanni Marco.

Flying high after Shantou wins the 1996 St Leger.

Nightmare in Kentucky as Swain throws away the 1998 Breeders' Cup Classic by hanging badly right-handed towards the stands, leaving Awesome Again (right) to beat Silver Charm.

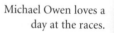

Michael Owen loves a day at the races.

Seventh Heaven. I still can't believe that Fujiyama Crest has just given me my seventh success of the day at Ascot in September 1996.

The old grey marvel Desert Orchid steals the show.

Trainer Clive Brittain and his wife Maureen pose for the cameras after the globetrotting Luso lands another big prize in Hong Kong.

Racing has never been more international, as this photo shows at the same Hong Kong meeting with riders from around the world.

In party mood after winning the first Young Jockeys World Cup in Japan in 1992. Spot a youthful Johnny Murtagh fourth from the right, in the rear.

Sheikh Mohammed leads me back in triumph on Cape Verdi after the 1,000 Guineas in 1998.

Sharing a joke with Her Majesty The Queen.

Below left: Collecting another Ritz Club trophy as leading jockey at Royal Ascot from the Queen Mother.

Pity the top one doesn't look like me!

Over the moon after winning the 1999 Breeders' Cup Turf on Daylami.

The best job in the world. Winning the Hong Kong Cup on Fantastic Light in December 2000 (top) and the Dubai World Cup nine months earlier on Dubai Millennium (left and below).

Longchamp on Arc day. As usual Paris was awash with English and Irish punters for a long weekend's partying. Many relied on her to pay for their excesses. They never had a moment's worry about collecting. Her start was explosive, her pick-up irresistible, and long before half-way she was running in a race of her own. We returned to one of those uplifting receptions that make Arc weekend such a special date in the calendar. Lochsong was on such a roll she had captured the affections of the racing public.

Considering my shocking start to the campaign, I was surprised to finish runner-up to Pat Eddery in the championship with 149 winners, but there was still work to be done before I could take a sunshine break. My earlier problems came back to haunt me when I was tipped off that the Japanese were reluctant to allow me to ride Misil in the Japan Cup. A spokesman for the Japan Racing Association indicated that it was not their policy to invite any person who'd been involved with drugs.

On the advice of John Gosden's wife Rachel Hood, an astute lawyer, I responded with my own statement the next day explaining that as I hadn't applied for a licence to ride in Japan I hadn't been denied one! Nor had I applied for or been refused an entry visa. Commitments elsewhere, I added, would prevent me going to Japan. It would take much longer than I expected to persuade the Japanese to change their minds.

While the door to Japan remained closed, there was a welcome change of heart in Hong Kong whose authorities agreed to allow me to ride Marina Park for Mark Johnston in the

Hong Kong International Bowl in December. I was free to take part as an international jockey but wouldn't have been able to stay on to ride on a short-term contract. All was not yet forgiven. It was almost a fairytale return, too, for Marina Park lost out by only a neck to Michael Kinane's mount Winning Partners.

It was just as well that I had other plans that winter. After a long chat with John Gosden I decided to take advantage of racing on the all-weather to kick start the new season on 1 January. Every winner now counted towards the jockeys' championship, so I hoped to build up a healthy lead by the time the big boys came back from their beach holidays.

I also wanted to show people that the new Frankie Dettori was a different, hungrier and much more disciplined professional than the one they'd seen make a fool of himself early in 1993. I'd messed up so badly then that I'd had to start from the bottom again, trying to build up a new clientele of trainers and owners. The more I thought about it, the more I realised that the winter all-weather programme offered a heaven-sent opportunity for me to get into the groove earlier than ever before.

I stayed on for a few days holiday in Hong Kong in mid December, then headed for my parents' house near Agadir in Morocco, to prepare myself for the ordeal that I knew lay ahead. For the next ten days, which included Christmas, everything was geared to bringing myself to a peak of physical fitness for 1 January. Back in Newmarket, Mattie Cowing was busy ringing all his contacts to make sure that they knew I was available to ride their horses once the New Year festivities were over. Thanks to him I had plenty of decent horses on stand-by.

Sacrifices had to be made if I was going to be serious about a fast start. The biggest sufferer of all was Catherine. To my delight our romance had progressed speedily over the past three months, but at the very time of year young lovers expect to be together, I locked myself away with my parents beside the beach in Morocco, oblivious of her feelings.

It was a cruel blow to Catherine. I was ruthless about it, a right so-and-so in the way I treated her that Christmas, but I had absolute tunnel vision then and no-one, not even the girl I would later marry, was going to interfere with my programme. I hoped she understood, and every couple of days I jumped on a scramble bike that I had rented, rode into Agadir and spoke to her on the phone. At the time I was like a racehorse wearing blinkers, solely concentrating on the task ahead of me.

Having my parents there was a huge bonus. They understood my need to prove myself again and supported my plan to make a lightning start in January. I knew it would be pretty much impossible to lose weight in the cold weather once I returned to England. That's why the dieting and the fitness programme had to be completed in the warmer climate of Morocco. Basically, I locked myself away like a monk, eating only fish once a day and drinking mostly plain water. The only alcohol I allowed myself was a half glass of champagne on Christmas Day.

Each morning I'd wake around ten, have one espresso with a sweetener and a large bottle of water, then doze or lounge around in the sun until two in the afternoon. Then, with a walkman clamped to my ears, I would set off on a long, lonely walk on the beach towards Agadir and back again, covering a distance of around ten miles in just over two hours.

The last hour late in the afternoon, walking and jogging with severe hunger pangs, was always the hardest. By that stage I would be absolutely starving. At times I felt like I was dying from malnutrition. I used to have a bath to revive me while my father cooked my one meal of the day, grilled fish, nearly always sea bass, a good two-pounder, on its own, without any oil, salad or potatoes. While I wolfed down my fish my parents kept me company. We'd chat for a while before I headed off on my bike to ring Catherine.

Then I took myself off to bed and read for a bit before trying to force myself to go to sleep. Within a few days I was lean and hungry like a championship boxer locked away in a remote training camp before a title fight. All the time I was trying to sleep so that I couldn't eat. Every now and then I'd pop onto my dad's scales. I weighed just over eight and a half stone when I arrived from Hong Kong, but within a week had starved myself down to 8 st 1 lb stripped, the lightest I'd been for three or four years.

To complete my tougher new image I had my head shaved, then flew back to England on New Year's Eve ready to take on the world. There was a tearful reunion with Catherine, though in my new spirit of self-denial I restricted myself to a glass of Perrier water and an early night since there was important business ahead the next day. I also called on my new boss John

Gosden at his home early on New Years's Eve. He told me later that he didn't recognize the tanned, slim, shaven-headed figure shivering on his doorstep.

'The little bastard has sent his cousin to make his excuses', he thought for a fleeting second, before realising his mistake and welcoming me like a long-lost son. We were ready to go to war.

fifteen

Champion Jockey

I was probably one of the few people at Lingfield on New Year's Day 1994 not suffering from a hangover. It's not a place I'd normally choose to visit in the depths of winter, but it felt pretty good by the end of an afternoon which yielded a double for me on the opening day of the campaign. I started as I intended to continue, by winning the first flat race of the year on Tiddy Oggie.

This was the first important step to prove to the people who'd helped my recovery in 1993 that I wasn't a one-hit wonder. This was going to be my pay-back time. That first week of the year set the pattern of what was to come in the next two and a half months. Mattie and I had mapped out every all-weather fixture on his calendar. I spent the time shuttling between Lingfield, Southwell and Wolverhampton.

Often on Saturdays I managed a double shift, starting at Lingfield in the afternoon before finishing with several more rides under the floodlights at Wolverhampton, where between races we crowded around the television in the weighing-room, making rude remarks about the girls appearing on Blind Date with Cilla Black. We'd go out to the paddock, freezing to death in our silks and riding breeches, complete a race, then rush back into the warmth of the weighing room which supplied a welcome supply of sausage and mash for the jockeys who weren't doing light weights.

Like most of the boys I had an assortment of clothes to help me keep warm, including ear muffs, gloves, thermal socks and tights. Many jockeys also wore face masks to protect them from having sand kicked in their faces. I tried one too, but found it so difficult to breathe that unless the temperature was really severe I preferred the discomfort of the sand stinging my face. It was unpleasant riding in conditions like that, but I was so angry inside I would have put up with much more. There were things to prove and nothing was going to divert me from my course.

I sailed through the early weeks of 1994 on a tidal wave of confidence. My first treble arrived at Southwell on 7 January, and there were further rewarding doubles at Lingfield before I ended that month with a four-timer at Wolverhampton on a bitterly cold Monday afternoon. Jason Weaver was my closest pursuer and we had a typically vigorous set-to that day on two hardy stayers which seemed to run into each other almost every week. I set out to make the running on Arc Bright. Jason then laid down a furious challenge over the final three furlongs on Milngavie. It was already beginning to get personal between us and I was more pleased than I should have been to pip his horse in a photo finish. Jason had become a close friend over the previous few years, but I couldn't shake off his shadow that spring and began to see him as an obstacle to my dream of becoming champion.

I started riding out for John Gosden at Stanley House at the beginning of February. As it was my first full year with him I was keen to make a good impression even though cold weather often restricted morning exercise to trotting endlessly round an indoor riding school. That way, at least, I got to know the horses and was able to build a rapport with his lads. I tried to make myself scarce when Rachel served up breakfast. Mostly I settled for half a cup of coffee. Then, most days, I'd be off racing after riding two lots.

One day early in March yielded five winners from twelve rides during a marathon that began at Lingfield at lunchtime, continued through the evening at Wolverhampton and came to an exhausting conclusion back at Newmarket on the wrong side of midnight. I took part in every race at both meetings, starting with a narrow success in the opening event at Lingfield on Letsbehonestaboutit. Later I added a second success on Spender, and was just denied a third in the final race on Plinth by Jason on Surprise Guest. That race started five minutes late at 4.45.

The moment after weighing-in, I sprinted to the car park in my riding clothes for the familiar Saturday evening dash round the M25 and up the M40 towards Wolverhampton, where I was due to ride the second favourite, Chairman's Choice, in the opening race at 7 p.m. We made it with a couple of minutes to spare. Chairman's Choice ran below form, but three more winners later in the evening brought my tally for the day to five and helped me pull further clear of Jason.

By this time I knew I would never have a better chance of becoming champion. The winners were coming along even faster than I'd expected. It was up to me to avoid the risk of suspensions that could halt my momentum. In the past when I found myself boxed in on the rails I would nudge my way out, maybe catching the attention of the stewards. Now I was prepared to sit and suffer, even if it cost me a winning chance. Better to live to fight another day than spend a week watching in frustration from the sidelines.

If the boys who regularly earned their bread and butter on the all-weather circuit resented my presence that winter they didn't show it. They knew I'd been dumped on my backside the previous year and was trying to re-establish myself. I felt I was just like the rest of them, chasing the winners, riding through the worst of the bad weather to give ourselves an edge when the turf season sprang into life.

The three all-weather courses offered surprisingly varied challenges. I rode plenty of winners at all of them, but felt at my best at Lingfield. Though I say it myself, I was sensational there at times. Horses hated the kick back so much it was vital to jump out a fraction quicker than the others to be sure you were in the first three. The lessons I'd learned in the States about making a fast start gave me a big edge over my rivals. Wolverhampton's new track had a distinct bias which favoured jockeys prepared to go really wide in search of better ground, while riding at Southwell was physically demanding because the surface was so deep that you would be pushing along for dear life five furlongs from the finish. Horses had to be exceptionally fit to win at Southwell. So did their jockeys.

When the turf season began at Doncaster on 24 March I was in a clear lead in the jockeys' table on 51 winners, with Jason Weaver trying hard to stay on my tail. The title already looked a two-horse affair and that's how it stayed for the rest of the year. Only bad luck or serious injury could prevent one of us becoming champion. The deficit was too much for the jockeys starting off at Doncaster, like the reigning champion Pat Eddery and Michael Roberts. While they were sunning themselves, we had pinched a massive advantage.

My association with John Gosden led to a request from Sheikh Mohammed to take part in a trial in Dubai involving Balanchine and State Performer, two highly promising horses who were part of a package of four bought by him from Robert Sangster for well over £1 million towards the end of the previous season. They had spent the winter training in Dubai in the infancy of the Sheikh's experiment under the Goldolphin banner. A year earlier Dayflower and Blush Rambler had been the pathfinders for Godolphin. Their success in England and France had convinced the Sheikh of the benefits of wintering his horses in the warmth of Dubai.

None of us realised the full significance of it then. We were just swept along by the enthusiasm shown by Sheikh Mohammed, known to everyone as 'the boss'. Initially the training set-up at Al Quoz in a spot in the desert not far from the City of Dubai was fairly modest, with one barn and a handful of horses. The only building you could see in the distance was the slender shape of the World Trade Centre reaching into the sky. Now dozens of tall hotels, apartment blocks and other buildings shimmer in the heat on the horizon and a new dual-carriageway passes quite close to our all-weather training circuit. Godolphin grew rapidly into a well-oiled machine with dozens of grooms from India and Pakistan living on the spot, the best of everything for the horses and the most modern veterinary facilities imaginable. Nothing is left to chance. There is even an immaculate little grandstand by the finishing line of our training track. It is a unique creation.

That spring Ray Cochrane and I were recruited to ride in a searching Guineas trial at Nad Al Sheba racecourse before an audience of half a dozen people or so – including the Sheikh, his three brothers, the trainer Hilal Ibrahim, his assistant Jeremy Noseda who is now training at Newmarket, and Simon Crisford who remains at the heart of Godolphin's operation. Although Balanchine had a big reputation as a two-year-old, I was aware that she hadn't been sparkling in her recent home work, so everyone seemed pretty pleased when we finished just behind State Performer. She gave me a lovely feel before tiring through lack of fitness and had plenty of scope for improvement. After-wards Sheikh Mohammed was anxious to hear what I thought of Balanchine. When I suggested that with any luck she should finish in the first three in the 1,000 Guineas he beamed with delight.

Once again the betting public had yet to appreciate the significance of Godolphin. On the big day at Newmarket,

Balanchine was dismissed in the market at 20–1. She didn't look much like an outsider as she came with a storming late run up the final hill to join the Irish filly Las Meninas on the line. Balanchine finished so well that for a few moments I thought she had given me my overdue first Classic victory. When a result is too tight to call you automatically glance down to check the number of your horse on the saddle-cloth. A few seconds later, to my dismay, the number of Las Meninas was announced first. It was a bitter blow. What irony that we should fail by the shortest of short heads to catch Las Meninas in the colours of Robert Sangster, the man who had sold Balanchine six months earlier.

A narrow defeat in any race is hard to endure. When it happens in a Classic you torture yourself, going over and over in your mind what you could have done to make the difference. This time I didn't entirely blame myself. The widest draw of all, out in the centre of the course, hadn't helped, and it was also clear that Balanchine would be even better at distances over a mile. She had the speed for the Guineas but would come into her own over further.

I wasn't so philosophical on Saturday after another short-head defeat in the 2,000 Guineas on Grand Lodge for Willie Jarvis. Once again I was drawn in the middle of the track, 22 of the 23 runners, but it didn't prove to be such a disadvantage because the first three were all out there. Over the last furlong and a half the race developed into a duel between Grand Lodge and Mister Baileys, ridden by Jason Weaver.

Mister Baileys had a handy lead at one stage but Grand Lodge finished to such purpose that you couldn't be sure which horse had won. This time I wasn't so confident and just prayed that we'd snatched the verdict in the final stride, but the evidence of the camera told against us. I rode over and gave Jason a pat on the back, but deep inside I was devastated. What the hell did I have to do to win a Classic? Lochsong briefly lifted my depression by carrying me to a blisteringly fast triumph in the Palace House Stakes despite Ian Balding warning me that she was only eighty percent fit. She felt stronger than ever as she shattered the course record by more than half a second.

After yet another photo finish went against me in the final race on the odds-on chance Night Bell, I felt a black cloud of depression envelop me as I left the course. I headed home on my own, locked the door, took the phone off the hook and went to bed at six in the evening, sick with disappointment, convinced that the world was against me. Nor did things improve much the next day when I finished second in a Classic for the third time in four days, on Blinding Speed in the Italian 2,000 Guineas.

The beauty about racing is that however low your spirits, there is always another day, another meeting, another ride that can lift your mood. The trick is to put the past behind you and look forward. But after that run of reverses in important races I felt a bit like a punch-drunk fighter who doesn't want to come out for the next round. It helped that my parents had again come over to stay in Newmarket for a few weeks to lend their support to my championship bid.

Catherine too was a tower of strength, but I wasn't the most cheerful of companions. Some evenings we'd snatch a few precious hours together, but often (too often she would say) I would ring her to cancel a date, explaining that I was tired after a long day or had to be up before dawn to ride work. I think she understood by then that it was hard for me to be lively company on a diet that consisted of little more than fresh air and small amounts of liquid. I knew that she was the girl for me, but it was tough for her to adapt to the demands of my crazy lifestyle as the season moved towards its hectic peak. There are compensations of course. One of the best is to ride horses like Lochsong who carried all before her that season at the mature age of six. Late in May we returned to Sandown to share another easy victory in the Temple Stakes.

Although the turf season was barely two months old I was already close to exhaustion from setting such a fast pace in the championship on a strict diet. On a flight to France from Cambridge one Sunday in May, I confided to John Gosden that I was on the verge of burnout. How could I go on? He knew that I wasn't exaggerating and generously gave me time off over the next few days to catch up on my sleep and refuel my tanks again.

John had rapidly developed into the father figure I sensed I had been searching for. He was proving to be a fantastic supporter and provided a timely shoulder to lean on, when necessary. He has just about the broadest shoulders in racing. The knowledge that he was there for me certainly improved my riding.

Another fleet-footed filly now emerged to test my loyalty to

Lochsong. At Epsom, Balanchine finally ended my hoodoo in the Classics with a determined winning run in the Oaks despite heavy rain. Others were preferred in the betting, but I had a good feeling about Balanchine after the Guineas and was confident that the step-up in trip to a mile and a half was just what she wanted. Most jockeys chose to use light, nylon gloves to give them more grip on the reins. I made a big mistake leaving mine in the weighing room. From the moment she jumped out of the stalls Balanchine pulled so fiercely that the reins were slipping through my hands. Because I couldn't hold her properly, I had to let her bowl along with the leaders and hope that she kept going. Luckily it turned out to be the right thing to do.

Aware that the ground at Epsom is always best on the stands side when it rains, I let her stride into the lead running down the hill so that we could ease our way across to the favoured stands rails. Walter Swinburn then took a narrow advantage on Hawajiss, but the more I asked, the more Balanchine responded. Walter gave us such a good scrap I thought 'Oh God, I'm going to finish second yet again', but we were back in front over a furlong out and then in the last hundred yards we pulled right away. It was a great joy, almost unbelievable though my first feeling was one of relief. I'd finally cracked it in a British Classic, a huge milestone in a jockey's career.

Looking back now, it was an ever bigger step in the development of Godolphin – the first of a century of Group 1 victories that would come in less than a decade. What had started as the glimmer of an idea a couple of years earlier by Sheikh

Mohammed had swiftly become an obsession with him. Taking horses to winter in Dubai was his brainwave, and the triumph of Balanchine offered early evidence at the highest level that it was a winning formula.

There was further cause for celebration that weekend when I agreed a three-month contract to ride in Hong Kong from late November. Little more than a year earlier I'd been banned from the colony. Now my rehabilitation was complete. Some people assumed that riding in Hong Kong would jeopardise my chances of becoming champion jockey. Certainly Jason Weaver, who was nine behind me at the time, and his agent Terry Norman redoubled their efforts when they heard the news, but I hadn't the slightest intention of leaving the country until the title was in the bag.

Within days of the announcement, I reached the fastest century of winners ever recorded in Britain. The one that took me to three figures was Winter Coat for John Gosden at York on 11 June. A year earlier I'd managed less than twenty winners at the same stage of the season. Now I was in rampant form, but it had been a tough campaign that stretched me to the limit and beyond. I shook my head in disbelief when I read that the great Sir Gordon Richards once achieved 100 winners for the season by 17 June . . . and he didn't start until the middle of March!

Once they score a ton the best batsmen take a fresh guard and press on remorselessly towards a double century. That was exactly my plan too, provided that I had the ammunition. I wasn't counting my chickens, because I was all too aware that one slip, one bad fall could put me out for weeks or months. I was determined to keep my head down, try to maintain the winning run and hope that nothing would go wrong.

On the eve of Royal Ascot, I received a welcome call from Luca Cumani. There was no mention of the year's ban he had imposed on me as he booked me for his filly Relatively Special in the Coronation Stakes. It would be my first ride for him for twenty months. Our feud was at an end and I was just pleased to be back in harness with the man whose belief and backing had helped me make my name. Relatively Special failed to deliver at Royal Ascot, but Luca's door was ajar again and in the subsequent years I've ridden plenty of winners for him, culminating in our fabulous triumph with Falbrav in Hong Kong in December 2003.

I was searching for new superlatives to describe Lochsong after she carried me to another stirring success in the King's Stand Stakes at Royal Ascot. On Ian Balding's advice I took her to post early, on her own to keep her cool, but she came back as if her tail was on fire in less than a second more than one minute. Lochsong was so dominant that day she was frightening.

There's no better life than a jockey's when the big races come thick and fast and you are involved in nearly of all of them. Next it was the turn of Balanchine to attempt an audacious Classic double in the Irish Derby. It came at the end of a manic weekend of high-speed travel which was typical of my routine that summer. On the Friday I managed a winner from five rides at Newmarket, took to the skies within ten minutes of the last race (4.30), and reached Bath in time to win the first race on Farnham at 6.20. Later I completed a double at Bath before heading back to Newmarket by car.

On Saturday I rode work first thing at Newmarket, before flying to Ireland where I landed the Pretty Polly Stakes on Del Deya at the Curragh for John Gosden. Then there was another mad rush to catch a plane which yielded a further success on Line Out at Doncaster that evening. On Sunday it was back to the Curragh for the Irish Derby. Nor was there any chance of a day off on Monday, which saw me add to my score at both Nottingham and Windsor. At times I must have been running on pure adrenaline.

I wasn't complaining about my schedule after Balanchine destroyed some of the best three-year-old colts in the Irish Derby – including King's Theatre and Colonel Collins, second and third behind Erhaab in the Epsom Derby. Four years earlier the Maktoums had achieved the same highly unusual double with Sheikh Hamdan's brilliant filly Salsabil, but she hadn't spent the winter in Dubai.

It cost Ir£60,000 to supplement Balanchine a few days before the race but that proved to be a sound investment. This time she was even keener with me through the race. She began pulling after three furlongs, tugged her way into the lead with half a mile to run, and when I let her go early in the straight she flew clear. Nothing could live with her. We were going so fast through the final furlong it would have taken a machine to catch us.

That was the first time I saw Sheikh Mohammed really excited after a race. Balanchine ran in the colours of his brother Sheikh Maktoum, but it was Sheikh Mohammed who rushed out to greet me, raised my hand like a boxer's after a fight, and held it aloft for several seconds as we walked in triumph in front of the stands. You could understand his emotion, too, because he hand-picked Balanchine in the deal with Robert Sangster the previous autumn and had been to see her at Godolphin's stables at Al Quoz most days during the winter. He is a fine horseman with a vital input into the way the horses are trained and had just seen his dreams for Godolphin become reality.

The sky seemed the limit for Balanchine after the way she slammed the colts at the Curragh. We were looking at all the major autumn races for her against the older horses, culminating in the Prix de l'Arc de Triomphe in Paris, but three weeks after the Irish Derby she nearly died from an attack of colic. The vets managed to save her life but it looked like her racing career was over. It was a body blow for everyone involved with Godolphin.

That summer Ian Balding invited me to his open day at Kingsclere. I ended up setting a land speed record on his gallops on Lochsong. Of course it wasn't meant to happen that way. The idea was to canter round a large field in front of hundreds of spectators. We jumped off uphill steadily enough, but after a furlong she was really tanking. As she approached a sharp right-hand bend before turning downhill towards the finish, things suddenly looked decidedly dodgy.

Ahead lay a thick hedge. Would Lochsong try to jump the hedge or manage to negotiate the corner flat out? Either way I didn't fancy my chances of remaining on her back much longer but she sped round the tight turn like a greyhound, found an extra leg from somewhere and dashed eagerly past her horrified trainer watching in disbelief with a group of his owners. I set out to give everyone a thrill and ended up surviving a nightmare. Ian still maintains that she covered four furlongs that day faster than any horse in the history of Kingsclere.

Sometimes I stayed with Ian and his family so that I could ride work in the mornings for him before heading off to local meetings at Salisbury or Newbury. Once he made the mistake of asking me to ride Lochsong over five furlongs on the valley gallop which is so twisty that you can't possibly go flat out. We ended up covering the best part of seven furlongs as she veered impatiently from side to side in her eagerness to get to the other end. I think that was the last time Ian took her to the downs.

There was a rare reverse for Lochsong that summer in the July Cup at Newmarket on the day that Willie Carson took over when I was claimed to ride Catrail for Sheikh Mohammed. Lochsong lost her chance by rushing down to the start much faster than Willie intended. Normal service was resumed at Goodwood, where she scorched through the rain in the King George V Stakes at a blistering pace which left me describing her as the fastest thing on earth. She dominated from the front with a ruthless display of power and found more when pressed by Mistertopogigo in the last furlong.

Lochsong was not the prettiest thing in the world. She was so strong and snappy she looked a bit like a refugee from

early days together I wasn't quite sure what to do. Once I learned to let her run she quickly became used to me and began to relax through a race. Then she saved something extra for the finish.

Lochsong had one more card to play. Unfortunately it was a joker. By then, to my relief, I had all but wrapped up my first championship with my lead over Jason Weaver sufficient to allow me the luxury of a late-season break. I was totally knackered, running on empty. To have continued the daily grind all through October would have been inviting disaster. Realising the extent of my exhaustion, John Gosden encouraged me to take my foot right off the throttle and coast through the final weeks of the season. I didn't need a second invitation. First, though, I badly wanted to beat my dad's record of 229. I just managed that, notched up a couple more winners, then ground to a halt with a total of 233 for the year. I couldn't go on.

That overdue break late in October left me fresh for the challenge of the Breeders' Cup held at Churchill Downs in Kentucky, which was pencilled in for the final public appearance of Lochsong. It proved to be a bitter farewell. Once again she boiled over in her anxiety to get on with things. This time it happened in her last piece of work three days before the Sprint which left experienced track observers checking their watches in disbelief as she covered the last three furlongs in 33.1 seconds. Apparently no horse had ever clocked fractions that fast. The plan was to breeze round the bend at a good strong canter before letting her stride on up the straight at no more than half pace, though with Lochsong there were no half measures.

Straight away we were going much faster than I wanted, but once she got up a head of steam there was nothing I could do about it.

It didn't seem like a disaster at the time but the seeds of doubt were sown. Had she left her race behind that morning? And how would she face the unfamiliar dirt surface if she was headed at any stage? Whatever the reason, Lochsong failed to fire in her final race. For the first time in my experience she wasn't anxious to jump out of the stalls, nor did she seem particularly interested in racing. Once the cause was lost, I eased up and allowed her to coast home last of the fourteen runners. X-rays later detected that she had chipped a little bone in one of her knees. More than likely she had done the damage in that famous work out. It was a sad end to a great career.

Lochsong came into my life at just the right time in 1993. She gave me a lift when I badly needed one and rapidly developed into a superstar. She was certainly the fastest horse I've ridden, a giant among sprinters. I'd love to have ridden her against the best American quarter horses because it was her initial early pace that set her apart. Five furlongs was plenty far enough while six furlongs was like a trip to Scotland for her. Lochsong was the people's favourite and mine, too. For me she was the ultimate sprinter.

I could hardly have made a worse start at Churchill Downs, but matters soon improved as I finished fourth on Belle Genius for Paul Kelleway in the Juvenile. Then came my reunion with Barathea in the Mile. It had been so long since I'd ridden him that I'd all but given up hope of ever sitting on his back again.

But out of the blue towards the end of October, Luca rang to ask me to ride work on him round a specially designed, tight, left-handed American bend on the gallops at Newmarket.

The first time he tried it Barathea sped round the sharp bend like a greyhound from trap one. Further practice in the days before he left for America left us both full of confidence that he'd handle the demands of Churchill Downs. I remember telling Luca that Barathea would win after his final sparkling piece of work.

I knew the key to his chance was making a sharp start and claiming the ideal position just behind the leaders. That's exactly how it worked out. He jumped every bit as quickly as I wanted, so didn't get killed in the rush by the others as he settled into position A, just where I planned to be, travelling like a dream. Round the bend and into the straight he was cruising on auto-pilot, the only one still on the bridle. It was just a question of when to let him go, so I made myself wait until the furlong pole then let him have it and he flew clear in a matter of strides like the champion Luca had always believed him to be. As we reached the line I experienced an amazing release of joy and saluted the crowd with my whip.

For some time I'd doubted that I would ever win a race at the Breeders' Cup. Barathea ended my drought in the most spectacular manner possible with the biggest win of my career so far. It was a fantastic feeling, partly because English horses had always seemed to struggle in the Breeders' Cup. As Luca rushed out to greet us I was so excited that I planted a kiss on his cheek, then warned him that I was planning to emulate my hero Angel Cordero with a flying dismount. It was something I'd been waiting to unveil for years. I'd been tempted to try it at home but always backed off aware that some people might consider it unacceptable behaviour. Now I had the perfect excuse. The way I felt at the time I wanted to jump fifty feet into the air.

When Luca asked what would happen if I broke my leg, I replied 'Who cares? It doesn't matter any more.' My mind was made up. I'd practised my flying dismounts almost daily as a teenager on my winter trips to Santa Anita. The time had arrived for a public performance. I slipped my toes out of the irons and launched myself skywards before landing nimbly on both feet beside Barathea. It might not have earned maximum points for artistic impression, but at least I didn't fall on my face. The reaction around me was one of surprise and then delight. This was an evening for celebration and I'd just set the tone for the rest of the night.

The Americans like a showman, but back home my flying dismount sparked a chorus of disapproval which included damning letters in the racing papers complaining about my actions. I thought it was curious that people reacted in such a critical manner. What was so terrible about celebrating a famous victory for England which restored my relationship with Luca Cumani? For me it was a fairytale.

As rain began to fall, I remember being marooned in the car park for ages with Barathea's breeder and joint-owner Gerald Leigh. We were both in ecstasy at the way his horse had annihilated the best milers from America and Europe on his last outing.

When we stopped off at the stables to check that all was well with Barathea, I took the chance to ring my father and talk through the race with him. Later I enjoyed a lively dinner with Gerald, Luca and some of their friends. I was still on cloud nine, much too alert to go to bed, so I joined Barathea's lad Keith Ledington and Luca's travelling head lad Ian Willows for a nightcap at their hotel. None of us wanted the day to end.

Back in England, behind the scenes, John Gosden and his wife Rachel were working overtime on my behalf so that I could ride Sheikh Mohammed's colt Zieten if the decision was taken to send him for the Sprinter Stakes in Japan in December. Aware that the Japanese authorities were still reluctant to allow me to ride there following my fall from grace in London in April the previous year, they composed a long, supportive letter to the Japan Racing Association emphasising that I was never charged with any legal offence whatsoever, let alone convicted of any breach of the law.

They further pointed out that the Hong Kong Jockey Club had allowed me to take part in the International meeting at Sha Tin in December 1993, and had also offered me a three-month contract. In the end, however, the horse didn't go to Japan and it would be another couple of years before I rode there again.

sixteen

A Lion in Paris

By the time I returned from America the season was over and I was champion with 233 winners, the biggest total since Sir Gordon Richards scored 261 in 1949. Of course the goalposts have been moved since then, especially with the introduction of all-weather and evening racing, but after working my backside off all year I was still thrilled and amazed to have won so many races. One record was definitely mine. Apparently I was the first to ride in 1318 races in the same year. I was also the sixth jockey in history to achieve a double century. Soon it would be seven.

Jason Weaver had been chasing me doggedly all year, intent on setting new marks of his own. For weeks he was in touching distance of his own double century and finally reached that landmark on Magna Carta under the floodlights at Wolverhampton on 12 November. It was not, he readily admits, his finest performance as a jockey. Aware of what was at stake he booted Magna Carta into the lead fully three furlongs out, then picked up his whip and chased him all the way home without another horse in sight. At the line they had won by the ridiculous margin of twelve lengths. Jason had finally joined the band of double centurions but in the process ruined the handicap mark of Magna Carta forever.

I was over the moon for my buddy and rang him straight away in the weighing room to offer my congratulations. I admired his pluck for keeping going once he knew the championship battle was lost. He then bought a bucket-full of champagne and was driven home to Newmarket on a cloud of bubbles. To this day we are the only two jockeys to have ridden a double century of winners in the same year. It was great for us and an even greater feather in the cap of Luca Cumani who masterminded both our careers. All those hundreds of bollockings had finally paid off.

My decision to call off my contract in Hong Kong gave me the chance to take Catherine on a Club Med holiday in the Caribbean. We had a fabulous time. I returned to England early in December in time to say farewell to Lochsong at a party for her at Kingsclere before she departed to Jeff Smith's stud. Everyone involved with her was there and quite a few of her supporters, too. There was plenty of champagne and laughter as we gave her a lively send-off. I thought I'd add to the entertainment by jumping on to her bareback, but it nearly backfired when she gave a huge buck and did her best to drop me. It could have been the end of a beautiful friendship.

Soon I was off to join my parents in Morocco to prepare myself for another arduous campaign on the all-weather at the start of January. The celebrations hadn't lasted very long and now they were over. With a title to defend I resumed the spartan regime which had done me so well twelve months earlier. Being champion was everything I'd hoped it would be, but I had to do it again to prove that it wasn't a fluke. This time it was harder than ever to leave Catherine behind in England. We were head over heels in love but had to make do with long chats on the phone late in the afternoon. We missed each other more than words can say.

Once again I was back for the opening day of the season at Southwell on 2 January. In the space of three days I rode seven winners, but this time Jason Weaver matched me stride for stride through the worst of the winter in January and February. Our long friendship became strained to the limit once he headed the jockeys' table for the first time. Until then we travelled to the races together whenever possible. Not any more. It wasn't possible once we were at each other's throats. There had been a bit of niggle between us a year earlier. Now it was out in the open. We were going hammer and tongs from day one, but once he took the lead in the jockeys' list I couldn't peg him back. That's when things got nasty.

It was all hunky-dory when I was in front, but from the moment Jason headed me I became really nasty to him. When I look back now I realise I was a horrible little bastard. It's terrible that you can be like that, and it's not normally the way I behave, but I was just reacting to seeing my champion's crown under threat. I consoled myself with the thought that if I managed a thousand rides in 1995 then, at my lowest strike rate of 20%, that should provide the 200 winners I needed to retain my title. In a duel as bitter as the one I was engaged in I knew that to achieve that target of a double century I couldn't afford suspensions.

The simmering resentment between us came to a head in a five furlong handicap at Lingfield on 16 March. I tried to make all the running on the favourite Nordico Express. Jason then locked horns with us on Dolly Face with two furlongs left. We raced head to head and toe to toe, cursing and shouting, whips banging, the pair of us going for it as though we were fighting out the finish of the Derby, not a Mickey Mouse event in front of a deserted grandstand.

Most of the time, Nordico Princess looked like holding on. Then Dolly Face nailed us on the line. My dark mood didn't improve when Jason began celebrating loudly before turning round inviting me to give him a high five. I am ashamed to admit that what he got instead was a torrent of abuse. That's how bad things had come between us. I certainly knew I was in for a long battle when the turf season began a few days later at Doncaster with Jason holding a useful lead of ten winners over me. As we sparred for the ultimate prize over the next eight months, we behaved like two fighting bantam cocks, snapping at each other at every opportunity, bad tempered, suspicious, and always jealous of each other's winners. Things improved in April when I was voted jockey of the year and Flat jockey of the year at the annual Lester's awards dinner in London. It was a big night for me and I was very proud that all the hard work that I'd put in during 1994 was recognized by my fellow riders.

Godolphin had a new trainer for 1995. When Hilal Ibrahim decided to step down he was replaced by my good friend Saeed bin Suroor, who until then had been in charge of a few horses in another yard. Saeed is a total enthusiast, speaks English well, has a great sense of humour and is a key member of the team. He made his mark immediately at the highest level when we shared the first of dozens of major triumphs together with Vettori in the French 2,000 Guineas at Longchamp. Further ahead we were confident of a big run from Moonshell in the Oaks at Epsom. For a filly with so much stamina in her pedigree she ran with promise to finish third in the 1,000 Guineas and had subsequently been working very well with one of Godolphin's best horses, Red Bishop.

I decided to be positive on Moonshell in the Oaks. Once I let her stride into the lead over two furlongs out we were never going to be beaten. Walter Swinburn came out of the pack with a strong run on Dance a Dream, but my filly held on well by one and a quarter lengths. Job done. That evening Walter gave me a lift back to Newmarket in his plane. As we chatted I realised he was still upset at my beating him in the Oaks, so just to cheer him up I suggested it would be his turn the next day on Lammtarra in the Derby. What happens? He goes and beats my mount Tamure.

People assume that I could have ridden Sheikh Mohammed's Lammtarra in the 1995 Derby, but it wasn't a straight choice between the two horses. At that stage I was still retained to ride the Sheikh's horses trained by John Gosden, and Tamure was our best candidate. Unbeaten in three races he was tough, consistent, improving and in form. We were all in the dark about Lammtarra, winner of his only race as a two-year-old, trained by the late Alex Scott. Soon after Lammtarra joined the Godolphin squad in Dubai he suffered from a blood disorder that almost cost him his life. He was out of training for a couple of months and totally out of the Derby picture. But Sheikh Mohammed had a feeling about the horse, owned by his nephew Saeed Maktoum. Most days that winter Sheikh Mohammed spent time at Al Quoz monitoring his progress.

Lammtarra was so ill in the spring that it was always going to be a race against time to get him to Epsom. I admit I was unimpressed when I saw him in two gentle pieces of work, ridden by Walter Swinburn. Frankly I thought they were mad to run him in the Derby. He'd raced only once in his life, nearly died afterwards, and had been rushed in his preparation. He wasn't a good work horse and you had to wonder how he would cope with the twists and gradients of Epsom on his first outing of the season.

For all those reasons riding Lammtarra wasn't an option for me. I was more than happy with Tamure, a 9–1 chance, who was handy all the way and turned for home in third place, poised to pounce on the long-time leader Fahal. But when push came to shove Tamure seemed to take all day to overtake Fahal. I was battering my horse for what seemed an age before he finally struggled into the lead a hundred yards from home.

Then, for the only time in my career, I experienced the heady feeling of knowing I was about to win the Derby. If only I could have bottled it up because it lasted for less than a second. I remember looking up to see how far we had to go, then sensed a shadow appearing on my outside and immediately saw Lammtarra rush past going three strides to our one. Walter had mugged me. Lammtarra only caught Tamure twenty yards from the line but he was travelling so fast he was a length clear at the line.

It was tough to take, particularly because for a fleeting moment I thought I had it won. But I was genuinely pleased for Walter who had come back bravely from life-threatening injuries to claim his third Derby. Tamure held on to second place by three-quarters of a length from his stable companion Presenting. But for the presence of Lammtarra, John Gosden would have had the first two in the Derby and I would have ridden the winner. Whatever our feelings inside we just had to take it on the chin. That night I joined Walter and the Goldolphin team for a celebration dinner at the Fountain, our favourite Chinese restaurant in Newmarket. My Derby dream was over for another year, though Lammtarra would pay me back much sooner than I could have imagined.

Two days later my spirits lifted again with my hundredth winner of the season on Persian Secret. I was back in front in my duel with Jason Weaver and well on track for another double century, but it wasn't all plain sailing. When the Coral-Eclipse Stakes came round at Sandown early in July I found myself on the wrong one for Godolphin. It was a real cock-up and so annoying. When the two worked together at home, Halling – who had been running in handicaps the previous year for John Gosden – absolutely destroyed Red Bishop. Though that was easy work, I could tell Halling was going to go better than Red Bishop at Sandown. But because Red Bishop was a battle-hardened globetrotter, and everyone assured me that he was a lazy worker who only came alive on the track, I ended up on him. What happens? Walter had an easy lead on Halling and made all the running. Singspiel was the only horse to stretch him while I finished three lengths further back on Red Bishop. With over £150,000 for first place, it was one of my more expensive mistakes.

Later in July my latest suspension allowed me to snatch a short break at my dad's home in Sardinia. I was lolling on the beach when Mattie Cowie rang, sounding more excited than usual. He warned me to sit down before announcing that I'd been booked for Lammtarra in the King George V1 and Queen Elizabeth Diamond Stakes at Ascot at the end of the week. That was a huge bonus because up to then Mattie and I had been scratching our heads trying in vain to find a ride in the race.

It was tough on Walter, but these things happen in racing. I'd be lying if I said I was embarrassed to be taking over from him on Lammtarra. The truth is that I was surprised and delighted. I think Walter had had a bit of an argument with someone over missing a couple of rides, but I don't know the full story. In our game it's often a case of dog eat dog. If somebody better than me comes along they will have my job with Godolphin just like that.

That's why you have to make the most of it at the time. If a striker falters and fails to score for Arsenal or Manchester United, the manager doesn't hesitate to drop him and bring in a replacement. Just look at the way Sir Alex Ferguson has shown some of his most famous players the door. One day it will happen to me, but for the moment I'm still holding my own.

In the days before the King George the press were up in arms about the change in riding arrangements for Lammtarra. Incensed that Walter had been jocked off a Derby winner, they took his side and by Saturday the pressure was well and truly on me. Only a win would do. Yet, knowing that I hadn't gone looking for the ride, Walter told me everything about the horse and that, crucially, he would keep finding more in the finish.

The first time I sat on Lammtarra was in the paddock at Ascot. Obviously I didn't know too much about him, and as we approached the final bend I was pumping away furiously without any immediate response. We were flat out turning for home. Then, as the race came to the boil, Michael Hills came past absolutely swinging on the bridle on Pentire. It looked all over but Lammtarra loved a proper scrap and for the next two furlongs we had a right old ding-dong. For most of that time Pentire looked to be cruising home just ahead of us, but when push came to shove he didn't find as much as Michael expected.

The more I asked Lammtarra, the more he responded and in the end we wore Pentire down to gain a famous victory by a neck. My horse dug very deep and showed himself a true champion in only his third race. I had shivers down my spine as we passed the post. It was one of the best feelings of my life. Sheikh Mohammed, too, was clearly overwhelmed by the gutsy style of his victory. I was surprised how much Lammtarra found under sustained pressure. He made me look as if I was smelling of roses, and up to this day the Sheikh says that was the best ride I've ever given one of Godolphin's horses. Of course he is entitled to his opinion, but I suspect Lammtarra's courage flattered me a bit. My view is that over ten years I've nicked better races for the boss.

My roller coaster season nearly came to an abrupt end early in August at Haydock with one of the worst falls of my career on an old favourite of mine called Wainwright. It was his last race before he was due to join me as a hack for Catherine. As the old horse had terrible feet, Sheikh Mohammed had agreed to let us have him as a pet. But his life was snuffed out in a horrible fall that day which left me out for the count for quite a few minutes. When he snapped one of his forelegs the first part of me that hit the ground was my head. Mike Tyson couldn't have inflicted more damage and when I came round I didn't know if it was Tuesday or Thursday.

I felt like I'd been flattened by a ten-ton truck, partly because the brutal force of the impact on my head had ricocheted through my neck and spine to the rest of my body. Though I was discharged from hospital the next day I knew instinctively that I'd struggle to be back in time for York in just over a fortnight. In desperation I turned to Andrew Ferguson, a gifted, workaholic masseur with magic hands who has no end of ballet dancers on his books. After confirming that I was in trouble, he tried to put me back together in double quick time.

But the first morning I rode out again for John, I turned blue with pain during a gentle canter and had to jump off and lead the horse back home. Since I was in agony it was still touch and go whether I'd make York. I was blowing like a train, unfit, my muscles ached, and I wouldn't have passed the vet – but I made it by the skin of my teeth to win the Nunthorpe Stakes on the Thursday. I was the most nervous jockey of all in the weighing room beforehand. It was like I was going out for my first ride. After such a terrible fall I was worried how I'd perform, whether I'd be able to push the same as before, whether my timing was still there. Luckily So Factual had plenty in hand and looked after me.

Suddenly I was closing on the landmark figure of 1,000 winners. It finally arrived at Doncaster on 9 September. Band On The Run took me on to 999 early in the afternoon, and then came Classic Cliche for Godolphin in the St Leger, a race I'd always wanted to win so that I could wear the floppy velvet cap which by tradition is always presented to the successful jockey. I wanted one for my trophy cabinet.

At one stage I was expecting to ride the ante-post favourite Presenting for John Gosden, but once Classic Cliche became a contender for Godolphin I was committed to him. When the rain came, Presenting was withdrawn. Up to that point in his career Classic Cliche was seen as a twilight horse, but he was always keeping on doggedly at the end of his races and I really fancied his chances because I was confident that he was going to stay the distance of one and three-quarter miles. He was a massive, powerful animal, like a giant charger. I hoped that once he got into a rhythm he would be hard to pass.

That's exactly what happened, though the other jockeys thought I was crazy when I kicked him into a clear lead with well over three furlongs left. He kept going strongly right to the line and could hardly have won more easily, though I dared not look round until the last fifty yards. I was so excited to achieve my thousandth winner in such a famous old race, and that I'd done it so quickly. It seemed like I'd been riding for only two or three years. I couldn't have stage-managed it better and threw my goggles into the crowd before unleashing a flying dismount from Classic Cliche. I then collected my cap with great pride before ordering bubbly all round for the boys in the weighing room.

Soon the Arc in Paris was dominating my thoughts. It was now the one race above all others that I wanted to win. As a small boy in Italy I watched it year after year on TV, more often in black and white than colour. Sometimes I saw other big races, too, like the Grand National and the Derby. The National was an amazing spectacle but I never expected to be riding in it, and I usually only showed any interest in the Derby as a youngster on the rare occasions my dad rode in it.

So, for me, the Arc was the race above all others. There always seemed to be thirty runners with a mix of French, English and Italian horses providing lots of drama in a beautiful setting. Naturally my heroes like Yves Saint-Martin and my dad had ridden in it. Now it was my turn. Initially I was tempted to ride Balanchine who'd made a comeback from the attack of colic that almost claimed her life the previous year. In September we'd only just been pipped by the previous year's Arc winner Carnegie in the Prix Foy. I thought she'd run a huge trial for the Arc that day.

Simon Crisford looked surprised when I confided that I was leaning towards Balanchine in preference to Lammtarra. I can remember sitting in his office as he rang Sheikh Mohammed for his verdict. It was a startlingly short conversation. 'Frankie rides Lammtarra', said the boss. Then the phone went dead.

I flew over to Paris with Catherine for the weekend and set myself up by landing two decent races on Saturday on Grey Shot and Flemensfirth. That evening we took in a show at the Crazy Horse with can-can dancers before a reasonably early night.

I get so excited before a big race that my heart was going a million miles an hour when I woke up the next morning. My hands were sweating and when I wandered into the bathroom I was amazed to see that my hair was standing on end as if I'd just had an electric shock. It could have been the boxing promoter Don King staring back at me from the mirror. I put on some clothes, wandered downstairs to collect a *Racing Post*, talked to some punters who wished me luck, read the paper in five seconds, gelled my hair and was champing at the bit ready to leave for the nearby racecourse well before 10 a.m.

Catherine protested that we had hours to kill, but the longer she took to get ready the more I became anxious to set off, concerned that we might be caught in a traffic jam. Finally I snapped. Bursting with impatience, I couldn't wait a moment longer. We rushed down, found a taxi and reached Longchamp shortly after 11 a.m. without a person in sight. Half of Paris was still asleep. Even the valets hadn't arrived. At least the weighing-room was open. I left Catherine to sort out her ticket, had a sauna, read the paper, enjoyed a leisurely massage and finally began to settle down.

For weeks my dad had been drumming into my head the importance of a sharp start in the Arc. We must have spoken a hundred times. The only thing that mattered, he repeated, was to jump out smartly like a sprinter, go flat out and get in the first three. He left me in no doubt that he'd go ballistic if I didn't follow his instructions to the letter. I was hardly about to argue since Ascot had taught me that Lammtarra was vulnerable to anything with a bit of zap because he couldn't quicken instantly. So my plan in the Arc was to be extremely aggressive, a bit like Andre Agassi going into the fifth set of a grand slam final. I'd get out there and kill them all off before anyone could ace me with a sharp serve.

Lammtarra jumped off so well I was able to settle him in the ideal spot in second place, three or four lengths behind Luso, who gave us a perfect tow. At the top of the straight, aware that the challenges would soon be arriving from all directions, I knew it was time to go. By making my move with three furlongs still left we enjoyed first run and helped take the sting out of our rivals. Lammtarra responded like a champion, pounced on Luso and set sail for home under full power.

It was a fantastic feeling to be clear in such a great race in the short straight with tens of thousands of racegoers screaming. I started to wonder what the horse was feeling. It was only his fourth run but I was confident nothing could catch us. As it was a cloudy day and I was wearing dark goggles everything seemed remote – dream-like. The horse and I were in a world of our own. Only we knew what was happening. It was all in slow motion, just like the movies.

I kept pumping away as hard as I could and one by one we saw off all the challenges – until out of the corner of my left eye I spotted my good friend Olivier Peslier appear with a sustained charge on Freedom Cry in the middle of the course. I was alarmed that we might not be able to hold on but Lammtarra found extra in the last one hundred yards and was drawing away at the line.

As a son of the peerless Nijinsky out of an Oaks winner, Snow Bride, he was bred to be a superstar and that's just what he proved to be that day, the best we'd seen for years. He was like a lion in victory, so tough, a born fighter who refused to be beaten. I heard the others coming but he kept finding more. It was his will of iron which helped him become the first un-beaten winner of the Arc since the great Italian colt Ribot back in 1956.

I was suffering from wax in one of my ears that weekend, so the emotion of winning while half deaf sent me completely over the top. I turned round, looked at the crowd and felt a bit like Neil Armstrong landing on the Moon. The buzz I got from winning meant that much to me. It was a cue for the highest flying dismount I've ever managed. That was the biggest leap in the world. Sheikh Mohammed then gave me a fierce hug which said more than a thousands words.

After the presentations I was running around like a lunatic giving high fives all round. Grasping my trophy in my left hand

I sprinted along the front of the grandstands. Down the long exit gangway punters were standing five deep, reaching over the rail to touch me. I slapped all the hands I could reach along one side, then switched the trophy to my right hand and repeated the process on the way back into the paddock. It was madness, of course, but I loved every minute of it. Later the Godolphin team had a knees-up as we all flew back in the same plane, drinking and spraying champagne around as though it was going out of fashion. I was still half crazy at what I'd achieved.

I was the proudest man in the world when I arrived at Pontefract races the next day, but the smile was removed from my face at the end of the afternoon after a ruling by the stewards that left me facing a hefty ban under the new totting up procedure. Riding a horse with the unpronounceable name of La Alla Wa Asa, I was found guilty of irresponsible riding. I thought the stewards were out of order. My horse was a big greenhorn, backward and inexperienced, didn't handle the bend, and took somebody out. Although it wasn't deliberate, it cost me a long holiday.

I returned to Yorkshire two days later for a treble at York. This included my two-hundredth winner of the season on Sheer Danzig, so I became the first jockey since Sir Gordon Richards in 1952 to claim back-to-back double centuries. A month later I ended the season as champion again with 216 winners, a decent enough figure given my injuries and suspensions. It rounded off the best year of my life to that point, but I made it clear that I wouldn't be chasing Gordon's record of 269 winners in the future. The championship rules were changing so that winners on the all-weather circuits would no longer count towards the title. Also, Sheikh Mohammed's fast-expanding Godolphin team had global ambitions which would require my presence regularly overseas. My days of riding flat out for ten months in this country were over. I can't say I was sorry.

That winter there was an even more significant change to my lifestyle. On Valentine's Day, 1996, I took Catherine to lunch at Scalini, my favourite Italian restaurant just behind Harrods. After the main course I suggested she placed her knapkin over her eyes. When she refused, my well-laid plans were briefly in disarray, but eventually she agreed to turn away. I dropped onto one knee, took her hands in mine and asked her to marry me. Thank goodness she said yes. What's more the diamond engagement ring I'd bought for her was a perfect fit. The waiters all started clapping and within seconds everyone in the restaurant was applauding us.

Asking Catherine to marry me was the best decision I've ever made. She's a beautiful girl, kind and generous and knows exactly how to handle my mood swings. There are no half measures with me, I'm either hyperactive or in a total strop. The highs are amazingly high and the lows are very low. She picks me up when I am down and brings me back to earth when I go over the top. And together we have produced five lovely bambinos. How lucky can you be?

seventeen

Godolphin Comes Calling

The start of the 1996 season saw a subtle change in my job description. I continued to ride for Sheikh Mohammed but the focus of his attention was switching dramatically. From now on the high-flying Godolphin team would have first claim on me. After that I would ride the Sheikh's horses with other trainers in England and France. My contract included a handsome retainer and a Mercedes which is replaced every so often. So in March, instead of the daily grind on the all-weather, I found myself commuting to Dubai, riding Godolphin's horses most mornings as the sun came up at their training centre at Al Quoz.

The band of Indian stable lads and experienced work riders are in the yard before six each morning, seven days a week, to bandage the horses' legs before first lot. However cool it is first thing, the sun is usually beating down from a cloudless sky by 9 a.m. Its certainly preferable to having sand kicked in my face at Lingfield, Wolverhampton and Southwell. The horses, too, appreciate the climate, their coats gleaming with good health after several months in balmy temperatures.

Sheikh Mohammed's determination to take on the world was evident when he announced details of the first Dubai World Cup to be run at Nad Al Sheba on Wednesday 27 March, three days before the Grand National. A first prize of over £1.5 million was more than enough to tempt the top American dirt specialists to make the long journey to Dubai. This included their best horse, Cigar, who was hopeless on grass but still unbeaten on dirt.

The build-up to that first Dubai World Cup was straight out of a show biz manual. There was a huge party in the desert attended by thousands of guests, but the highlight of the week for me was a private concert given by Mick Hucknell and Simply Red at the Hilton Beach Club with the waves lapping on the shore only yards from the stage. Naomi Campbell was there with a couple of beauties from *Baywatch* and a galaxy of stars from stage and screen. Mick chose as his opening number that evening one of his big hits, 'Money's Too Tight to Mention'! At the end of the concert I had a few drinks with Mick and his dad who turned out to be a racing fan.

On paper, Godolphin had assembled a decent home team with four runners in the big race, including my mount Halling. But, crucially, none of our turf-bred horses was used to having sand kicked in his face in race after race, which proved to be a huge disadvantage. It is a totally different discipline. All of a sudden in the World Cup they were going to find themselves unable to lie up early on because they couldn't match the early speed of the American horses. Then when they tried to close they would resent the dirt coming back in their faces every bit as much as a boxer having pebbles thrown in his eyes.

Although Halling had won his warm-up race on dirt, it didn't help that he had a poor draw in the World Cup on the inside close to the rails. That's a very hard starting position because you are either burning up too much gas by attempting to stay close to the leaders, or you are receiving all the kick-back by giving them a chance sitting in behind. A European horse drawn in any of the three stalls on the inside next to the rails is just about finished even before the gates open.

So it was hardly the greatest surprise that the three American horses had the race to themselves. Cigar kicked for home early in the straight, then held on in a titanic struggle with Soul Of The Matter. It was a fantastic race to launch the Dubai World Cup, but I was much too far behind on Halling to appreciate it at the time. My old sparring partner Pentire did best of the European horses, finishing fourth. We all had much to learn about dirt racing, though Halling would show his true form in Europe that summer back on turf.

Better times lay ahead back when the Godolphin horses returned to England late in April. We struck immediately with Mark Of Esteem, one of the horses at the centre of a well-publicised split between Henry Cecil and Sheikh Mohammed. Godolphin had already profited the previous year from horses previously trained by Henry. Moonshell, Vettori and Classic Cliche had all started their careers with him. Now he lost out again as I gained the tightest possible victory in the 2,000 Guineas on Mark Of Esteem.

He came to us with a big reputation, but when a horse spends all winter working on a dirt surface you can't always tell how he will run on grass. On dirt you tend to build up a momentum because it is so difficult for a horse to start and stop without the necessary grip on its feet. But when horses have a decent footing on turf they can produce a burst of acceleration that wouldn't be possible on dirt. What we saw from Mark Of Esteem on our training track was totally misleading. It disguised the truth that he had a searing turn of speed.

Unaware of this, I made my move earlier than I should have done in the Guineas and snatched a lead of perhaps a length on Mark Of Esteem who then held on by the skin of his teeth. It looked like Even Top and Bijou d'Inde were finishing fast, but I was coming back to them having been in front too soon. My horse ended up having a really hard race because I had to get stuck into him to hold on. He was knackered at the end. I thought we'd won, but Philip Robinson was equally convinced he had nailed us on the line on Even Top.

All three horses were made to wait out on the course, circling round and round, until the result of the photo was announced. When Mark Of Esteem's number was called first I leaped into the air with joy and landed in the arms of our travelling head lad, John Davis. It was an instinctive expression of delight that I'd won the same famous race which my father had twice captured in the seventies, but that moment of exuberance later cost me a fine of £500 for making illegal contact with John before I'd weighed in.

I was guilty at worst of a technical breach of the rules. It seemed a harsh penalty for a harmless bit of fun, but nothing compared to the suspensions the stewards then handed out for whip offences to the three jockeys involved in the tightest finish to the Guineas that anyone could remember. Jason Weaver on Bijou d'Inde got two days, Philip got four and I was stunned to be hardest hit with eight days. It was a ridiculous punishment. The way the race was run I thought I'd done really well to hold on. Instead I was pilloried in the papers as a butcher and left facing a lengthy holiday. For what? Just doing my job.

My horse had scrambled home by no more than an inch. If I hadn't been hard on him he wouldn't have won, but it was done to encourage Mark Of Esteem, not punish him. When you flick a horse quickly, as I did that day, you don't make nearly as hard a contact as when you strike him every four or five strides with full force. I consoled myself with the thought that it would have been much harder to bear if I'd ended up with eight days for being beaten.

Mark Tompkins, the trainer of Even Top, was not a happy bunny either. Nobody likes to finish second in the Guineas but some of his bitter comments were picked up by the press. Mark described me as 'most unprofessional'. At the time I was a bit wounded about some of the things he said, but he's a nice fellow and I didn't take it all to heart. One of his suggestions was that I should be working in Chipperfield's Circus. I didn't mind that. If the circus was good enough for my mother it was certainly good enough for me.

My record in the Vodafone Derby would hardly set the world alight, but that didn't prevent United Racecourses signing me up late that spring for a fee of £5000 to promote the race. I was delighted to do my bit for the Derby because it means so much to me. Every jockey wants to win it more than any other race, but it is also the people's race. The bonus was that I met up with Vinnie Jones who soon became a good friend. I think Epsom called me in to help boost their decision to switch the Derby to Saturday from its traditional slot on the first Wednesday of June. A Saturday Derby made sense to me with so many more people free to go racing at weekends. Because the world is smaller now the race had lost some of its glamour. Other sports like soccer were invading the media space previously devoted entirely to the race. Once, punters bet solely on horses and greyhounds. Now they can gamble on a dozen sports at the same time.

The people in charge at Epsom were anxious to use me to raise the Derby's profile. My role involved press conferences and a photo call with my friend David Platt at England's training camp at Bisham Abbey near Marlow. I first got to know David when he was playing for Sampdoria in Italy, so you can imagine my delight when he signed for my beloved Arsenal in 1995. Most footballers I've met love a bet. David took it a stage further by becoming a racehorse owner with John Gosden and has had a fair bit of luck with horses like Handsome Ridge.

Promoting the Derby came naturally to me because ever since I came to England I've understood its significance in the sporting calendar. Godolphin didn't have a serious Derby candidate that year, so I was free to ride Sheikh Mohammed's colt Shantou, a 25–1 shot trained by John Gosden. Shantou was so difficult at home he used to train on his own. He was a gangster really, a man's ride. In short he was a zero bastard, but he had ability and I knew he would stay the trip even though he'd only won a maiden at Sandown. I thought he ran out of his skin in finishing third to Shaamit. At first he struggled to go the pace, so coming down the hill I was further back than I wanted to be. I was in good company with Pat Eddery beside me on Dushyantor. It was such a rough race with Pat and I zig-zagging on our horses, looking for daylight. Dushyantor eventually claimed second place with Shantou just behind him.

Pricket was beaten out of sight by Lady Carla in the Oaks the previous day, but Swain made sure I didn't leave Epsom empty-handed by taking the Coronation Cup in a thunderous finish against Singspiel with Michael Kinane on board. That was one of my first rides for the French wizard André Fabre. I was honoured that he wanted me. French trainers tend to like you to drop a horse in behind to conserve energy for a late run. To my surprise André asked me to jump out in front on Swain, kick him in the belly, give him a breather at the top of the hill then set sail for home. I carried out my instructions to the letter and just gained the day in a ding-dong battle with Singspiel over the final quarter mile. It was a fantastic race between two brilliant horses.

The twelfth of June was one of those days that made me want to keep riding until I was fifty. It began at dawn on the gallops as we gave some of the Godolphin horses their final pieces of work before Royal Ascot the following week. Then I flew to Yarmouth for a rewarding treble. Soon after winning the 4.45 on Fatefully, I took to the skies once more for a swift flight to Kempton where another treble took my tally of winners for the day to six. One way and another I was absolutely flying. As I would be riding at Newbury the next day I'd arranged to stay with Ian Balding at Kingsclere so that I could put some of his two-year-olds through their paces in the morning.

Ian must have been going soft by then because he allowed me a lie-in during first lot. By the time he woke me with the papers at around 8.30 the sun was offering promise of a glorious summer's day. It was so warm I rode four of his nicer two-year-olds in a tee-shirt and jeans. Life couldn't have been sweeter. Later at Newbury racecourse I spent an hour before racing with youngsters from the Fortune Centre of Riding Therapy based in Dorset. It is one of my favourite charities which gives pupils with special needs the chance of further education, with horses at the heart of their activities. The Centre runs a residential course and also holds weekly riding therapy sessions for a further fifty young children. It does a terrific job and I try to help whenever I can.

Then it was down to business. One of my trickier rides that afternoon at Newbury was a highly strung grey filly called Shawanni for Godolphin in the Ballymacoll Stakes. In our previous race in the French 1,000 Guineas she had nearly pulled my arms out, took charge after two furlongs yet still finished close behind the placed horses. She was a great big filly with a nasty side to her, one of those girls who spell trouble. In the preliminaries Shawanni was in a particularly vile mood. She froze the moment I jumped on her back in the paddock and wouldn't move. I quickly slipped my feet out of the irons and asked her lad to take a half-turn behind some of the other horses as she didn't seem to appreciate being out in front on her own.

She took a couple of steps, froze again, then without warning reared over backwards on top of me. If my feet had been in the stirrups I might have been able to use my legs to thrust myself away from her before the moment of impact. Now I had no means of escape. When fillies freeze like that they mean to squash you when they somersault backwards. That's just what Shawanni did to me. I fell underneath her in a sickening crunch on the tarmac path in the paddock.

She was going to break my pelvis but in a desperate effort to move away from her at the last moment I landed on my left elbow. Immediately I felt a searing pain. I knew I'd smashed my elbow. I lay in a crumpled heap, in terrible pain, already suffering from the first onset of shock. One of the first to reach me was the trainer's wife, Jane Chapple-Hyam, who asked for the pin on my collar to be removed to assist my breathing.

At first the medical people didn't appreciate the severity of my injury. One doctor even declared that I was only suffering from bruising. Through gritted teeth I assured him that I'd shattered my elbow. Soon I was on my way to Royal Berks Hospital by ambulance, but the casualty department was overrun that day and it was another hour and a half before I was taken down to X-ray. By then I was in bits. The pain was unbelievable.

The X-rays confirmed my worst fears and showed that the

bone from my upper arm had been forced right through my elbow joint. Only then was I given a pain killing injection and wheeled into a private ward. John Gosden was straight on the case, arranging for Andy to bring Catherine down to see me that evening. I was so lucky that Richard Dodds, the consultant surgeon, was free to operate the next morning. I knew I was facing a long spell on the sidelines, but Richard's skill gave me a realistic chance of salvaging something from the wreckage of my season.

Watching Royal Ascot at home on TV was a grim experience for me. So many of the horses I'd expected to be riding ran well, starting with Charnwood Forest who took the opening race on Tuesday. My spirits descended to an all-time low when Italy were knocked out of the Euro 96 championships. After missing three more winners on the Thursday – including Classic Cliché in the Gold Cup – I was like a bear with a sore head. On the spur of the moment on Friday I decided to cheer myself up by going to Ascot for the final day. Aware that I was making everyone around me miserable, I had to get out of the house. I borrowed a morning suit from Bruce Raymond, cut off an arm from one of my shirts and hitched a ride to the races with John and Rachel Gosden.

The best part of the day was meeting the pop legend Ronnie Wood, one of John's newer owners. Ronnie proved to be a great racing fan. I've never known anyone keener on the sport. It was strange talking to him about horses like any other racing enthusiast. Here was one of the biggest names in rock music looking up to me as though I was some kind of idol. On the same day Sheikh Mohammed told me that he'd retired Shawanni. Apparently the first time she'd been ridden after Newbury she dived under a running rail on the gallops at Newmarket with her lad still on her back.

Soon it was time for Mr Dodds to check on the progress of my elbow. Eleven years earlier I'd fainted when the plaster had been removed from my broken right elbow in Milan. This time I took Catherine with me to hold my hand in case I collapsed again. The prognosis was encouraging so, to speed up my recovery, we flew to Gran Canaria where my dad has an apartment. To while away the time I read a book on Fred Archer, one of the greatest flat jockeys of all time. Despite being 5 ft 10 in tall and using the most drastic methods imaginable to keep his weight down, he was champion jockey thirteen times in succession and won twenty-one Classics before he shot himself in a fit of depression at the age of 29.

At first I spent every afternoon by the toddler's pool, crouching under the water, trying a few gentle movements with my arm. After five days I was swimming busily in the pool, and as my confidence increased I progressed to swimming in the sea alongside my dad who was masterminding my training regime. The temperature was ideal and with Catherine to comfort me I briefly stopped worrying about all the winners I was missing. My frustration at my injuries rose to the surface again when I saw on teletext that Halling, one of my favourite horses, had won the Coral-Eclipse Stakes. I rushed straight down to the pool and completed twenty-five laps in a new personal best time. It was a signal to return to England. I was impatient to be riding again but Mr Dodds wouldn't hear of it. The broken bones in my elbow had still not healed completely.

We headed for the sun once more, this time to Sardinia, where I worked on the muscles in my left arm by lifting big, black shiny stones above my head. I also wore weights on my wrists. By that stage I was strong enough to swim half a mile across the bay. After a week I felt ready to go. Initially Richard Dodds had given me a time scale of between four and six months for my comeback. That's fine if you are dealing with people who haven't done any physical work.

I was thinking more in terms of two months. You have to start somewhere because however long you wait it will always hurt at first. Once the bone has healed in four weeks or so you have to get it moving. Of course it hurts because the limb is rusty and all the muscles and ligaments are slack. You just have to go through the pain barrier. That's the part that people don't understand. It's true that all injured jocks come back too early, but in such a competitive sport we have no choice.

During Goodwood I rode out for the Sussex trainer Lady Anne Herries to help the BBC's racing correspondent Julian Wilson put together a feature on my progress. At breakfast I sat next to her husband Colin, a large, genial man I'd not met before. Julian, who fancies himself as a spin bowler, soon started banging on about all the wickets he'd taken for the Newmarket trainers' XI. As my eyes glazed, he turned to ask if I was keen on cricket. I replied that it was the most boring sport on earth, even worse than watching paint dry.

Julian was stunned, absolutely horrified. Judging from his

expression I was guilty of high treason at the very least. In total contrast Colin seemed highly amused by my views. He couldn't stop laughing. Julian soon put me straight. By the time he'd finished I had to agree I'd made a right fool of myself. Then again, how was I to know that Colin was the cricketing legend Sir Colin Cowdrey, once captain of England and one of the finest batsmen of the last century? No-one enjoyed the joke more than him. We quickly became friends and by the end of the morning he was giving me bowling lessons on the lawn.

Despite the lingering pain from my elbow I was determined to resume at Newmarket on 9 August. It would swiftly lead to the best three months I've ever enjoyed as a jockey. But to my dismay I needed almost a week to play myself in and ended up in the headlines for all the wrong reasons after finishing third at Windsor on an ancient old campaigner called Cape Pigeon. Perhaps if I'd been race sharp we might have finished closer. I'd ridden Cape Pigeon a fair bit over the years but he was eleven by then and liked things his own way. Because we had a right old battle with another horse for the lead over the first two furlongs, he was knackered at the end as he finished third behind Talatath – who provided Walter Swinburn with a fairytale winning ride on his own return from injury.

The stewards held an inquiry and accepted my explanation that I had burnt Cape Pigeon out by going too fast too soon. That should have been the end of the matter, but his owner Eric Gadsden created a terrible fuss by writing to the newspapers claiming that I hadn't ridden to orders. He called me a disgrace, lashed the stewards for not taking action against me, and ended up by saying he'd be selling all his horses. It was no more than a storm in a teacup, but fuelled by Mr Gadsden's fury it rumbled on for days when I was desperately in search of a winner to boost my flagging confidence.

Aware that I was trying too hard in those first few testing days as I struggled to regain my touch, John Gosden advised me to be natural and not to force things. The tide finally turned on 16 August at Newbury, the very course where I'd smashed my elbow. By the end of the afternoon I was flying again after a treble which included two winners for John. I followed that with a double on Saturday.

Further success came my way on Sunday on Bahamian Bounty for David Loder in the Prix Morny at Deauville. Now I was really motoring. The winning streak continued at York with a stunning victory on Halling in the Juddmonte International. Then the wheels came off. My headlong rush to comeback hadn't prepared me for the demands of a hard three days in the saddle at York.

My problems began with a disagreement with jockey Richard Quinn which cost me a four-day ban in the Yorkshire Oaks. Not for the first time he was all over me like a rash on Whitewater Affair. Only when his filly weakened and began to drop back was I able to get out on Russian Snows. The two fillies just touched as we pulled out. It was the sort of thing that happens every day, but the head-on camera made the incident look so bad that I copped four days for irresponsible riding.

The next morning I needed to lose weight in a hurry to do

8 st 6 lb on North Song for John Gosden. I made it with barely an ounce to spare after running round the track and spending longer than I wanted in the sauna. After three consecutive rides I was feeling hot and sweating freely, drained of all energy as I left the paddock on North Song. In the race he was up there all the way, pulling eagerly, yet still rallied to finish second, but when I tried to pull him up he bolted with me towards the stables. His mouth was dead and he was out of control as disaster beckoned.

I remember thinking the end was coming as we headed straight for the starter's car. This was going to be my big accident and I could do nothing about it. Just when a collision seemed inevitable he stopped all by himself. I took a deep breath, turned him round and aimed him in the direction of the unsaddling enclosure. The drama was over but I felt dreadful, and then had to listen to John telling me I'd given the horse a poor ride.

I should have called a halt because I was in no condition to hold a child's pony, let alone a hard-pulling thoroughbred. My arms had been pulled out of their sockets by North Song and my left elbow was as weak as a baby's. I struggled through two more rides in a swirl of exhaustion before being taken to the ambulance room where they plied me with Coca-Cola and sugar in an urgent attempt to kick start my battery. In the next forty-five minutes I also downed five cups of tea liberally laced with sugar.

I bounced back two days later at Goodwood on Mark Of Esteem who showed his true colours with a brilliant victory in the Celebration Mile. A week earlier he had worked like a champion. In racing we talk excitedly of the best horses catching pigeons. That morning Mark Of Esteem passed the pigeon after three furlongs, cooked it after five and was already suffering from indigestion by the time he reached the seven furlong marker.

For all our success there was one big omission from the partnership between John Gosden and myself. We finally put that right in the 1996 St Leger with Shantou. It proved to be one of the most emotional triumphs either of us had experienced. John is a big guy with broad shoulders, but in the weeks before the race he'd been getting plenty of grief in the press about his lack of success in the Classics. Outwardly he seemed unaffected but I knew he was hurting inside, mainly because the criticism was unfair.

I owed so much to John. He was the man who put his faith in me when others hesitated. I don't mind admitting that when he walked up to the podium to collect his trophy at Doncaster my eyes were full of tears of pride at what he'd just achieved. I'll never forget that moment because I knew it meant everything to him to win a prize like that.

Shantou was a right old bruiser, who knew how to handle himself. Just as at Epsom three months earlier, we ended up in a sustained scrap with Dushyantor and Pat Eddery. Dushyantor looked sure to win when he cruised into the lead two furlongs out. Then we locked horns and went at it like two street fighters trading punches, looking for the knock-out blow, Pat with his stick in his right hand and me with mine in my left hand.

A piece of grit in my eye was driving me mad at the same time. It is so hard to concentrate when you are blinking half the time, but in a tight finish every little piece of gamesmanship helps. Aware that Dushyantor was ultra genuine and responded to a challenge, I let Shantou drift right-handed away from him into the centre of the course before giving him three or four quick cracks with my whip in the last fifty yards. He responded by lunging forward and heading Dushyantor in the last ten strides. It was the only time he led throughout the race.

Winning the St Leger on Shantou was a magic feeling. I remember screaming and waving to the stands, but most of all I was thrilled for John. Once again there was a backlash as Pat and I were suspended for our use of the whip. He ended up with two days and I got four. Just like a motorist with several speeding convictions, I knew I was heading for a lengthy ban under racing's totting up procedure.

In my opinion it's a crazy system. Did the stewards really expect the pair of us to put down our whips in the last dramatic stages of an epic duel in such an important race? Was anyone who understands horses honestly offended by our actions? If so let me put the record straight because people watching on TV who have never seen a horse in real life tend to be the ones who make all the fuss.

I've been riding since I was a toddler and the truth is that one strike with the whip is one too many on one horse and a hundred times is not enough on another. Shantou definitely comes into the second category. Hitting him had about as much effect as hitting a rhino. Cruelty didn't come into it. He was a big, heavy colt, weighed nearly a thousand pounds, and would kill you given half a chance.

Yes, technically I was guilty of excessive use of the whip but you can't hurt horses like Shantou. In the St Leger you have to go for it. It was exactly the same scenario for me on Mark Of Esteem in the Guineas back in April. As a result I earned the dubious distinction of becoming the first jockey in history to collect separate whip bans in winning two Classics in the same year.

eighteen

The Bookies Were Crying for Mercy

Wall Street came first on the day that turned my world upside down in 1996. I wasn't in the best of moods as I arrived at Ascot on Saturday 28 September for the Festival of British Racing, one of the highlights of the racing calendar. A long afternoon's toil at Haydock 24 hours earlier had drawn a blank – six rides and nothing to show for it except a lousy journey on the way home on a Friday night.

At least Ascot looked more promising. I really fancied Wall Street in the Cumberland Lodge Stakes. He was entitled to be favourite, as close to a certainty as you can find. I was also hopeful that Mark Of Esteem could see off the mighty filly Bosra Sham in the most important race of the weekend, the Queen Elizabeth II Stakes. Some of the others had chances, but on a glittering card like that any jockey would settle for one winner.

Since Wall Street had plenty of stamina I planned to sit close behind the obvious danger, Salmon Ladder, then press for home once we hit the straight. So it was a bit of a surprise to find myself in front after a few strides. As Wall Street seemed happy making the running at a sound pace, I let him bowl along before quickening it up on the home turn. Salmon Ladder pressed us hard over the last two furlongs but Wall Street kept pulling out more and won well by half a length. My ace had delivered the perfect start.

I could have ridden three or four in the next race, the Diadem Stakes over six furlongs, but ended up on Diffident, my only mount of the day which I thought had no chance. I told Godolphin's travelling head lad, Sam Avis, that I would bare my bum under Newmarket's clock tower if he managed to win. It was a very tough contest and we had our doubts about the horse after the way he let us down the time before at Newmarket where he was far too keen and ran a stinker. He was one of those frustrating horses that have lots of speed but refuse to settle.

At one point earlier in the week Diffident was far from being a certain runner, so it looked as though I might be on Lucayan Prince for David Loder. Leap For Joy was another on my short-list, but once Diffident was declared of course I had to ride him. He turned out to be my luckiest winner of the season. I still can't really believe that he won.

I dropped Diffident in close behind the leading bunch, as Averti took us along at a smart gallop. He half settled for me and it probably helped that a horse in front of us was weaving around, blocking our path. When I tried to edge past him on the left he closed the door and then the same thing happened when I switched to try to squeeze through on the right. Time was running out fast. Eventually I managed to get through on his left. The winning post was looming but Diffident quickened up so smartly that I felt we still had a chance of catching Leap For Joy.

When sprinters are jostling for position races are won and lost in a split second. As Diffident put his head in front of Leap For Joy in the only place that matters, Lucayan Prince suddenly burst through to join us. The three horses crossed the line as close to a triple dead-heat as you are likely to see, but I was confident we weren't beaten. One thing's for sure, with any sort of run Walter Swinburn would have won decisively on Lucayan Prince. The photo confirmed that Diffident, a 12–1 chance, had stolen it by a short head from Lucayan Prince, with Leap For Joy another short head away in third place. It couldn't have been any closer.

Little did I know that in her room at the Holiday Inn in Mayfair, Mary Bolton, wife of a Somerset cattle dealer, watched the finish with more than a little interest. As part of a romantic break in London to celebrate their nineteenth wedding anniversary, the Boltons had backed all seven of my rides in a complicated bet involving twenty-one £9 doubles and a £5 each way accumulator. They laid out a total of £216.91 including betting tax in a nearby Ladbrokes betting shop.

Mary obviously has her priorities right. Once the result of Diffident's race was announced on television she set off on a shopping trip and didn't see another race all afternoon. Elsewhere around the country many others who had put their faith in me with hard cash were equally unaware of what was developing at Ascot. One of them, Darren Yates, boss of a joinery firm from Morecambe in Lancashire, was feeling pretty miserable after the local football side he played for had been thumped 4–0. He had placed a £54 accumulator in his local William Hill shop on my seven mounts.

Back at Ascot I was winding myself up for my most testing ride of the day on Mark Of Esteem, aware that the falling out between Henry Cecil and Sheikh Mohammed at the end of the previous season added spice to the occasion. Henry had trained Mark Of Esteem as a two-year-old and was relying on Bosra Sham to give him the victory that could seal the trainers' championship over Saeed bin Suroor.

There was so much at stake I couldn't help feeling the tension. The Sheikh's faith in his warrior was unshakeable. In the paddock he told me to wait, wait again and then wait even longer before reaching for the rocket booster on Mark Of Esteem. The only tricky moment came when Michael Kinane appeared on my outside on our stable companion Charnwood Forest just as I was about to edge out to make my move. Luckily Michael let me out.

Bosra Sham was a champion filly in her own right and when Pat Eddery set sail for home on her he must have thought he had the race in his pocket. He certainly had a shock when my horse went by him as if his was standing still. I knew Mark Of Esteem had this tremendous turn of foot but also suspected it lasted little more than a furlong.

Once I did ask him, the delivery was like the kick-in from a fuel injection car. It almost knocked me out of the saddle as we rocketed into the clear. I've never had a feeling quite like it in my life. That was the best performance of any miler I've ridden because a tip-top field was lined up against him and he slaughtered them. On the way back to unsaddle I was uncontainable. My first three rides had yielded victories in a Group 3, a Group 2 and now a Group 1 race, all for the team that retained me. I would have settled for three winners there and then. Surely it couldn't get any better?

After all the fuss about my flying dismount from Mark Of Esteem after the 2,000 Guineas I was in two minds about doing it again in this country. Was it worth all the hassle? I knew we had a great horse in Mark Of Esteem but hadn't expected him to blow the filly away like that. If ever there was a perfect excuse for another flying dismount this was it – but at that moment, as if reading my thoughts, an official walked alongside and warned me not to do it. Then as I reached the winner's enclosure Sheikh Maktoum called out 'Go on Frankie, jump.' So I did.

Aware that the pressure was off, I enjoyed the moment to the full, running around screaming and shouting in the weighing room, driving everyone nuts, giving interviews left, right and centre before rushing out to the paddock for my fourth ride of the day on Decorated Hero – known affectionately in John Gosden's yard as Square Wheels because he was such a bad mover. The omens were not good. Decorated Hero was giving weight all round and a 5 pound penalty for a recent success left him carrying the welter burden of 9 st 13 lb. Also, John and I felt he had just about the worst draw of all in stall 22 in the middle of the course.

No wonder we didn't think he could win. Frankly I thought it was an impossible task yet amazingly he proved to be the easiest of all my winners. When the leaders set off too fast they played into my hands and the race somehow landed in my lap. I decided to do my own thing and was so far back early on that we were last. This allowed me gradually to ease Decorated Hero all the way over to the stands' rails and creep into the race. The horses in front were looking a bit tired as we moved stealthily into the action with a quarter of a mile left, and when I launched him on a powerful late run he swept to the front a furlong out.

Decorated Hero finished so well that he was three and a half lengths clear of the runner-up Kayvee at the line. This time I came back with four fingers raised before John Gosden stepped forward to shake my hand. Looking back now, I suppose Decorated Hero must have been a certainty because he won decent races abroad on his next two starts and wound up finishing third in the Breeders' Cup Mile the following year.

Now I had four in the bag and was back in the royal blue colours of Godolphin on Fatefully, a red-hot favourite in the mile handicap. She was well drawn in stall six over the straight mile and I thought she had a decent chance of being placed, but 7–4 seemed a ridiculous price in such a tight race with eighteen runners. Later I realised the skinny odds were created by the sheer weight of money rolling forward from multiple bets on my mounts.

Once again luck in running played a vital part. As the field bunched near the stands rails soon after half-way I was trapped behind a wall of horses searching desperately for a bit of day-light. When the split finally appeared it wasn't very big, but if I'd waited any longer it might have disappeared. As I kicked Fatefully forward I heard Jason Weaver on Ninia shout 'Go on Frankie, go and get 'em.'

But as Fatefully squeezed through she drifted a little left, causing Pat Eddery to slightly check on Questonia who was dropping back at the time. Fatefully shot forward into the lead on the rails with just over a furlong to run and then I heard a horse coming with a furious late run on my outside. It was Abeyr ridden by Ray Cochrane. For a moment I thought they were going to pip us on the line, but Abeyr wouldn't go through with her run and we held on by a whisker.

There was barely time to celebrate my fifth win of the day and my fourth for Godolphin before a stewards' inquiry was announced – though once I saw the head-on film I was very confident that the result would stand. Pat helped by telling the panel that his filly was beaten at the time the two touched. Luckily for me the stewards concluded that the interference was accidental.

I felt totally numb when the inquiry was over because I suddenly realised that I was within touching distance of match-ing the long-time record of six wins at the same meeting. I knew that I'd never have such a good chance again, with Loch-song's sister Lochangel to come in what was virtually a match against Corsini and Pat Eddery in the Blue Seal Stakes. The pair were inseparable in the betting ring at 5–4.

In the paddock Ian Balding was looking worried, wondering

if I had used up all my magic. He explained his fears that Lochangel was so fast she might not last six furlongs on a stiff track like Ascot. He told me to be patient, drop her in behind the leaders and give her every chance to stay the distance. That was easier said than done in a field of five runners. Lochangel was both strong and keen, so when she jumped out of the stalls in front it made sense to let her run. Nobody was taking me on, so I thought 'Sod it, I'll let her bowl. Why take her back and forfeit an early advantage?' So much for my orders.

As Lochangel sailed along eagerly in the lead I tried to save a bit, aware that she might hit a brick wall towards the end. Then with a furlong and a half left I asked her to quicken up and we were still out in the clear on our own. I was expecting Pat to arrive on Corsini at any moment, but when they did finally appear it was all too late and Lochangel held on cosily by three-quarters of a length. As we crossed the line I punched the air with delight, acknowledging that I'd matched the record. It was an astonishing feeling.

I could see that Pat was fuming as we walked back together. Perhaps he was getting fed up with chasing my tail. Certainly he wasn't the happiest man at Ascot. Later he explained that he felt he was beaten by the instructions he was given to drop Corsini in during the first part of the race. If he'd made more use of him Pat felt he could have beaten Lochangel. I'm glad he didn't.

All hell broke lose as we returned to unsaddle. My feet hardly touched the ground as I was pushed and pulled in all directions for interviews and presentations, including some champagne from Sir Michael Oswald, the Queen's representative at Ascot. I even made a little speech to the crowd that threatened to engulf the winner's enclosure. When I spoke to Julian Wilson on BBC TV, I warned him not to touch me because I was red hot.

I knew there was work still to be done on Fujiyama Crest in the final race and thought there was no chance of a fairytale ending. Well, it was impossible to win all seven wasn't it? Yes, he'd won the same race – the Gordon Carter Handicap – with me twelve months earlier as a progressive three-year-old, but he'd been running like a dog all season and had shot up in the weights. The handicapper had him by the throat and this time the task must be beyond him.

Although I didn't realise it at the time, there was already blind panic in the ranks of the nation's bookmakers. Some faced ruin, whatever happened to Fujiyama Crest who had generally been on offer at 12–1 in the morning. In the weighing room I remember Walter Swinburn telling me to concentrate and pull my finger out in the last race, clearly believing that I could win that, too.

I looked at him as though he was stupid before replying 'Walter, I'm on a twelve or fourteen to one shot with far too much weight who is hopelessly out of form. We can't possibly win.' But he persisted, badgering me to be positive. Other jockeys, too, were egging me on and all the while I'm thinking: 'Come on boys, wake up here, get real. Just look at the form book and then you'll see why you are wasting your breath.'

As I walked out to the paddock through a crowd of well-wishers I felt a huge sense of achievement. I'd done what I had to do. Now, at last, the pressure was off. For the first time that day I felt relaxed. In the paddock I told Fujiyama Crest's trainer Michael Stoute 'If this one gets beat, I'm going to blame you.' The horse's lad Derek Heeney was quick to add his own warning: 'Don't forget Frankie that this horse is bone idle. He'll pull himself up given half a chance, so don't be afraid to give him a smack' he suggested as he led us out onto the course.

What happened next left me covered in goose pimples. As we cantered steadily past the stands towards the two mile start near the final bend the racecourse erupted with a thunderous standing ovation. People were hanging over the rails shouting, cheering and applauding me. It was a deeply moving experience, one that left me so full of emotion that I couldn't even remember what I'd ridden in the first race. I felt as though I was on the verge of completing a three-day event in one long, exhausting afternoon. Mark Of Esteem came at the end of day one, the next three winners filled up day two, and now I was embarking on the final one.

John Bolton, whose wife Mary was still shopping in London blissfully unaware of the drama, took up his position on the grandstand steps close to the finishing position. He'd watched the odds on Fujiyama Crest, his final selection in his accumulator, tumble from 12–1 in the morning to 2–1 and was too dazed to consider the implications for his bet.

When I glanced up at the giant screen opposite the stands I couldn't understand why Fuji was such a short price. I remem-

ber thinking that as I'd won six races already, I wasn't going
to let defeat in the final race spoil my day. I'd made all the
running a year earlier on Fujiyama Crest in the Gordon Carter
Handicap, but this time we had the worst draw of all in stall
one, on the stands' side, with another large field of eighteen
runners. It was a 'big ask' to make my way across without
encountering trouble, but the way I felt I had nothing to lose.
Maybe if I'd known upwards of £40 million was running on
the result I'd have panicked and made a mistake.

I kicked Fujiyama Crest out of the stalls, let him find his
stride and immediately began to edge ever so quietly right-
handed across the runners nearest to us. It took the best part
of two and a half furlongs to get across to the far rail and claim
the narrowest of leads. Just as we did so Fuji briefly lost his
back legs as another horse clipped his heels, but by then neither
of us was in the mood for compromise. We had the lead and
the rail and were not going to give them away lightly.

We free-wheeled down the hill towards Swinley Bottom,
moving comfortably out on our own. Then as we turned right-
handed for the long climb over the final mile I heard a
spine-tingling noise emerging from the stands in great waves
of sound. Normally in a race you don't notice the crowd. This
was different. Seeing me in front so far from home on Fuji,
tens of thousands of racegoers were willing us on in a way I'd
never experienced before. Then I began counting down the
furlong markers ahead of us. With half a mile to go I knew it
was time to stretch the lead and as we raced over the road
crossing with three furlongs left I started to hunt Fuji along,

and pinched an extra length or two. All the time I was wondering how much longer we could hold on until the cavalry arrived.

Turning for home I heard a massive roar as the huge crowd sensed that the impossible was unfolding in front of their eyes. Then Northern Fleet emerged from the pack driven with grim determination by Pat Eddery. For Pat it was becoming personal. Even above the noise of the crowd I could hear the frequent crack of his whip as he got stuck into Northern Fleet.

Few jockeys have tried harder in defeat than Pat Eddery that day, but despite all his efforts Fujiyama Crest still held a slender lead as we entered the final furlong. Then we hit the wall. Fuji was beyond tired, barely managing to put one leg in front of the other as Northern Fleet closed in remorselessly. I was praying for the winning post to come but more than once I was certain he was going to beat us.

In the final 100 yards Fuji was numb with exhaustion. The weight on his back was anchoring him, the last weary strides were like a mile and he was running on empty. With twenty five yards to go the distance to the winning post seemed to lengthen. Keep going, keep going, for God's sake concentrate. Fuji was almost unconscious, drawing deep on a reservoir we didn't know he possessed. Somehow he conjured up a little bit more and was still a neck in front as he staggered over the finishing line.

I've never been as happy in my life as that moment after we passed the post. Fujiyama Crest was an awkward thing to ride, a bit like a dinosaur, tall and narrow, with a big long neck. I was so tired, too, so I almost fell off his back as I tried to punch the air. Everything went dark as though I was in a world of my own, then I let out a huge scream.

I couldn't begin to understand what had happened. I suppose it was like Eric Cantona scoring seven times for Manchester United in the FA Cup Final, a total fluke, impossible. It was all too much, far too much to take in and I felt numb for the next two hours. So many times since I've wished that I could go back, relive it all and really milk the occasion. One thing I do know for sure, if the last race had been first I wouldn't have dared be so positive on Fujiyama Crest and so he would almost certainly not have won.

But when you are on a high you have an edge and I doubt if I've ever been higher after winning the previous six races. That made the difference between victory and defeat. Perhaps Pat knew it too. He's such a ferocious competitor and I could see from his face that he was absolutely furious. He wasn't angry with me, just upset at finishing second to me for the third time that afternoon.

I've heard it suggested that the other jockeys gave me the last race. That's complete rubbish. We might all be friends in the weighing room but once we are out on the track there is no quarter asked or given. None of them had glimpsed so much as a sniff of a winner until then. I'd been taking bread from their mouths all afternoon. The seventh race was their chance to make up for lost time and you only had to see Pat's reaction to realise what losing-out again meant to him.

As I returned on Fujiyama Crest a sea of people, thousands of them, seemed to be blocking our path, cheering and waving, overcome by the occasion. It was mass hysteria on a scale I'd never experienced before in racing. Imagine how I felt! John Reid shook my hand and Jason Weaver rode over on Flocheck before raising my hand as if I'd just won a world title fight. I certainly felt as if I'd just gone fifteen rounds.

I was greeted by sheer bedlam in the winner's enclosure. Everyone was going mad. I leaned down, gave Fuji's neck a heartfelt hug, then managed one final flying dismount. It was another personal best on a day of records. As a result I dropped my whip and nearly fell on my backside.

I flung my arms around my friend John Ferguson, Fuji's racing manager, and fielded a huge hug from Michael Stoute who was behaving as if he'd just won the lottery. Maybe in a way he had. The crowd then gave me three cheers and I responded by throwing my goggles among them, then grabbing some champagne and rushing round the enclosure like a Grand Prix driver, spraying the bubbly in all directions. No-one seemed to mind.

Next I leaped into the arms of my trusty valet Dave Currie who has looked after me ever since I came to this country. What a coincidence that Dave's dad Fred had looked after Alec Russell when he equalled the record of all six winners at Bogside in 1957. Now Dave had helped me on the day I became the first jockey in history to ride all seven winners at the same race meeting.

My feet hardly touched the ground over the next hour while I was dragged, pulled and shoved as everybody seemed to want a piece of me at the same time. I was pretty much in a trance as I gave a series of interviews watched by thousands of punters and racegoers who stayed on, long after racing ended, reluctant to leave the scene. Nobody wanted to go home.

I had important calls to make, too. Catherine had watched the first three races before going out, and my father in Tenerife was thoroughly confused after noticing on the teletext that I appeared to have won all seven races on the card. He assumed there was some mistake and took some convincing that it was true.

Then came the autographs. Still wearing the blue and pink silks of Fujiyama Crest I must have signed several thousand racecards, newspapers, scraps of paper and backs of envelopes as racegoers waited patiently in a surprisingly orderly queue. One of them was John Bolton who estimated that he and his wife Mary had won around £300,000 from Ladbrokes on my seven winners. The correct figure was £500,000, and later they presented me with a calendar in a lovely silver frame enscribed with the words 'Frankie, Thanks for a day in a Million'. Naturally the date is set permanently on 28 September 1996. Hundreds of others, too, told me that they had just enjoyed the biggest wins of their lives by putting their faith in me.

I think the cleaners had all finished by the time I left the course in the gathering gloom to meet Andy who was waiting in the car park. Overwhelmed with exhaustion I collapsed into the passenger seat, closed the door and immediately began to feel upset with the world. Andy was impatient to go but I made him wait for ten minutes while I collected my thoughts.

I should have been the happiest man on the planet and still can't explain the onset of my bad mood. Perhaps it was a combination of emotion and tiredness, or maybe the events of the past few hours were just too much for me to handle. Whatever the reason I felt grumpy and miserable, drained of all feeling. It didn't help that my mobile phone never stopped ringing all the way home. Friends were calling offering me congratulations on setting a new record and all I wanted to do was hide myself away from view.

I perked up a bit later at home when Simon Crisford and my business manager Pete Burrell came round for a glass or two of bubbly as we watched the video replay of the day's events at Ascot. We talked briefly about the implications of what I'd done, but none of us was prepared for the avalanche of publicity that overwhelmed me in the next few days. My mood blackened again when Catherine announced that we had to go to a party in Cambridge given by one of her old boyfriends. I needed that like a hole in the head. I was tired, irritable, the phone was going non-stop and I knew I had another long day ahead at Ascot the next afternoon. All I wanted was a meal before collapsing into bed. Some chance!

Eventually I reached an uneasy compromise with Catherine. I did go to the party with her, reluctantly, but we didn't stay long and by the time we reached home I was so bad-tempered the tension between us was unbearable. The greatest day of my life ended with the pair of us sulking in bed, lying back-to-back, not speaking.

Four years later I completed a deal which guaranteed that Fujiyama Crest would stay with me for the rest of his days. It was the best day's business I have ever done. Late in 2000

Where's my parachute?

I knew I was going to die – but a miraculous escape for Ray Cochrane and I in 2000 (above and right).

AND THEY GOT OUT ALIVE

MIRACLE: This is the tangled wreckage of the plane carrying jockeys Frankie Dettori, right, and Ray Cochrane that crashed at Newmarket yesterday. They survived but the pilot died.

FULL STORY: PAGES 2 and 3

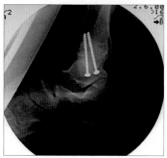

Leaving hospital with Catherine (above), and my broken ankle (right).

Ray Cochrane deservedly collects an award at the Lesters in 2001.

A change of dress code for me as I sit out Royal Ascot 2000.

L Dettori MBE. It's got a nice ring to it.

Insets: A morning session in amazing light (far left), and the A-team: Sheikh Mohammed and Saeed bin Suroor (right).

Left: Leading the string back in Newmarket with Saeed on his hack.

Main: Working at Godolphin's training track in Dubai.

Studying form with
Sir Alex Ferguson.

With my hero, Angel Cordero.

Squaring up to
Vinnie Jones at a press
conference in 2001
to promote the
Shergar Cup.

Spot the odd man out.
Tiger Woods on the
fairway in Dubai with,
from left, me, John
Carroll, the Hills twins
Michael and Richard, and
Kieren Fallon.

Three legends of the turf:
my dad (above left),
Lester Piggott (above)
and Pat Eddery (below).

Sparring with California's
Governor Arnie Schwarzenegger
at the 2003 Grand Prix at
Silverstone while Bernie
Ecclestone keeps the peace.

Kazzia bravely holds off
Snowfire (Pat Eddery) in
the 1,000 Guineas at
Newmarket in 2002.

Attending weight-watchers, with
Michael Kinane.

I salute the incredible jumps
champion Tony McCoy as he
retains his title once more at
Sandown in April 2003.

I heard that he'd been entered at the Malvern Bloodstock Sales. The lad who used to look after him for Michael Stoute alerted Pete Burrell and he rang me straight away. This was the chance I had been waiting for to give Fuji a secure home. I'd briefly considered buying him when he appeared at the Newmarket sales a few weeks after carrying me to the last of my seven victories at Ascot. Unfortunately he was always going to make too much money at that stage and was bought for 65,000 guineas by the jumping trainer Nicky Henderson. However he failed to make the grade over hurdles, changed hands twice more and had been struggling in point-to-points, racing for about £100 in prize money before he was entered in the Malvern Sale.

Knowing that I would never have a better opportunity to make Fuji my own, I moved swiftly to contact his owners. At the back of my mind was the awful fear that if I didn't buy him then he might make so little money at the auction that he could end up in the wrong hands with someone who would sell him to a knacker man. That was something I wasn't prepared to allow because he was the horse above all others who made me famous. Negotiations weren't easy, because his owners weren't prepared to give him away, particularly when they heard that I was the one who wanted to buy him, but I struck a deal before the auction and brought the old horse back to my home at Stetchworth.

It was the least I could do and now he has a home for life. He wasn't given away but what I paid for him was peanuts compared to what he had done for me four years earlier. From the moment he arrived here I was determined his racing days were over unless Catherine fancies riding him in the annual Newmarket Plate for charity. Now it has gone round in full circle. He has served his time and is part of my history. On quiet days at home I sometimes go out to the paddock to talk to Fuji, who reminds me a little bit of the French actor Gerard Depardieu. He's big and gangly and not a thing of great beauty but to me he will always be priceless.

At first I gave Fuji a few months off to let himself down. Then one morning in September 2001 I saddled him up and rode him along the roads for about five miles. It was something I had been promising myself for a while and I was thrilled that I finally seized the chance. That morning he seemed as big as an elephant and was full of fun, screaming and yelling like a young colt. But he looked and felt brilliant, a million dollars, and I knew then that buying him was without doubt the best money I have ever spent – apart, that is, from Catherine's engagement ring! He was also hopelessly unfit after many months turned out in a paddock at home with a few friends. So we just walked and trotted from Stetchworth to Kirtling to the yard of Mitch Doyle, the girl who was going to prepare him for a rare public appearance back at Ascot's Festival on the day a bronze of one Frankie Dettori was to be unveiled.

The plan was for me to canter down the course on Fujiyama Crest in front of the grandstand as part of the proceedings. I was extremely touched that Ascot had arranged this as a permanent reminder of that great day. Looking back now to 1996 I think what I did is even more unbelievable, total fantasy. It's impossible to win six races at a minor track, let alone seven at one of the biggest flat meetings of the year.

That Festival was the start of me, really. Those seven winners pitchforked me onto a worldwide stage into the view of millions of people who don't follow racing. I have the pictures of the seven horses above the door at home, and sometimes I pause and look at them and ask myself 'How did I do that?' People who were there probably remember a lot more about the day than I can.

Late one evening last summer at a barbecue at home someone asked about the horse grazing quietly out in the field next to the garden. It was probably the wine talking when I offered to ride Fuji. I collected a bridle, put it on him as he munched some grass, and flicked myself onto him bareback like an Indian before galloping round and round the paddock in the dark until we were both dizzy. I must have been mad.

nineteen

Nobody Had Done It Before

In the weeks that followed the magnificent seven I was pitched into a swirl of celebrity, which, to my amazement, continues to this day. It began early on the Sunday morning when I woke, wandered downstairs in my tee-shirt and underpants and discovered a reporter from the *Daily Mail* who had walked straight into the house at some unearthly hour. That's when it hit me that my life would never be the same again. Until then I'd been doing well, but Ascot took me to another level. In racing terms it launched me into a David Beckham type of scenario.

I popped out to collect all the newspapers and only then began to realise how much I'd cost the bookies. The papers were full of it on the front pages, the back pages and everywhere else, too. I certainly picked the right day. It was a bit like winning all the season's Formula One grand prix on the same afternoon. Racing had been going for more than 300 years and nobody had done it before.

In Lancashire, Darren Yates had won £550,000 from Hills.

Apparently his wife told him not to waste his stake money on me. They would probably be divorced by now if he'd listened to her! Darren's father picked up £10,000 on a similar bet, while John and Mary Bolton had collected £500,000 from Ladbrokes.

One punter who scooped £247,000 from Corals for a stake of £32.70 turned out to be a bookie called Peter Saxton. Dozens more had picked up in excess of £100,000 and even the smallest punters with 50p accumulators earned many thousands of pounds. Anyone putting together my seven winners in an accumulator was rewarded with combined odds of 25,095–1. As a serious and frequently skint punter myself in my early days as an apprentice I was thrilled to have helped them all clean up.

It had been a black Saturday for the bookmaking industry. Some bookies would never recover from their decision to stand against Fujiyama Crest as his odds plunged to 2–1. One of them, a genial character called Gary Wiltshire, a formidable rails layer, lost over £1 million. He explained: 'When a horse that should be 12–1 starts at 2–1 you have to lay it all day long. If you don't you shouldn't be a bookmaker. It was the opportunity of a lifetime to make proper money. Laying 2–1 about a 12–1 chance should have been the best day's business of my life. Instead it left me in the poorhouse. I'll be paying for years.'

Early on Sunday I took time out to attend Newmarket's Catholic Church to thank the Lord for my fantastic day, then set off once more for Ascot where there was still work to be done. Earlier in the week I'd spent two days of a short suspension with Catherine at Henlow Grange, a health farm in Hertfordshire. It was a great way to tone myself up. Naturally the staff there pressed me to give them my banker for the weekend before I left. The horse I tipped them was Sunbeam Dance in the opening race at Ascot on Sunday. I honestly thought he'd win and take my sequence to eight, but he ran poorly and the dream was finally over. I had to wait until the last race for my only success of the day on Altamura, but I could hardly complain.

All Sunday morning I fielded calls and messages on my mobile phone asking for interviews and requesting endorsements. It was time for an urgent summit meeting with Pete Burrell before racing. Suddenly he needed about four assistants. We decided to take full advantage of the situation, to milk it for all it was worth – provided any contracts we agreed didn't interfere with my racing schedule. We knew we'd never have the same opportunity again. We grabbed every sensible deal that came our way, believing it was helping our sport, too, and I hope someone else in my position would have done exactly the same. I don't think people minded too much because it was taking racing to a different audience.

First there was a series of publicity photos with bookmakers like Mike Dillon from Ladbrokes and Mike Burton from Hills cheerfully trying to throttle me. Ascot chipped in by giving me a methuselah of champagne. You need a big crowd to drink that much bubbly, but I've always loved a party so after racing on Sunday I solved the problem by taking Catherine and some of my friends to the Chinese in Newmarket. It was the first chance I'd had to eat properly in two days.

Early on Monday I found myself on the couch at GMTV's studios with Anthea Turner, presenting a cheque for £550,000 to Darren Yates. It was great to meet face to face the man who had won more money on me than any other punter on Saturday. He confided that he wanted to buy a racehorse or two of his own. Naturally he called his first horse Seventh Heaven! It didn't win, but later Darren did enjoy success with Royal Dome and Natsmagirl.

That morning Peter's mobile phone burned out from constant use, so he threw it in the Thames. We were waiting for a helicopter at Battersea to take me to Bath, where I won the opening race in the Queen's colours on her filly Sabina. A few days later I was working my way through hundreds of telegrams and cards from well-wishers. One was signed Elizabeth R. I turned to Catherine and asked 'Who on earth is Elizabeth R. Do I know her?' If I'd taken the time to read the telegram properly I could have answered my own question. The message ran 'My warmest congratulations on all eight wins. Elizabeth R.'

Catherine and I also attended a reception given by Prime Minister John Major at 10 Downing Street for a variety of sportsmen, including Frank Bruno, the Olympic gold medal winning rowers Steve Redgrave and Matthew Pinsent, the boxer Naseem Hamed, and most of the England soccer team including my good friend David Platt. I was struck by the sheer size of the premier's residence. When we arrived we had our photos taken knocking on the front door. The policeman guarding it welcomed me with a big grin. He'd backed two of my winners at Ascot.

It's a little front door but the house is huge behind it, with photographs and paintings of all the previous prime ministers lining the walls of the staircase. Once we entered the big room upstairs John Major greeted us with the news that he'd watched six of the seven races on TV. Later in the evening I teased him that for a jockey on a strict diet the honey roast sausages were a bit scary. He even offered to find me something else.

It was a memorable night. In his speech to all his guests the Prime Minister gave us a history of the house. If he ever comes round to mine in Stetchworth I'll do the same for him! Looking back now I realise I had something in common with John Major and I regret not asking him about his father who worked in a circus just like my mother. The reception didn't seem to last long, which was probably just as well, because the problem with being a jockey during the season is that you can't party in London like other sportsmen. You are always thinking of tomorrow's rides and the need to shed a couple of pounds in the morning, but that doesn't stop me breaking out whenever I can!

So the celebrity, the promotional work and the parties had to fit round my schedule as an international jockey which extends to seven days a week at the height of the season. It means that Pete turns down all requests for me to do daytime chat shows, though we were delighted to accept an offer for me to appear on Parkinson in the evening. Michael seemed happy to see me, too, until I told him I'd be taking over his job when I retired from riding. As it turned out, the last three months of 1996 produced a bonanza for me on and off the racecourse. Whatever I rode was winning. Maybe God was paying me back for those two months I missed.

On the commercial front, one of the best deals Peter concluded was with Alfa Romeo. For a limited amount of work for them we received three cars, twice a year, one for me, a second for Catherine and a third for my speed-loving agent. I also picked up a contract to help promote the Tote for £50,000 a year, later renewed at £60,000. Over a period of time I filmed advertisements for various companies including McDonalds, One 2 One T-mobile, and Royal Doulton. Invitations also poured in to attend any number of film premiers in the West End. I tried to go whenever I could.

The most surprising request to come my way after Ascot was to host Top of the Pops. I'm game for just about anything, but working on that programme was nerve-wracking. I spent a whole day writing and rehearsing my links and managed to survive the show without any obvious mistakes. Then again, they didn't ask me back.

Sometimes my English let me down. It happened when I was interviewed by Sybil Ruscoe on BBC Radio Five Live shortly after Ascot. Why, asked Sybil, was it necessary for jockeys to carry whips? I did my best to explain. A jockey without a whip, I suggested, was like a carpenter without a spanner. I think she knew what I meant! My spelling is another problem. I can remember my irritation when Barney Curley and Bruce Raymond couldn't understand the name of a hotel I was recommending to them. Eventually they asked me to spell out the name. I looked at them with pity in my eyes. 'It's simple. O for hotel, T for Tommy', I began. The rest was lost in howls of laughter.

My injury in mid-summer had put paid to my hopes of being champion again, but in the week after Ascot I added two more Group 1 victories on Bahamian Bounty in the Middle Park Stakes at Newmarket and Ryafan in the Prix Marcel Boussac at Longchamp. Both won narrowly but life wasn't all a bowl of roses as Classic Cliche ran a stinker in the Prix de l'Arc de Triomphe. A week later I picked up yet another major prize on my old friend Shantou in the Gran Premio de Jockey Club in Milan.

The Breeders' Cup, held for the first time at Woodbine in Toronto, Canada, provided an unexpected reverse for Mark Of Esteem who failed to fire for me on his farewell performance. My international tour next took me to Rome in mid November where I won four out of five races on a damp winter's afternoon. Then I was on my way to Japan for Singspiel in the Japan Cup. Partnered by Gary Stevens the horse had run up to his very best in finishing a close second to his stable companion Pilsudski in the Breeders' Cup Classic. Now Michael Stoute had asked me to ride him for the first time.

One of the reasons Michael is such an outstanding trainer is that he leaves nothing to chance. Singspiel had looked like winning in Canada until faltering inside the final furlong. That rather confirmed Michael's view that the horse barely stayed twelve furlongs. He impressed on me the need to be patient.

'When you want to go, count to ten before making your move', he advised me. I saved ground all the way, cut the corner, moved inside and remembered Michael's instructions just as I was set to launch Singspiel on his run. I paused for a moment, counted to two then thought to hell with my orders, I'm not waiting any longer.

At the line we held on by a nose and I had landed the biggest prize of my career with Singspiel collecting £1,093,662. In addition to my cut I also won a new car which I sold at cost price because I couldn't take it out of the country. The next morning I woke up shortly after 4 a.m., wandered down to collect the newspapers and headed for the coffee shop where I ran into Michael who was also unable to sleep. Only then did I admit that I'd disobeyed his orders.

My golden late autumn harvest continued in Hong Kong with yet another Group 1 success on Luso. A few days later I was brought down to earth in a horrible fall at Sha Tin that ended the life of Magic Power, the horse I was riding. We'd travelled barely a furlong and a half when another runner clipped heels, unseated his rider Jackie Tse and pushed Magic Power onto the running rails. The impact sent me tumbling to the ground before Magic Power struck my wrist as he somersaulted past me. He fractured his off foreleg and had to be put down. I was carried from the course on a stretcher and taken to the nearby hospital for X-rays. Although shaken and bruised, I was able to head for the airport in time to catch my flight to London so that I could attend the BBC's Sports Personality of the Year review.

Some observers were speculating that I might be the first jockey ever to win the award, but since no-one from racing had ever featured in the first three, I wasn't getting carried away. I was just pleased to arrive at the studios in one piece. I remember telling Sue Barker, the presenter, that I felt like I'd just gone two rounds with Evander Holyfield and Frank Bruno who were both sitting in the audience.

Willie Carson and Walter Swinburn appeared from nowhere with a cake in the shape of a horse's head with 26 candles to celebrate my birthday a day late. Somebody was playing games because I couldn't blow them out. The best part of the show for me was being given the chance to wear the number 7 shirt of Arsenal in a celebrity penalty shoot-out with the former England goalie Peter Shilton between the posts. The programme devoted a chunk of time to the magnificent seven but it wasn't enough to clinch the award for me. That was won by Damon Hill. I was thrilled to finish third.

The hardest part of my engagement to Catherine was finding a date for our wedding which didn't clash with the racing programme. When I turned to Simon Crisford for help, he pulled out his desk diary for 1997, spent a few minutes flicking through the pages, then sat back with the satisfied air of a man who'd just completed a difficult crossword. 'Here it is,' he declared happily. 'Sunday 20 July. That's the only free date in the summer.'

So 20 July it was. I signed off in style with a double at Newmarket the previous afternoon – and a three day suspension which, as it happens, was very convenient because it allowed me to take Catherine away for a brief honeymoon in the South of France. I tried to avoid a stag night, partly because I didn't have time and also because I didn't fancy somebody dumping me in handcuffs on a train to Glasgow in the middle of the night. Of course I was outvoted and we had a right old jolly on the Saturday night. We ended up in the same club as the girls enjoying Catherine's hen night, spraying champagne at each other.

I'd been staying at the Bedford Lodge Hotel for the previous two months while work continued on renovating the house I'd bought in Stetchworth from Barney Curley. I felt awful on the morning of my wedding and even worse after devouring a large fry-up. Aware that I was in urgent need of fresh air, my best man Colin Rate took me for a walk in Newmarket High Street.

When we returned to the Bedford Lodge the man in reception handed me a fax. It read 'My congratulations to you both. Elizabeth R'. Suddenly I felt a whole lot better. Later, after a swim, a jacuzzi, and a swift gin and tonic I was ready for anything. Catherine looked lovely when she walked up the aisle at the Catholic Church in Newmarket. The hardest part was getting the ring on my finger. That seemed to take five minutes and when we left the Church we were surprised to find at least 500 people waiting outside.

The reception seemed to last all night. Catherine and I led off the dancing. We'd hired a ten-piece orchestra but the high-light was an unforgettable solo by Ronnie Wood even though he didn't have any of his own equipment with him. He spent twenty minutes tuning up a guitar he borrowed from the band, fashioned a plectrum from the top of a broken bottle, and launched into a spell-binding rendition of Amazing Grace. We were all crying by the end.

Eventually we left the reception in a taxi at around two in the morning and headed for our new home in Stetchworth. I carried Catherine over the threshold before we both collapsed into bed and fell asleep with exhaustion. So much for romance. The next day we realised we'd forgotten to pack a change of clothes. So with me in my morning suit and Catherine in her wedding dress we jumped into the car and drove to her parents' home in Cambridge. What a carry on. It was hilarious.

My timely suspension allowed us to sneak away for a short honeymoon eight days later in the South of France. I tried to rent a Mercedes convertible at the airport, but they decided that at 26 I was far too young. We had a brilliant time in lavish surroundings before rushing back to England for the second half of Glorious Goodwood.

Mattie Cowing's poor health worried us all that summer. He'd been struggling for a while, getting increasingly breathless and the outlook was grim unless he had an operation for a heart by-pass. Time wasn't on his side: if he waited for it to be done on the National Health it might be too late. Nor could he afford to go private. I solved the problem by paying for surgery to be carried out straight away. At first he protested but it was the least I could do in return for all his hard work for me. I'm pleased to say the operation gave him and Rita five more years together. It was money well spent.

Nineteen ninety-seven was the year that another of my close

friends, John Gosden, won the Derby with Benny The Dip. The way he was going in the spring convinced me that he was a serious, uncomplicated Derby horse. I got him ready with John and but for a late change of plan it would have been me, not Willie Ryan, on his tough colt when he held off Silver Patriarch in a nerve-tingling finish to the race. I'd won on him as a two-year-old and felt he had progressed into a decent horse when he carried me into second place in the Thresher Classic Trial at Sandown in April. With Godolphin short of serious Derby contenders that year, I fully expected to be on Benny The Dip at Epsom. Everything changed when Bold Demand won a maiden for Godolphin at Sandown eleven days before the Derby. Aware that we had nothing else for Epsom, Sheikh Mohammed decided to let Bold Demand take his chance. As his retained jockey I would have to ride him. End of story. That's life. Normally my commitment to Godolphin works in my favour. Not this time.

At the last minute John was left searching for a new partner for Benny The Dip. With nearly all the big names already committed he turned to Willie, a stalwart of Henry Cecil's team for years. It proved to be a wise choice as Willie gained the biggest triumph of his career by a short head from Silver Patriarch. I missed most of the action as I finished far behind in ninth place on Bold Demand, a 20–1 shot, who ran well up to a point before fading in the straight.

So another Derby had passed me by. In racing you'd send yourself round the bend if you spent too much time worrying about what might have been. Obviously I was disappointed not to be sharing John's great triumph. But as the photo finish was announced and Benny the Dip was confirmed the winner I was thrilled to bits that my staunch friend had won the prize he had wanted for so long. We celebrated with a few drinks at his house that night.

My runaway victory on Singspiel in the Coronation Cup provided some compensation. By this stage of his career he had developed into a truly formidable racehorse. He proved the point with a breathtaking success from the front, so I had no intention of deserting him for Swain in the King George VI and Queen Elizabeth Diamond Stakes in July. Given the chance I'd make the same choice again. We were undone by a monsoon two hours before racing which flooded the track and produced the unusual sight of a swamp at Ascot in high summer. Our doubts about Singspiel's ability to last home in such testing ground were all too soon confirmed. He tried as hard as ever but the wings on his heels were weighed down by mud as he finished a weary fourth to Godolphin's second string Swain who relished the conditions.

Back on a more suitable surface at York, Singspiel once again displayed his true class with a defeat of the two Derby winners Desert King and Benny The Dip in the Juddmonte Stakes. For all-round performance and guts he had to be the best horse in the world because he'd done it at every trip, and in every country. You could set your clock by him he was so reliable. For a top-class horse he was such an easy ride, he didn't pull and you could do what you liked with him. He had resilience, too, in bouncing back from such a punishing race at Ascot 24 days earlier.

Sadly the Juddmonte proved to be Singsiel's swansong. In November he was flown to America for a tilt at the Breeders' Cup in California but broke down during a routine canter at Hollywood Park a couple of days before the race. By the time he reached the safety of his barn he could barely walk. X-rays confirmed that he'd fractured the cannon bone on his foreleg but happily he was saved for stud duty.

I ended the season with 176 winners and a controversial ban that left me on the sidelines for 21 days, though part of the ban was suspended. I knew it was coming under the totting-up procedure. But now, for the first time, I will admit that by deliberately getting myself into trouble at Newmarket at the end of the year, all I missed were some meaningless outings on the all-weather in November and one day's work in Japan. It was a small price to pay for the comfort of knowing that I wouldn't have a stiff sentence hanging over me at an important time the following summer.

It's always seemed unfair that we can get penalised twice for the same offence, once when it happens and again when you reach fifteen days' suspension over a period of time. To be banned when you do something wrong and then punished further for being banned is crazy. And without wanting to blow my own trumpet, because of my high profile I seem to end up with six days when less well known jockeys get four. So I tend to reach fifteen days quicker than most, often from only three offences.

All that year I'd been trying to stay out of trouble, not always successfully. So it felt a bit strange setting out with the intention of catching the eye of the stewards in a maiden race at Newmarket on 31 October. As the race came to the boil I pulled my whip through to my left hand and made my mount Baajil drift sharply right across the horses on his inside. When I heard Michael Hills, his brother Richard and John Reid all shouting in alarm I knew I'd achieved my purpose as Baajil hampered all three.

Afterwards the boys were mad at me in the weighing room. No wonder they looked baffled when I explained I'd done them on purpose. Nor, as I wanted a ban that would take me past the threshold, did I want them speaking up for me in the subsequent inquiry. The stewards obliged by referring me to Portman Square under the totting-up procedure. My little wheeze had worked a treat.

Later in London I collected the three-week 'holiday' as expected, but in doing so it wiped my slate clean for the next season. Publicly I made a bit of a fuss about missing out on the Japan Cup, but privately I was delighted at what I saw as a satisfactory outcome. Some people might not approve of my tactics, but really I was only playing the game by the Jockey Club's rules.

twenty

A Brief Encounter at Epsom

Cape Verdi was my type of girl, attractive and willing in equal measure, brave, versatile and supremely talented. I just wish she'd stayed around much longer in 1998 so that I could have got to know her even better. Bought, like Balanchine, from Robert Sangster at the end of her two-year-old career, she gave Godolphin's season a perfect start with a storming victory in the 1,000 Guineas. We knew she was a star from the way she was working at Al Quoz early that spring, and she confirmed it by breezing up in one of our trials. Cape Verdi flew in from Dubai with a batch of our horses on the Monday before the Guineas and was still flying as she sped home unchallenged five lengths clear of the runner-up Shahtoush six days later at Newmarket.

What a performance! I don't think I've ridden a more professional racehorse. She hacked down to the start as though it was a morning workout, was so cool in the stalls she didn't blink, moved through the race like a well-oiled machine, then pulled up after the finish as if nothing had happened. I felt nothing could touch Cape Verdi in the Oaks, but Sheikh Mohammed had other plans and took the bold option to take on the colts at Epsom in the Vodafone Derby.

We had a fine substitute for the Oaks in the shape of Bahr who was unlucky not to beat the Irish-trained outsider Shahtoush. That was one Classic which slipped from our grasp. If I rode the race again I'd probably win because I'd pay more attention to her, but Bahr travelled so beautifully I decided to wait until the furlong marker before taking on the favourite Midnight Line. Unfortunately for me, Mick Kinane then stole first run on us on Shahtoush. Their momentum was quicker than ours and we couldn't quite get back at them in time. I thought I had everything covered until Mick caught me by surprise. In trying to target the favourite Midnight Line without going too soon, I made the mistake of handing the advantage to Mick. If I'd kicked earlier it might have been different. I helped put things right at Royal Ascot by winning the Ribblesdale Stakes on Bahr.

Cape Verdi wasn't so lucky. She was never the same again after she came off worst in a prolonged barging match in the Derby with my old foe Richard Quinn on Courteous. I don't know what he was trying to do. Obviously he didn't want to go wide but all he seemed to achieve was knocking my filly all over the place.

What Richard did was right out of order, totally shocking and to this day I am upset about it. Courteous kept on bashing Cape Verdi, the poor filly, until it got to the point where she'd had enough after being whacked in the ribs every couple of strides. Most jockeys get on well enough with each other. Racing's too dangerous for feuds, though Kieren Fallon famously once got six months for pulling Stuart Webster from his horse. You'd be mad to try it today because every yard of every race is under the microscope with cameras watching your every move. Most exchanges in the heat of battle are quickly forgotten, but from time to time I've clashed with Richard and I don't think it's all coincidence. He is one of those guys who always seem to be in the way when you want to make your move.

Things came to a head between us when he murdered Cape Verdi in the Derby. I had a right go at him afterwards but as he's deaf in one ear I'm not sure he took much notice. The race had gone and Cape Verdi's chance with it. The stewards looked into the matter and agreed that interference took place, but to my amazement they took no action against Richard. As a person I don't dislike him but it's surprising how often we've ended up on the wrong side of each other though we've never come to blows. Maybe it's a clash of personalities. At least we've moved on but in the early days we didn't get on at all. The upshot of the Derby was that Cape Verdi hurt herself quite badly in finishing ninth behind Luca Cumani's winner High-Rise and failed to find her form when she came back the following year.

Royal Ascot in high summer is a fabulous meeting. It is like having our own Olympics each year and means so much to me. There is a continuous buzz throughout the week and you never tire of it because you feel you have a chance in every race. It is beautiful. The 1998 Royal meeting passed in a blur of blue. Godolphin had four winners, I rode three of them, won a couple more in Sheikh Mohammed's colours, and ended the four days as the runaway winner of the London Clubs Trophy for the meeting's top jockey. The highlight had to be the gutsy victory of Kayf Tara by a neck in the Gold Cup after a ferocious battle with Double Trigger, whose brave style of running and flaxen mane and tail made him deservedly one of the most popular horses in training.

Kayf Tara was just beginning to realise his potential that summer. Knowing that Double Trigger liked to dominate and relished a scrap I made certain I came wide to challenge, hoping he wouldn't spot us until it was too late to react. Sure enough Double Trigger saw off the others one by one. We then caught him with the last punch of the fight and it proved to be a knock-out blow.

Godolphin's good fortune continued with a clean sweep in the Coral-Eclipse at Sandown. This time, unlike two years earlier, I chose the right one – Daylami – who came home half a length clear of his stable companion Faithful Son, with our other candidate Central Park in third place. Daylami was a powerful attractive grey but not yet at the peak of his powers – in contrast to Swain who, being two years older, was a battle-hardened campaigner. That's why I picked Swain in preference to him when the King George VI and Queen Elizabeth Diamond Stakes came along three weeks later. Plenty in the Godolphin team thought I'd got it wrong. Some thought the horse had gone after his recent defeat at Royal Ascot.

I felt like a boxer in the ring without any cornermen. Nor was I sure. Swain had chinned me a year earlier when I preferred

Singspiel, but that was hardly his fault and he was one of those horses that kept coming back for more. The King George is a tough race and they don't come any tougher than Swain. He proved to be the oldest winner of this famous old race which provides an annual collision between the best Classic horses and the older generation. The 1998 King George was a vintage renewal: Swain beat the Derby winner High-Rise by a length, with another three-year-old Royal Anthem third just ahead of Daylami.

Very few horses keep delivering in the highest league like Swain. Either their wheels give out, or their appetite for the fight begins to wane. Not Swain. The furious early pace set by Daragh O'Donoghue on Happy Valentine was ideal for him. While others cried 'Enough!', Swain quickened into the lead over a furlong out. As usual when he hit the front he didn't let me down. When we crossed the line a length clear of High-Rise I gave a whoop of joy at the sheer excitement of what we'd achieved. For a horse of his age to win this great race for the second year running was unique. Nor was his summer of excellence at an end. Six weeks later he made light of dropping back a quarter of a mile by landing the Irish Champion Stakes.

Sometimes in this game you take one step forward and two steps back. At York I was involved in one of those spine-tingling finishes that leaves everyone present gasping for breath. Three horses crossed the line locked together in the Juddmonte International. No-one would have complained if it had been called a triple dead heat, though the photo showed that Pat Eddery had prevailed on One So Wonderful by a short head from my mount Faithful Son, with Kieren Fallon on Chester House the same distance away in third.

Minutes later we were on the mat before the stewards who handed out suspensions for whip offences to all three of us. It was both predictable and pitiful. We knew as we pulled up that we were heading for trouble. It was one of the biggest races of the year, so none of us was likely to ease up in the closing stages and wave the others through. We were not beating up our horses, just using our whips to encourage them to do the job for which they are bred.

Jockeys have an impossible job when they are tied down by so many restrictive rules. We do what we have to do in the heat of battle and aren't going to worry then about ridiculous whip rules which we know might cost us dear in the future. Whatever the penalty we will go out and ride in exactly the same way tomorrow. The rules still aren't perfect but after some tinkering by the Jockey Club there is less chance of wholesale suspensions after epic races like that one at York.

As each autumn unfolds, agents for Godolphin leave no stone unturned in their pursuit of promising young horses who might benefit our team – provided, of course, that they are on the market. That's how Balanchine, Cape Verdi, Daylami and many others came to race in the light-blue colours. As the better two-year-olds began to emerge at the back-end of 1998, word began to spread of a truly exceptional colt which was burning up the gallops in Newmarket. This one, however, already belonged to Sheikh Mohammed, who'd bred the horse himself.

Named Yazzer, he was exciting his trainer David Loder in a

way no other youngster had done before. At some point before he made his racecourse debut the boss took the bold decision to change his name to Dubai Millennium. Nothing ambitious, then! Dubai Millennium was finally ready to run at Yarmouth towards the end of October. Although Godolphin was represented in the same race by the second favourite Blue Snake, I was thrilled when Sheikh Mohammed agreed that I could switch to Dubai Millennium – who winged home with me in breathtaking style. When he was switched to join our team in Dubai shortly afterwards we all hoped we had a champion on our hands. But events over the next few months would leave me perilously close to walking out on the job with Godolphin.

twenty-one

Nightmare in Kentucky

The crisis erupted without warning when I was beaten narrowly on Swain at the Breeders' Cup early in November. I wasn't feeling at my best at the end of the long haul across the Pacific Ocean after riding in the Melbourne Cup on 3 November. On the way from Australia we all stopped off in Buenos Aires and spent a fun day out on the ranch, riding with the boss, galloping across miles of open country. It was so dusty I picked up a dry cough that I couldn't shake off when we reached Kentucky on the Friday. After a long season, I was tired, run down, and coughing my head off.

Swain had already proved a superb globetrotter for Godolphin and we hoped he would go out in a blaze of glory in the Classic, the highlight of a glittering card at Churchill Downs. The one we had to beat was Silver Charm who had just pipped Swain in the Dubai World Cup in March. We all knew the last thing we needed was to get into a prolonged duel with Silver Charm, so it was agreed that when the time came I'd try to challenge as far away from him as possible.

At half-way I couldn't have been happier in a beautiful position not far behind the leader, Coronado's Quest. As the tempo quickened racing off the bend into the short straight, Gary Stevens began to move up on Silver Charm and edged into the lead just over a furlong out. I was confident we had him covered as I asked Swain to go after him three or four horses wide, but when I reached his quarters I couldn't get by him.

That's where my troubles started. In my eagerness to beat Silver Charm I probably hit Swain a few times more than I should have done in double-quick time with the whip in my left hand. I caught him with seven proper cracks and that gave him the excuse to duck away sharply right-handed towards the stands.

Usually experienced horses don't do that. But it was dark inside the track and there were plenty of lights around the winning post. That, combined with my hitting him so hard, made him dart instinctively towards the grandstand. I tried to straighten him up but we still ended up on the outside of the track and our chance had gone. Awesome Again nicked the race by three-quarters of a length from Silver Charm with Swain a neck further back in third place.

I could sense the first flutter of vulture's wings as I came back to unsaddle. Aware that we'd tossed away a winning chance I was ready for the abuse that was about to come my way. I could smell the atmosphere. Even so I was shaken by the venom of the onslaught. The press crucified me. When I explained that Swain ducked when he saw the floodlights I could see the disbelief in their eyes. They'd been waiting ten years to batter me and now they had their chance. It was horrible. Everybody jumped on me by judging me on one ride. They gave it to me big time.

I was tried, convicted and found guilty without any mitigating circumstances. Then they buried me. At first I fought my corner because I still believed I was right, but eventually I lost it, declaring if they wanted me to say I'd ridden a balls of a race, then that's what happened. I took the rap. I was told by everyone that I should put up my hands so I did. I hope it made them all happy giving me a good kicking.

That was the first serious reverse since I'd joined Godolphin and it nearly finished me. Maybe I did make a mistake but the horse didn't help me, either. How many times do you see an experienced horse swerve suddenly like that? Normally Swain ran as straight as a gun barrel and never ducked away from the whip. Was it the whip or the floodlights? I'm still not sure, but it's clear on the video that he pricked his ears and dived right. Maybe he was going for a gap. To this day I believe that something strange happened, that he must have seen something because I'd already given him four hard smacks and he was running straight and true. As it happens Silver Charm came across to the middle of the track but no-one said a word about that. I still think I didn't do much wrong, apart from hitting him once or twice too often.

I was so upset at my treatment after the race that I fled from the course as soon as I could and headed for the airport. On the flight to London I broke down in tears in Catherine's lap, fearing that my job was on the line. Ten years in the limelight had been destroyed by one luckless defeat. I was in bits because the intensity of the criticism was so underserved.

The next day Sheikh Mohammed rang me at home, telling me not to worry about all the criticism in the newspapers. Everyone at Godolphin, he added, was behind me, yet with the season at an end I had all winter to chew over what happened. To my dismay when I arrived in Dubai at the start of February I could see that the wounds from the race hadn't healed. One person in particular at Godolphin gave me a very hard time, making me ride out four lots every morning instead of one or two. If anything went wrong in the yard I was the one picked on, just to show me up in front of the others. I went along with it for almost two months. Whatever I was made to do, I did without saying a word.

Outwardly I seemed fine. Only Catherine knew how the torment was tearing me apart. At night I was usually in tears, saying I couldn't handle it any more. Eventually I cracked when we were out to dinner with half a dozen friends. During the meal I suddenly started crying my eyes out. The unfairness of the situation all spilled out. It was time to lance the boil.

Next morning Catherine took me to see my good friend Simon Crisford in his office. I explained that I was so miserable I couldn't go on because my confidence was in pieces. Simon arranged for me to see Sheikh Mohammed straight away. I remember saying to the boss that I wasn't happy at the way things had developed since Swain's defeat and if he wasn't happy with me then I was prepared for the parting of the ways. To continue the torture of the past two months wouldn't be fair to either of us. He stopped me in full flow by telling me I must never forget that I was the jockey who rode all seven winners at Ascot, then encouraged me to carry on with the promise that I had his full backing. The nightmare was over but it took time for the scars to heal. Looking back, the crisis over Swain's defeat probably made me a better person in that I can take situations like that in my stride now.

It was just as well I didn't walk out because 1999 was the year Godolphin moved into overdrive as a global force. We enjoyed eighteen Group 1 winners around the world, the most we've ever achieved in a calendar year. I couldn't ride them all because some clashed on the same day in different countries. Nor was I always on the right one, but that's the nature of the job. At the start of 1999 it was touch and go whether I would still be riding for Godolphin, so I wasn't going to complain after winning thirteen Group 1 wins for them by the end of the year.

I began the campaign by finishing last on High-Rise in the Dubai World Cup way behind Almutawakel. Things could only get better and they did when I landed the 2,000 Guineas at Newmarket on Island Sands, a Godolphin recruit from trainer David Elsworth. That was a bit of a surprise, but once he jumped out smartly I felt I had nothing to lose, so I let him bowl along in the lead and somehow we pinched the race from the front.

All my life I'd dreamed of emulating my father by winning the Italian Derby in Rome. I finally did it on Mukhalif late in May, but I wasn't so sure about the chance of our new superstar

Dubai Millennium six days later at Epsom. Once he recovered from an early setback he was working like a champion. On the track he breezed in at Doncaster and then won easily enough at Goodwood over ten furlongs – though, even with a pace-maker to help, I had the devil of a job to hold him and didn't feel he really finished his race properly.

Dubai Millennium was probably too quick for the Derby and it was a bit of a rush getting him there. We all had doubts about his stamina. On the day I felt he should be at least a 10–1 shot, not the 5–1 he started, but you don't know for sure unless you try. Once again he pulled like hell with me and by the time we reached the straight I was already struggling to hold my position. So many good horses have been ruined in the Derby, but I made sure I looked after Dubai Millenniun when he got a bump. After that he had nothing more to offer so I let him finish in his own time. Now we knew for certain he didn't stay.

Daylami was in superb form that year and completed a swift Group 1 double at the height of the summer in the Coronation Cup at Epsom and then the King George at Ascot. At Epsom he had to work hard to wear down Royal Anthem. Next time at Ascot he was a sensation as he sailed home like an ocean liner in full flow by five lengths from our second string Nedawi. It was billed as the highlight of the racing season but quickly developed into a lap of honour for Daylami. Until then I hadn't realised he possessed a turbo under his handsome grey coat. He was one of those horses who need a furlong to find top gear. You'd be scrubbing away on his back for a couple of hundred yards, then whoosh he'd take off and fly by the others as though they were standing still. Once we were clear at Ascot I enjoyed the rare luxury of watching our progress on the giant screen on the inside of the course near the winning post. It was an amazing experience.

Our rich haul of important races continued remorselessly through July, August and September. Aljabr, Diktat and Kayf Tara all played their part, but the pair who quickened my pulse the most were Dubai Millennium and Daylami. Late in July, back at a more suitable distance of ten furlongs, Dubai Millennium strolled home at Maisons-Laffitte. He then repeated the dose against some of the best milers around at Deauville before completing his season with an unforgettable triumph in the Queen Elizabeth II Stakes at Ascot.

Jockeys live for days like that, when the horse you are riding is invincible and you know the best still lies ahead. He had the raw power of a jet plane, although by then I was afraid of him because I couldn't really control him. If he woke up on a going day you couldn't stop him, yet he was one of those rare horses who pull like hell and still find more at the finish. I didn't want to take on the free-running Gold Academy in the lead, but Dubai Millennium resented restraint and did his best to tug my arms out of their sockets.

I was losing the fight from the start, struggling to hold one side of him. Soon I couldn't wait to give my aching limbs a rest. In the paddock the boss had encouraged me to give him a kick in the belly and enjoy myself. Shortly after half-way I had no choice. I had to let him go. Dubai Millennium immediately swept clear in a matter of strides. One moment we were involved in a horse race, the next we were out on our own.

The winning distance over Almushtarak was six lengths but it could have been twelve or more if I'd chosen. It was a performance which inspired Sheikh Mohammed to go public with the views he'd been expressing in private for months. He was not pulling any punches when he declared that Dubai Millennium was the best Godolphin had ever had. No-one involved with the horse was inclined to argue.

Daylami was in equally rampant form in the Irish Champion Stakes, which unfortunately again clashed with the St Leger won for Godolphin at Doncaster by Mutafaweq ridden by Richard Hills. Consolation at missing that ride was provided in spades for me by Daylami who dismantled the opposition at Leopardstown with murderous ease. It looked a match between Daylami and Royal Anthem, so impressive at York the previous month. He was a good horse in his own right but I felt he stole the race at York with the help of a canny ride from Gary Stevens. The key was not to let him have things his own way.

The pace at Leopardstown was furious as Royal Anthem took the field along, but crucially this time he was unable to establish a clear lead. Turning for home I was poised on his heels, waiting to pounce with Daylami. The moment a gap appeared next to the rails we were through it in less time than it takes to tell. I called out to Gary, asking how much he had left. When he didn't answer I knew we had him cooked. Once in the clear Daylami sprinted home to record an astonishing winning margin of nine lengths over Dazzling Park. It was a brilliant performance by a horse who had improved by countless lengths at the age of five.

On that display Daylami should have gone on to win the Arc in Paris. I really thought he would win, but everything seemed hard work for him in the soft ground at Longchamp and he began to gurgle at the top of the hill five furlongs out. It was one of those mystifying reverses that so often occur in racing.

Catherine didn't join me in Paris for the very good reason that she was about to give birth to our first child. When she rang me that night she sounded worried that the baby had stopped moving in her tummy, so I flew home first thing on the Monday morning and took her to hospital in Cambridge for a check-up. That's when the decision was taken to induce the baby. After she'd had an injection we thought we had plenty of time to go for a short walk, yet as we turned to come back Catherine began having spasms. In the end they were coming so fast it was a struggle to make it back to the maternity ward.

I found the next two hours torture, so scary as I stood beside her bed, watching the birth of our son Leonardo. I felt helpless and frightened in turn for my wife and my child. I was a bag of nerves and couldn't see anything good about the experience except the end result. It was a case of mopping Catherine's brow or holding her hand through the worst of the pain until I was overcome with a mixture of happiness and relief when Leo popped out.

I nearly fainted when the nurse passed me a pair of scissors and invited me several times to cut the umbilical cord. I couldn't begin to do it. Catherine's powers of recovery were remarkable.

One moment she was in agony. Two hours later she was strolling around the ward showing off her newborn son in his pram already decorated with balloons. I couldn't believe it.

Anxious to wet the baby's head I drove to the nearest off-licence, bought a bottle of champagne and rushed back to share it with Catherine. She isn't much of a drinker at the best of times and sipped perhaps half a glass while I polished off the rest. Overcome by the excitement of the birth, and by the bubbly, too, I was soon in serious need of sleep. Of course a moment after crawling in beside Catherine in the narrow hospital bed I was out for the count.

Later I was woken by a sharp nudge on my shoulder to find her squashed uncomfortably into the corner of the bed while I'd taken over most of the covers snoring loudly. It was hilarious but Catherine didn't think so. She pointed out that she was the one urgently needing a rest after the long ordeal of having a baby. My place, she concluded, was in a camp bed on the floor and that's where I spent the rest of the night.

I returned to action at York in mid week after two days off for good behaviour. The English season was winding down and my sights were already focusing on Daylami's next assignment in the Breeders' Cup Turf race at Gulfstream Park in Florida early in November. People say revenge is a dish best enjoyed cold. Mine would be positively icy after the mauling I'd suffered at the hands of the American press the previous year.

First, there was another testing challenge four days earlier in the Melbourne Cup. I was already half-way to Australia when our chief hope, Kayf Tara, was pulled out of the race after a setback. At the last minute it was decided to run Central Park in his place. He was widely dismissed as a no-hoper but gave the Aussies a real fright by leading until the last twenty yards under a big weight that anchored him at the end. It's a hell of a long way to go to finish second, but I was encouraged that Central Park's spirited run showed that our horses were holding their form at the end of a hectic year.

None had been campaigned harder than Daylami who raced in five countries in 1999 and seemed over the breathing problem that troubled him in Paris. The disaster with Swain was never far from my mind during the build-up in Florida. Even so, given luck in running, I was confident of ending the European hoodoo which stretched to 34 consecutive losers in the Breeders' Cup series at Gulfstream. No wonder. The sharp track, tight turns and exceptional, steamy heat were far from ideal for our horses at the end of a long domestic season. Even in the late nineties a lot of English runners were entered in the Breeders' Cup as an afterthought though we've learned with the years to plan these expeditions more carefully.

Naturally the American press kept reminding me of Swain twelve months earlier. They couldn't wait to tell me to watch out for the lights. There were plenty of other cheap shots, too, at my expense. They weren't exactly nasty, but as I was from out of town they threw as much shit at me as they could and didn't care one bit if they upset me. Two earlier rides on the card put an edge on my game. They both finished in the money. I was grimly determined to ram the words of my critics right down their throats, and in Daylami I had the ideal accomplice

– though I was worried about his habit of taking at least a furlong to find top gear. The team in the paddock was unusually edgy. Simon Crisford was a bag of nerves, the boss looked anxious, too, and my heart was pounding like a drum as I was led to the start. I was praying that God would give me a clear path because there were sure to be plenty of people out there waiting for me to mess up.

With fourteen runners spread across the narrow course in the stalls, it was vital to get an early position close to the rail. Once we managed that we dropped in just behind the leaders and the race unfolded like a dream. It was up to me to prevent it turning into a nightmare. The pace was good, Royal Anthem eased past us and I started pumping away, winding up Daylami. It might have looked as if I was in trouble, but I knew he would soon respond.

As we moved onto the heels of Buck's Boy and Royal Anthem round the final turn I had to take a couple of deep breaths to contain my excitement. If the split came the prize was ours. When it appeared I gave Daylami a couple of smacks and he took off with me, shot to the front like a cork out of a bottle and put the result beyond doubt in a style I will never forget. He coiled his legs, lowered his head, and surged clear with an irresistible display of power and speed which left the Americans for dead. In the last fifty yards we were going that fast I knew nobody could pass us. It was there to enjoy, the best race he'd ever run.

After the race I lost it completely. 'What about Swain now, you bastards! What about Swain?' I screamed at the waiting pack at the press conference. 'You want to talk about Swain now boys; OK let's talk about him.' Oh yes, I lost it big time and you know I don't regret a single word. I felt great, absolutely great at what I'd just achieved because it's so hard to beat the Americans in their own back yard. It took a year to get my own back on those bums but I knew it could have taken me a lifetime.

twenty-two

A Horse in a Million

On a night of pure fantasy under a starlit Arabian sky late in March 2000 it took me a fraction under two minutes to earn £219,000. We all believed in Dubai Millennium by then but I was still shocked at the way he demolished the opposition in the Dubai World Cup. He was unbelievable that night. Nothing I can say can adequately describe his performance. He was the best in the world and the best I've ridden.

The boss decided that he should have a warm-up race at Nad Al Sheba before the World Cup to get used to the kick-back from the dirt surface. At the time he was burning up the gallops so fast it was scary, doing timed fractions that nobody could believe. So when he raced on dirt for the first time in the Maktoum Challenge early in March we ran two pacemakers. I spent half the race anchoring him behind horses to make sure he caught plenty of sand in his face from the hooves of the front runners. Then I let him go and he cantered home unextended, four and a half lengths ahead of Lear Spear. Although I'd ridden him with restraint, he set a new course record of 1 minute 59.6 seconds.

After that the boys didn't let me near the horse in case I squeezed him too much in the morning. So I didn't sit on him again until his final bit of work before the World Cup. It was sensational, mainly because I couldn't stop him! He covered five furlongs on his own in 59 seconds and afterwards everyone at Godolphin was furious with me. Simon, Saeed and Tom Albatrani were all convinced he'd left his race on the gallops by going too fast. They were still fuming when I protested that I couldn't hold him, but no-one could have stopped him that morning. For most horses the pace of that final gallop would have been disastrous. Damage would have been done. But for Dubai Millennium it was no more than a walk in the park.

For the last few years I'd just been a nuisance in the Dubai World Cup but I knew I was on the right one this time and even persuaded my dad and Christine to fly over for the race. Catherine was there too with Leo, who was only a few months old. We all had a great time. I was even more confident when we drew an outside stall which ensured we could have a clear run without much kick-back. The Americans had sent over a strong team as usual but there wasn't a horse in the world who could have troubled Dubai Millennium that night.

We jumped out smartly, took a good position and found ourselves in front after a furlong. It wasn't quite what I planned, but once we got into a rhythm there was no point in hauling him back. He was doing it all so easily out on his own, sailing along, and as we free-wheeled round the bend already totally in command I could imagine people in the stands questioning my tactics at letting him go at such a blistering pace. It might have looked crazy but I wasn't mad and saw no sense in fighting him.

Sometimes in a race you have to adapt to the cards you are holding. I had no doubt I was on the best horse in the race, he was in front, so I pressed on. Dubai Millennium was like a rhino with his horn down, pointing at the ground, thundering along. As we reached the crown of the bend I could hear slapping and banging behind me as the other jockeys, knowing they were already in trouble, desperately tried to change gear to chase us.

Then this incredible roaring sound came echoing down the course from the stands as people began to realise they were watching one of the great moments in sport. Dubai Millennium was already out on his own and when I leaned forward and asked him for a bit more his response was electrifying. I remember having a little peep round with a hundred yards to go. To my amazement we were so far clear I couldn't see the others. He had turned the richest race in the world into a lap of honour, and in covering ten furlongs in 1 minute 59.5 seconds he'd smashed his own course record.

You wait all your life for a horse like Dubai Millennium. Everything about him was exceptional. He had the lot – power, stamina, courage, attitude, an amazing turn of foot – and was equally brilliant on grass or dirt. He also had a mind of his own and that night he wanted to go. Three of my previous rides in the race had finished last, so once I had the chance to set the record straight I wasn't going to wait for the others. As a result he won a championship race in a style that had never been seen in Dubai before. It was magic.

No wonder the crowd went ballistic as we fought our way back to the winner's circle. Wherever I looked people were stampeding to acclaim the wonder horse they felt belonged to all of them. They swamped the paddock in their thousands trying to get close to him. I had tears in my eyes as I gave them one of my best flying dismounts, disappeared to weigh-in then jumped onto him again bareback and paraded him in front of the grandstand.

In addition to collecting £219,000 as my percentage of the first prize of £2,195,122, I also received a gold whip, covered in diamonds, which I carried proudly in my hand the next morning when I arrived at the airport for the flight home. It caused quite a stir as it passed through the X-ray machine and is one of my proudest possessions as a permanent reminder of the evening that fantasy overtook reality.

Once I was back in England I was racing again every day. In the mornings I'd put on the video of the Dubai World Cup in my gym, have a little jog, and watch the replay while running on the treadmill like Forrest Gump. I thought it was great and couldn't wait to ride Dubai Millennium again in a heavyweight campaign that would culminate in the Breeders' Cup Classic in November. We knew he was a world champion and were ready to take on all-comers. Defeat was not an option.

twenty-three

A Miraculous Escape

Every colour was grey when I stepped outside the house on 1 June. It was one of those horrible cold, wet and windy days that felt more like March than close to the height of summer. If I'd had any sense I'd have stayed in bed. I rang Richard Hills offering him a lift in Godolphin's plane to Goodwood, but he'd chosen to go by car so that he could buy some lobsters for his supper at a special shop the boys use in Sussex. Darley Stud's adviser, John Ferguson, also cried off to have treatment on his back. Thank God they did.

Then Ray Cochrane called me asking if there was a spare seat in the plane. Ray used to travel everywhere at great speed on his Honda motorbike, but the forecast was for rain all day and he didn't fancy getting drowned on the way down and back again. We arranged to meet at the air strip beside the July course at Newmarket.

The plane used regularly by Godolphin was being serviced that week, so our regular pilot Patrick Mackey had been flying us in a rented six-seater Piper Seneca normally based at Oxford.

From what I could see the substitute aircraft was in urgent need of servicing, too. The previous day Patrick Mackey had done a double shift in it with me, first to Yarmouth, then on to Newbury's evening meeting. After racing we refuelled at Oxford before arriving back at Newmarket shortly before darkness fell.

Both of us were unhappy at the way the plane seemed to bunny hop just before we took off. It would stagger into the air for a few yards, then touch down again through lack of power, then take off once more. While we were refuelling at Oxford on the way home from Newbury I asked Patrick when our usual plane would be back in action. I'll never forget his reply.

'As soon as possible I hope, because I don't like this one', he said. I shared his sentiments as we lurched and staggered into the air prematurely once more from Oxford. The next morning we met up with Ray at the strip shortly after eleven. I sat more or less behind Patrick on the left side of the plane with Ray beside me near the right-hand window.

As we accelerated down the grass runway we were bumping along uncomfortably, just as the day before. Then, without warning, the plane tried to take off before it had the power to do so. It jumped a couple of feet into the air before sinking to the ground again with a hefty bump. Ray gave me a concerned glance and immediately tightened his seat belt. When it happened a second time we knew we were in for a white-knuckle ride. The third time the plane tried to take off it did manage to climb a few feet into the air before thudding down once more with a sickening thump.

One winter a few years earlier Ray spent several weeks learning to fly in the south of France. Now sitting beside the right wing he saw to his horror that the right propeller and engine were seriously damaged, probably as a result of the suspension collapsing. A moment later his worst fears were confirmed when smoke and then flames started to emerge from the engine on the right wing as we finally clawed our way unsteadily upwards at around 85 mph.

Soon we had reached a height of sixty or seventy feet, maybe more. Normally when taking off at Newmarket we continued straight ahead as we rose into the sky. Not this time. The engine that wasn't working was dragging the plane increasingly right-handed towards the Devil's Dyke, the ancient grass bank and ditch that divides the July course from the main racecourse at Newmarket.

Since we were flying higher than the bank I imagine Patrick was hoping we had enough power to clear it before making an emergency landing on the other side. If we'd missed the bank it's just possible that we might all have escaped unscathed. But as we tilted ever more right-handed on our side and plunged towards the ground I knew with absolute certainty that I was going to die. People say in moments like that your life flashes before your eyes.

I didn't experience any of that, just an overwhelming sense of disappointment that I was never going to see my lovely wife and little son again. As the right wing tip of our plane caught the top of the bank and sent us spiralling into the ground, I remember screaming something at Ray.

The shattering noise of the impact will live with me forever. It was just like the chilling echoes from a war movie when a ship starts to break up after being struck by torpedoes. The terrifying sound continued for several seconds as we cartwheeled end to end before coming to rest the right way up in a shower of sparks and smoke just beyond the Dyke.

At times in your life you seem to have 180-degree vision. You are staring at everything but cannot focus on a particular thing. I remember the initial impact, the first almighty explosion of noise, but not the conclusion of it. All I could see once I came to my senses was the bank, Patrick lying unconscious with his head on the dashboard and the two engines on fire.

It was all a bit like a slow-motion nightmare and I remember wondering if I was on the other side. Was I in heaven or hell or somewhere else? Then all of a sudden, boom, it was as if someone had woken me up. Nobody really knows how long we lay in that plane before we came round. Ray was knocked out, Patrick was definitely unconscious, and at first I was out of it too.

Ray was the first to react. He began shouting at me to get out before the plane exploded, but I could hardly move because the door on my side was jammed in on top of me. Basically it didn't exist any more. Even more alarming, my right leg was hurting so badly that I knew I was in serious trouble. So much blood was pouring down my face that I thought I might have been blinded in my right eye.

As we searched desperately for an escape route we spotted a small gap in the left-hand side of the plane behind us where the bags are stowed away. The little baggage hatch was half-open. God had left us a way out. Ray screamed 'get out, get out' and when I was a bit slow to react he grabbed me by the scruff of the neck, bundled me over the back of our seats and started to push me through the narrow hatch.

Time wasn't on our side, so Ray sent me on my way with a kick and a shove which left me rolling in agony on the ground as I landed on my broken leg. Lying in a crumpled heap just in front of the tailplane I was still far from safe. Unable to move and aware that I could be trapped by the flames at any moment I screamed at Ray to help me. At the time he was moving forward through the wreckage to try to release Patrick.

When he heard me calling out he turned back and started clambering through the broken baggage hatch. As he did so I heard him say 'That's it, I've had enough. I'm not riding any more.' He put his hands under my shoulders and dragged me thirty yards or so to safety in the direction of the Dyke. Both my eyes were pretty well covered in blood from cuts to my head and right eye-lid, but through my tears of pain and shock I saw him go back once more to rescue Patrick. First he forced open the pilot's door on the right-hand side of the plane and was in the process of leaning in to undo Patrick's seat belt until he was forced to retreat by the sheer force of the fire from a fresh explosion under the wing. Everything he touched was red hot by then, yet despite his burns Ray wouldn't give up. Some of the flames reached up as tall as a tree. Ray responded by taking off his jacket and using it to try to beat them out single-handedly. In the process he was burned even more seriously.

Beaten back by the intense heat and smoke, he rushed round to the other side of the plane in a desperate final bid to reach Patrick from the route that we had used to escape. But by then the remains of the plane were an inferno brought on by upwards of sixty gallons of fuel spilling from the ruptured tanks. He went ballistic, crying and screaming in frustration at the knowledge that he couldn't save Patrick and was inconsolable as he stumbled over to join me. I found my mobile phone in my pocket, handed it to him and watched him dial 999.

Then I rang my wife Catherine, told her not to worry, and explained that we'd survived a plane crash. She immediately dropped everything and drove over to the racecourse with Leo. They arrived pretty much at the same time as the ambulance. My leg was killing me but as the medics gave me oxygen they seemed more concerned about my head. I was trussed up as tight as a sausage with belts, bandages and a neck brace, barely able to breathe, then lifted gently by stretcher into a large army helicopter which had landed nearby.

As Ray was carried in beside me the pair of us looked like a pair of mummies. After surviving such a horrific crash the last thing either of us wanted was to have to take to the skies again. But our pleas fell on deaf ears and soon we were on our way to Addenbrooke's hospital in Cambridge.

The next few hours were a blur as we were treated in emergency. I didn't really know how seriously I was injured but my emotions were stretched to breaking point. For a split second as I lay in my hospital bed I felt, like Ray earlier, that I'd had enough and considered giving up riding. I was in terrible pain, hurting all over, in shock and feeling negative about the whole thing. I had a lovely wife, a lively young son and my second life was just beginning. Why bother about racing? But I soon realised that you can't retire at 29. What would I do for the rest of my days?

Over the next 24 hours I had surgery to pin my ankle, which was badly broken, and plastic surgery to repair the gashes on my forehead. It was my good fortune that the plastic surgeon who specialized in this type of injury was at the hospital when I was brought in. He did such a brilliant job on me that you can hardly see the scars anymore.

Ray was just generally badly beaten up with pains in his back, blurred vision in one eye and numerous burns on his hands, arms and face. We shared a room, our beds facing each other. For the first time since the crash I laughed as I said 'Look at the state of you Ray.' I was hardly in a position to talk and in truth there wasn't much to smile about. Yes, we had both escaped from a plane crash. But our friend Patrick Mackey had perished in tragic circumstances after saving our lives.

It wasn't until much later, when we'd both fully recovered, that we spoke of the few minutes that changed our lives. While we lay hurting in hospital, neither of us wanted to bring up the subject. I didn't thank Ray in as many words for pulling me to safety but he could see in my eyes that I was eternally grateful.

Hidden away in the safety and comfort of our ward we were unaware of the public interest in our ordeal, but within hours of the accident dozens of photographers, cameramen and reporters besieged the hospital. Several dressed up as doctors and nurses in a desperate bid to smuggle their way into our room to snatch a photo or a snap interview. At first the hospital's defences held firm because we had 24-hour security on our ward.

Eventually the sheer number of invading paparazzi threatened to undermine the efficiency of the hospital. Visitors like Catherine, Colin Rate, my business manager Peter Burrell and Sheikh Mohammed had to run a gauntlet of flashing cameras. At the same time the hospital's press office was fielding hundreds of calls requesting hourly bulletins on our condition. Things became so difficult that eventually I agreed to give a press conference on the day of my release on the Monday. I'm still not sure if it was the right thing to do. I just hoped that by talking openly to reporters at the hospital on the day I left I might encourage them to leave me and my family in peace when I was allowed home.

By now I felt like an old hand at dealing with the press, but with stitches in my head and over my eye and my leg encased in an air cushion I was hardly at my best as I was wheeled before the media scrum. Really I was still in shock at what had happened. I tried to answer all the questions as best I could and was mightily relieved when it was all over.

Ray was well enough to leave hospital after three days and I followed 24 hours later. By then we were torturing ourselves with the question I dared not admit to the press conference. Why were we alive? Why were we saved while the pilot was killed? What if Richard Hills and John Ferguson had travelled in the plane with us? Would any of us have escaped? And why do we ride horses for a living just so that people can have a bet? How silly is that?

In the end you get into such a muddle trying to make sense of it all, but one thing's for sure. I dealt with it a hundred times better than Ray. He is a quiet, self-contained sort of guy who doesn't readily display his emotions, so the questions going round in his head were killing him. Ray needed to talk it out of his system but didn't know how to start.

I've always tended to be more open in my dealing with people, so I was able to cope with the press conference, and by talking constantly about the accident with my family and friends over the next few weeks I gradually came to terms with what happened. Looking back now it all seems like thirty years ago. I'm not saying it hasn't left any scars. For a start I will never fly in a small plane again. But I learned to deal with it and move forward.

I was so lucky to survive. Ray, too. We were two in a zillion who walked or crawled away from a fatal air accident. Normally when a plane falls out of the sky everyone dies. You are dead, finished, end of story. That's what I thought was going to happen to me as we plunged towards the ground. You are waiting to die, for the pieces of metal to rip your body to bits.

As I escaped I feel I don't have to put myself through the torture of riding in a small plane again because you can't live in fear all the time. I appreciate being given a second life. I got lucky once. That was enough. If you start worrying what might happen every time you climb into a little plane, you will arrive at the racecourse totally washed out, like a horse in a muck sweat in the paddock that has already run his race. Our sport is already dangerous enough. Why risk more?

Since I recovered I've flown in umpteen transatlantic jets and any number of helicopters. I've also flown in forty-seater propeller planes but I don't feel at ease in them. My worst moment came in a helicopter last year on the way to Ascot for the Shergar Cup. Helicopters usually fly quite low but for some reason this one travelled at 3,000 feet, maybe more, and I was terrified by the sensation of being really high up in the sky. When I felt a panic attack coming on I buried my head in the *Racing Post* until my heart rate eased.

The doubts will always be there in my mind, nagging away, when I walk into an airport. I know I will be shaking with fear for an hour if the engine makes a funny noise on take-off. That is the hardest part of flying, whatever the size of the plane. Until we are well up into the air I remain a bit tight and tense, and my hands are sweaty. It might be with me all my life. We are the only sport apart from motor racing where every race is followed closely by a posse of ambulances. Travelling by car can be hairy too, particularly at the speed jockeys drive, but I'm prepared to take that chance.

Exactly a week after the crash Ray and I attended Patrick Mackey's funeral near Newbury. Neither of us was in great condition to travel but we both badly wanted to pay our respects to the man we felt had saved our lives. Once again the press turned out in force. I'd have preferred to slip quietly into the church unseen, then leave in private, too. Obviously that wasn't possible but I hope our presence helped comfort Patrick's widow Gill.

While he was in hospital Ray announced that his career as a jockey was over. His decision sounded final but I wasn't convinced. I know that after a couple of days I wanted to ride again and felt that once he had time on his hands he would feel the same. It wasn't until a year later on the anniversary of the crash that we both talked frankly about it. We had a round of golf, he came back to share a bottle of bubbly at my home, and our memories of that awful day came spilling out. He hasn't been in a small plane since either.

For so long in my life the Derby has been the focus of my attention, yet nine days after the crash I watched the race unfold on television in a fog of indifference. I was thinking the Derby, great, but who cares? Trauma does that to you. I suppose it's natural to think like that when you are hurting mentally and physically. I was in bed, feeling lousy, in pain from surgery and the loss of a friend. My emotions were still running out of control, everything was negative and my ribs were also aching like hell. Although X-rays failed to pick up any damage I'm sure I cracked some of them in the crash because I couldn't breathe properly for three months.

I was pleased that my great friend Johnny Murtagh won the Derby for the first time on Sinndar. Beyond that I was still licking my wounds. Godolphin ran four in the race that year with Best of the Bests finishing closest in fourth place. Although we didn't expect him to stay I can't imagine how I'd have felt if he'd won the race that has always eluded me. Probably suicidal.

Catherine was brilliant in the days after the accident. I

couldn't have pulled through so quickly without her, but after a week or so she cracked. I think it was the grim realization that if I hadn't survived she would have been left a young widow with a baby son. The whole episode brought us even closer than before.

When you've been through the torment I suffered, you need an excuse to pull you round and focus your mind. Mine was the thought of returning in time to ride Dubai Millennium at Deauville in mid August. It was going to be an impossibly tight schedule but I was willing myself to feel better and my desire to ride him increased when, partnered by Jerry Bailey, he turned the Prince of Wales's Stakes at Royal Ascot into a procession.

That morning I decided on the spur of the moment to go to Ascot to cheer him on. Catherine said I was mad but nothing would change my mind. Despite my horror of flying again I hitched a ride in the boss' helicopter and spoke to Jerry in the paddock. I warned him not to rush Dubai Millennium out of the stalls and to try to save a bit of energy on the way round. It wouldn't have mattered what he'd done because they pulverized the opposition. Just being there to watch Dubai Millennium win in runaway fashion did me more good than a bucketful of pills. I don't mind admitting I had a huge lump in my throat as he came home a mile in front of serious Group 1 horses. We will never see a performance like that again, not for a long time anyway.

As the afternoon wore on I was much too lame to keep up with the Godolphin team as they strolled to the paddock for one of the later races. By the time I got there I was tailed off fifty yards behind them. People started clapping as I entered the paddock on my own. Assuming the Queen was right behind me, I ducked out of the way as best I could and turned to greet her but there was no-one there. To my astonishment the reception was for me. Everyone gathered round the paddock was giving me a right cheer. I was overcome by the warmth of it and ended up with another lump in my throat.

The most persistent problem in the early stages of my recovery was caused by the huge blisters that developed on my palms from constant use of crutches. The skin on my hands was rubbed raw in those first weeks after leaving hospital. Soon I was on my way to my father's home in Sardinia to speed up my recovery. The flight from Stansted wasn't as bad an ordeal as I feared, though I experienced a wave of relief through my body when we landed safely. Although my leg was healing well, I was unable to do much more than bathe it in salt water for hours and walk gently on the sand. That was painful enough but I knew I had to keep pushing on if I was to make my appointment with Dubai Millennium.

To push matters I flew over my local masseur Michael Rogers and his wife for a week. Michael usually pops in at home in the mornings to work on my back, shoulders and legs, but this time he concentrated on massaging my ankle to help reduce the swelling. Soon I reached the point where I could just about run on the sand. My weight had risen to almost 9 stone but it would come off once I started riding out again.

It was while I was in Sardinia that I heard I'd been recommended for an MBE in the coming New Year's Honours list.

Naturally I was touched by the news but also surprised because it never occurred to me that foreigners were eligible for awards like that. It turned out that I was in good company because Peter Schmeichel was also honoured at the same time. At first I suspected that someone was winding me up but the letter looked authentic enough. I also wondered whether the MBE was for surviving the plane crash or doing well as a jockey. I still don't know the answer to that one. The hardest part was keeping quiet until 1 January.

I was preparing to return from Sardinia with Catherine when Ray made a triumphant comeback on Glowing at Newmarket on 21 July. So much for his retirement! We spoke on the phone most days so I was aware that his back was still giving him trouble, but jockeys have always come back sooner than they should. When a doctor tells us it will be six months before we ride again we usually halve the timescale. You can't afford to wait until everything is working properly. So you rush back like a lunatic and hope you don't aggravate your injuries as you play yourself in.

Riding out was horribly painful at first. Naturally I was coming back too early but I protected my right ankle by putting all the pressure on my left leg. Wrapped in a special boot with a zip, the ankle was still swollen. I was frightened of putting any weight on it. When I did, it hurt like hell but I reached the point where I felt that if I didn't make a start, I wouldn't be able to do justice to Dubai Millennium.

Two days before my comeback I rode him in his final piece of work with Best Of The Bests before his next race at Deauville.

It was nothing short of sensational. Best Of The Bests was a decent horse in his own right, a top-class miler. The plan was to let him lead us before closing up to him in the final stages of the gallop. At half-way, when I was still three or four lengths down, I leant forward, gave him a squeeze and encouraged him to move up. Maybe I'd forgotten how good he was.

Dubai Millennium took off with me and shot past Best Of The Bests as if he was standing still. I was no more than a helpless passenger. He was so big and powerful, once again like a rhino in full stampede. He would have smashed straight through a wall if there had been one in front of us. Given the calibre of the horse we beat out of sight it was an astonishing piece of work, quite the most electrifying I've ever experienced. Two days later, on Saturday 4 August, I was more nervous than I'd been for a long time. So much was at stake. Had I rushed back too soon, I wondered, as I put the final touches to my preparation by running in my sweat gear on the treadmill in my gym.

Then the phone rang and my world collapsed. Dubai Millennium had fractured a bone in his hind leg on the gallops earlier that morning. His career was over. I sat down in stunned disbelief, devastated that the best horse I'd ever ridden would never race again. Overcome with self-pity I thought 'sod it' and decided then and there that I'd go out with him. I'd retire, too. What was the point in putting myself through torture every day to keep my weight down when he wouldn't be there for me? Why bother?

I stumbled into the garden where Catherine was playing with

Leo and told her the shocking news. The thought of riding Dubai Millennium had been the only thing that kept me going over the previous nine weeks. Now he was finished and I was stunned, totally distraught. Catherine tried to console me but at first I was beyond help. What else did fate have in store for me? My mood was so black that for the next half hour my career was in the balance. What was the point of going on?

Then Catherine began to talk me round. So many people had helped me recover from my injuries, she pointed out. I couldn't let them down nor all the racing fans on their way to Newmarket to see me ride again that afternoon. One exceptional horse had gone but there were still hundreds of other good ones to ride. Catherine's talk was enough to start turning the tide, and by the time I arrived at the July course I was in a reasonably positive frame of mind.

I felt even better after receiving a tremendous reception from the crowd gathered round the winner's enclosure before racing. They all seemed genuinely pleased to see me and greeted me with banners, kisses and loud cheers. It was great to be alive. Among my guests was Fred Robinson, the surgeon who had put my ankle together so skillfully barely two months earlier. He cautioned me against trying a flying dismount, though I wasn't really expecting a winner – but from the ovation I got on the way to the seven furlong start on my first mount Atlantis Prince you'd have thought we'd already won.

As we neared the stalls I looked across to my right towards the point where we'd crossed the ditch in the doomed plane. My thoughts went back to the accident and to poor Patrick. I needed to look at the exact spot where it happened. Then it was down to business. Atlantis Prince seemed beaten when Crazy Larrys took up the running over a furlong out, but then all the familiar old feelings came rushing back. Wanting to win more than words can say, I kept pumping and pushing, Atlantis Prince got the message and provided me with a triumphant winning return. It was a fairytale straight out of Hollywood.

I was greeted by rapturous applause and told the waiting press corps that I felt blessed to be there, and that I was planning to enjoy it all the more the second time around. I was still blowing when I came out for my second ride on Dim Sums who did his bit by giving me the second leg of an emotional double. By then I was absolutely knackered, mainly because my broken ankle had prevented me running my way back to fitness. I wasn't as prepared as I thought on the first, most important day of my second career.

I dedicated my two wins to Catherine who'd been so strong for me through the darkest days and never had any doubt that I would return as good as new. I also outlined my fresh philosophy that I wouldn't be riding on Mondays and Tuesdays which would allow me to spend more time with my family. But my well-intentioned plans to cut back on my hectic schedule were in tatters within months because the demands of racing suffocate people in this business.

Even if I wanted to do things differently, racing left me no choice. I have to do it the way racing wants me to do it. Hard as I tried, I was unable to change. The truth is that from the moment I leave home in the morning I am on the stage riding horses mornings, afternoons and sometimes evenings. That's my job. You can't be a part-time jockey. As a result of all this I'm busier than I've ever been. The day after Newmarket I finished second in a valuable race at Deauville on Lend A Hand. Soon I was on the treadmill again, rushing around the country as busily as ever. Two more visits to Deauville yielded lucrative successes on Best Of The Bests and Muhtathir, an able substitute for Dubai Millennium.

By the time I arrived at York for the Ebor meeting the strain of my frantic schedule was beginning to tell. Things came to a painful conclusion when my saddle slipped backwards on Ski Run in the second race of the opening day. To avoid being dumped abruptly on the ground I eased my feet out of the irons and rode virtually bareback for three furlongs. Normally I could have managed that without too many problems but I wasn't ready for that kind of drama.

York is very demanding on jockeys with seven races a day, long canters to the start in boiling hot weather, and horses pulling more than usual because they are wound up from being led across the Knavesmire from the stables. My setback on Ski Run convinced me I couldn't cope over the next two days. I was tired, in pain, and had come back too soon. After one more uncomfortable ride I had to stop.

A short break from racing gave me the chance to treat myself to the Ferrari that I'd planned to buy when I was thirty. That timescale had now gone out of the window. As a small boy in Italy I'd been brought up in the era when Niki Lauda and Gilles Villeneuve dominated Formula 1 with Ferrari. My leg was still in plaster when I borrowed a Ferrari from Clive Garrard, my partner in the pizza business we have built up together. He must be a good friend because I asked to take it out for a day and didn't return it for two weeks! By then I was hooked, but I soon discovered that buying a Ferrari in this country isn't easy. People have to place their orders months in advance.

I had everyone on the case when I heard that a guy who'd ordered one eighteen months earlier no longer wanted it. That was all the encouragement I needed. I tracked him down, did the deal in record breaking time, and for £110,000 I became the proud owner of a scarlet, two-seater Ferrari Modena coupe with a 3.58 litre engine. Later, in July 2002, I swapped it for a similar one with a soft top. It's a fantastic toy with stunning acceleration from nought to 60 mph in four seconds, though I don't use it as much as I would like. It's been to Yarmouth a couple of times, to Leicester and to London, but most weeks it stays untouched in the garage. Even now it has little more than 4,000 miles on the clock.

The roads in this country aren't ideal for such a powerful car. You don't just jump in, turn the engine on and pop round to the village shop for a loaf of bread. You've really got to be in the right frame of mind to want to drive it. So I treat my Ferrari a bit like a mistress and only take her out on special occasions.

A petrol strike in the late autumn of 2001 gave me the chance to put it through its paces on the way to Yarmouth with Richard Hills as navigator. The roads were empty of cars and police so I gave it a kick in the belly on a stretch of dual carriageway and wound it up to 155 mph. We were going so fast that the broken white lines on the road merged into one. I wasn't so brave when I let Richard have a go behind the wheel. Talk about a nervous passenger. I begged him to slow down.

Richard's great hobby is collecting furry friends. He has an amazing assortment of wild animals at home, so on the return journey we stopped off to buy a red squirrel to add to his collection. One thing's for sure: by the time we reached Newmarket Richard owned the world's fastest squirrel.

While I was recovering from my setback at York, Ray was having his own problems. He tried to soldier on after a bad fall at Salisbury in August but I could see how badly he was hurting. He was locked into a torture chamber without any sign of an exit. Some days he was green with pain as he walked out to ride, and I remember him confiding his fears that he was one fall away from being paralysed. Things were so bad that I suggested he retire from riding and become my agent. At the time he wasn't sure that I was serious, because he was aware that Andrew Stringer had done well for me after taking over the job from my great pal Mattie Cowing when he became too ill to continue. But after the events of 1 June at Newmarket my greatest loyalty lay with Ray. He'd been my guiding star in my early days with Luca and in the past few months we'd forged even closer bonds. So I was thrilled when he decided to hang up his boots and become my agent. It was a decision I've had no reason to regret. He's red hot on the form book and is a wily old bird to turn to when I need advice.

Naturally Ray was one of the star guests when Catherine

arranged a surprise thirtieth birthday party for me a few days before Christmas. I wasn't best pleased when she informed me that I had to attend a charity dinner with her in Newmarket that night. I was so tired at the end of the season all I wanted to do was chill out eating and drinking. I protested but Catherine wouldn't take no for an answer. I had to go, so I told my friends that I wouldn't be seeing them that evening. I delayed our departure as long as I could, then set off grumpily in the car with her. We strolled through the door of the M club to be greeted by a sea of people singing Happy Birthday. Wow, was I scared! I felt really weird. It was all so unexpected, I didn't have a clue. But I calmed down when a Marilyn Monroe lookalike sang a little solo to me and I was given a huge birthday cake in the shape of a Ferrari. It was a brilliant night.

twenty-four

In the Grip of Lester

I've been on the end of thousands of bollockings as a jockey. One of the longest and most deserved came from the red-shirted figure of Jack Berry, once he caught up with me. It must have lasted twenty minutes. Jack was a legend in the north of England as a trainer of sprinters. In July 1993 Jack ran two of his speedsters in a five furlong handicap at Chester. He booked me for the favourite, Laurel Delight, in the favoured stall next to the rail while his stable jockey John Carroll rode Press The Bell. In the paddock Jack told us that both horses were good enough to win – it just depended which one had luck in running. What we must do at all costs was avoid taking each other on from the start and burning them out before the finish.

The pair of us jumped out so sharply that we instantly locked horns, lengths ahead of the rest, running flat out like Linford Christie and his shadow in an Olympic final. We must have been mad. John and I were in a race of our own, our orders long-forgotten, fully a dozen lengths clear of the rest at half-way. You can imagine what Jack was thinking as the two horses tied up badly in the closing stages and finished out of the money. As we came back to unsaddle, the trainer's face matched one of his trademark shirts. John was unwise enough to approach him first and was immediately silenced by a torrent of abuse. I slunk away before Jack spotted me, and buried myself in the weighing room.

Once I felt the danger had passed I took a long, hot shower. The next moment a large hand at the end of a red-shirted arm appeared through the shower curtain and seized me by the throat. 'What have you got to say for yourself, you little Italian prat? Call yourself a bloody jockey?' he started, before making it clear that if he had his way I would never ride for him again. I had nowhere to hide as he continued to call me every name under the sun for minutes on end. It was just about the most one-sided conversation of my life.

I'd arranged to stay with John that evening. He was also giving me a lift, so once I'd recovered from my mauling at the hands of Jack Berry I begged him to smuggle me away from the course to avoid another confrontation. 'There's only one problem', he replied, 'Jack is coming with us. I've got to drop him off on the way home!'

So for the first half-hour of the journey we had to endure a rambling monologue from Jack on our many failings as jockeys. He would probably still be ranting and raving now if I hadn't interrupted him in full flow. John nearly choked and drove off the road when I suggested, 'Look Jack, you've had your say. I've already apologized. Let's leave it now.' Later John and I celebrated our narrow escape in style, with the result that I had so much to drink I didn't have a clue where I was the next morning.

John had already left to ride out when I woke up in a strange house in the middle of nowhere. I wandered out into the garden in my underpants, completely lost, then spotted a neighbour cleaning his car. When I asked him where I was he looked at me as though I was daft. A moment later, John got a frantic call on his mobile phone. 'There's a madman in your garden in his underpants asking whose house it is. And he sounds like a foreigner. Do you want me to call the police?' My hangover didn't do me any harm because I ended the day with a treble at York.

The boys in the north always seem to be a bit more relaxed than the jockeys on the southern circuit. In the days before breath tests at the races, packs of beer and bags of chips would be handed through the weighing room windows at evening meetings north of the border. Once when I was riding at Hamilton Park as a kid I was dragooned by Dandy Nicholls into driving him and Lindsay Charnock to Glasgow for a night out. At the time Dandy was a senior, if rather overweight jockey who used to lose up to 8 pounds in one session in the sauna. He didn't seem to mind one bit that I couldn't drive nor that I hadn't taken a test. I set off nervously at the wheel of his immaculate BMW on the way to a lively night in the clubs before the three of us shared one large double-bed in a hotel.

The Western meeting at Ayr in September is the highlight of the Scottish season. That week as many as six, eight or even ten of the boys share one room to cut their costs if they can hoodwink the hotel staff. Gary Bardwell was the chief sufferer one time when he was found out. Until he retired late last year, Gary – nicknamed 'the angry ant' – was a fiercely determined lightweight. Most of the time he was so quiet in the weighing room that he didn't say a word, but after a few drinks he wanted to fight the world. Afterwards he always used the same excuse: 'It wasn't me. It was Trevor', he would explain mysteriously.

Late one night the staff at Gary's hotel tried to restrain him from running up the stairs to share a room with half a dozen of his mates on the eve of the Ayr Gold Cup. He reacted by seizing a tall plant and wielding it like a sword so that no-one could get near him. Eventually the police were called. Gary responded by trying to head butt one of them in the knee.

As he was led away in handcuffs he was heard to ask, 'Will I be out in time to ride work for Linda Perrett in the morning?' What a pro. I doubt if he was in any fit state to ride out when he woke up in his cell, but he did arrive at the course in time for the first race. As he walked into the weighing room we all gave him a standing ovation. When the applause died down he muttered 'It wasn't me. It was Trevor!'

Many jockeys based in Newmarket prefer to let the train take the strain on the long journeys to northern tracks. Sometimes, for a laugh, they buy a child's ticket for some of the smaller jockeys. It happened the day I travelled up from Peterborough station to Newcastle with a group including Kieren Fallon and Jimmy Quinn. The joke was on me because I was the one handed the junior ticket. I wasn't exactly unknown at the time and sat squirming with embarrassment in my seat when the collector came along. I made sure I had the correct ticket on the way back.

By the time we reached Peterborough the park where Kieren had left his car was closed, so I jumped out to help him lift up the barrier. At first it wouldn't budge. Then it suddenly shattered into pieces with a noise that must have woken up the entire neighbourhood. As I looked up in alarm I found myself staring straight into a security camera. We all jumped back into the car and raced away from the scene of the crime.

In the days when he was still riding, Lester Piggott fully enjoyed his reputation for keeping a very tight hold on his finances. I'm not saying that he was mean, just that he was unbelievably careful. One of his regular tricks was to make someone else pay for his taxis and ice-creams, but he surpassed himself the day we flew back to England after riding in Hamburg.

As we rushed through the airport lounge to catch our flight he was stopped by an elderly English woman seeking his autograph. Lester gave me one his looks as if to say watch this, before replying 'All right, but it will cost you £20.' I was horrified at his response, even if, at first, I thought he was joking. Then the woman handed over a £20 note and he scribbled his autograph on a piece of paper. Amazingly she was delighted with the transaction but Lester, being Lester, was left rueing a lost opportunity. 'I made a mistake there, I should have asked for £50', he confided as she walked away! For once I was speechless. As usual he didn't do it for the money but just to see if he could get away with it. If he senses an advantage he goes straight for the jugular. He gets a kick out of it. That's his game. He can't help trying it on.

Nor did he believe in forking out on new clothes if he could pick them up for nothing. Because our riding boots are so small and close fitting, lots of jockeys use tights, or pop socks underneath them. Not Lester. One day at the races I fell about laughing at the sight of him wearing a pair of thick, grey woolly, British Airways Club class socks with wrinkles on the bottom. Once his valet had washed them a couple of times they grew a beard like tennis balls that have been used for fifty games. It was hilarious. Did I give him some stick about those socks.

Lester's appetite for racing was amazing. He was still riding plenty of winners in 1994 as he advanced on his fifty-ninth birthday. As a private person, he tended to keep his own counsel in the weighing room. All the jockeys looked up to him with a degree of awe. He had this great talent to get horses travelling sweetly for him, yet in so many ways he was twenty years ahead of his time. I spent a lot of time teasing him. Quite often I suggested that he'd end up in the British museum, stuffed with straw. I know at times I really pissed him off because he must have felt I was trying to destroy his reputation.

Lester finally took his revenge at Goodwood in one of those tight handicaps with two dozen runners fighting for position on the bend into the straight. Goodwood is one of the hardest of all courses to ride because of all the changing cambers, so you need eyes in the back of your head. Half-way round the bend as we turned for home I sensed rather than saw Lester a neck or so behind me. Then he struck like a cobra.

I suddenly felt my balls enclosed in a vice like grip. It was so painful and unexpected it brought tears to my eyes. As the grip tightened, I heard a familiar voice mutter 'That will teach you to be so cheeky, you little so and so.' I was in too much discomfort to argue. Once I'd recovered after the race I told a couple of the other jockeys what had happened. We looked time and again at the video but couldn't spot any evidence of the crime. The cunning old fox had caught me on the blind-spot where the camera angle changes.

No-one was laughing when I ended up with concussion after bailing out from a dodgy horse called Move With Edes at Epsom in 1997. One or two of the boys warned me about him in the weighing room but it was too late by then. He had all sorts of gadgets on his mouth to help control him as we cantered to the mile start at the top of the hill. He stopped for a second when we got there, suddenly gave two flying leaps, ran into another horse nearly knocking him over, then set off downhill towards the mile and a half start going a million miles an hour. With his reputation I didn't want to find out what would happen at the bottom, so I jumped off, banged my head and concussed myself. That should have been the end of the matter, but when I called the horse a yak his trainer Bill Turner threatened to sue me. He must have forgiven me because I rode for him again early in 2004.

I had another fright at Epsom the day Vinnie Jones and some of his old team mates from Wimbledon took their revenge on me for tipping them a loser. Before racing, I popped up to their box on the third floor and suggested that Selhurstparkflyer was a decent bet in the sprint. What happens? I came and beat him on the line on Lord Olivier. When I joined them for a drink at the end of the afternoon they lifted me over the balcony, hung me upside down by my ankles fifty feet above the ground and threatened to drop me if I gave them another bum tip. Some friends.

It's hard to be cheerful when you are always struggling with your weight, but I seem to manage it better than most. Over the years I've tried various dire methods to lose unwanted pounds including laxatives and pee pills. They all work for a time but the horrible side-effects make you pay and can seriously damage your health. Most mornings I need to lose three pounds before going racing. I do it with a mixture of running, walking, sweating in the sauna and working out in the new gym I finished at home towards the end of 2003.

When I had to lose weight in a hurry as a youngster the first thing I tried was laxatives. They work fine by clearing you out quickly. But you end up feeling a bit weak and light-headed, and if you use them regularly you start to suffer from the most agonising stomach cramps. So at some point on one of my first trips to California I tried lasix which is the same as a pee pill. You take a tablet – the same type used to stop horses breaking blood vessels. It's easy, too easy that way because you can lose 4 pounds of body fluid in an hour. Compare that to the four or five hours you'd need to spend in a sauna to have the same effect.

But lasix also has nasty side-effects, including sudden cramps, particularly in your feet and calves. I'd be asleep at night and wake up with an attack of cramp in my leg. After a while you have to take four or five lasix pills to achieve the same results that you initially get with one. I could see I was fighting a losing battle, but when I stopped using the pills after a fortnight I blew up like a balloon and it took the best part of a month to return to normal.

The problem is even harder for jockeys in America because the race weights there have hardly changed in fifty years. The fat-cats in charge of the sport enjoy large breakfasts, lunches and dinners but don't care if all their riders have to starve and throw up to make the weights. They argue that raising the weights by even a fraction would cause hundreds of horses to break down, but that's bullshit because all we are talking about here is the equivalent of an extra bag of sugar on their backs.

So a lot of jockeys in the States are in the habit of throwing-up, or flipping as we call it, after a meal. It's a drastic method of eating well and not putting on weight afterwards. Steve Cauthen used to do it from time to time when he was here, and I throw up occasionally, too. When you are wasting hard all the time you get to the point where you will go nuts if you don't eat a proper meal. So you dive into a big plate of food aware that you will then have to lose 4lb in a hurry afterwards. Flipping is the easiest way of doing it.

In Europe the weights have been raised several times over the years in recognition that people are heavier these days, but I still have the problem of shedding unwanted pounds every morning. If you are disciplined, drink only water and eat small pieces of fish you will stay reasonably light, but it is so difficult to strike the right balance. If I locked myself away like a monk, day after day, I'd soon go round the bend.

You deprive yourself of the pleasures of life because you are riding horses, which is one of the most beautiful things in the world – but you will damage yourself if you aren't careful. We are all human and can't resist looking for a way out. You want to eat and enjoy life but you can't afford to put on weight, so you compensate by eating sparingly, working out, sweating and keeping busy. It's been a nightmare for jockeys ever since racing began. Boxers go through it for a short spell before a fight. I deal with it 48 weeks of the year. That's why it's so hard. People don't understand just how hard. They tend to think we are just the guy who sits on top of a horse and beats the hell out of it. My constant battle with the scales is tough enough, but heavier-built jockeys like my friend Johnny Murtagh put themselves through hell to continue riding.

A jockey is not just the person riding a racehorse. He has to be a pyschiatrist, too. To get the best out of a horse you have to become its friend or you will not win. You climb into the saddle and you feel how it walks, how it places its feet and how it looks at you and you must understand. When I sit on a horse I can tell its character within five seconds, its nature, its temperament and best distance, even whether it has got a kick or is one-paced. That is something I was born with.

I will tell you something else that people don't appreciate. A horse is a ball of energy but when we go into the stalls he doesn't know if he is going to run five furlongs, a mile, two miles or even ten miles. Nor is he aware where the winning post is. So it is down to me to make sure we become friends so that he will respond to whatever I ask him. You must work to build a bond. He has to have that trust in me to slow down or quicken up when I ask. Only then can you control the release of that huge potential energy during a race. If you have that understanding then you have an edge over some of the others.

So the most important thing between man and horse is trust. You find it by body language and feeling. Horses have a sixth sense about the person on top, they can even feel you blinking. If they realise you are frightened they are just as likely to drop you straight away and bury you. It's their natural instinct. They won't stand for just anybody on their backs.

In any year I've never seen or touched 50% of the horses before I ride them in races. I don't even know what colour they are. That's the truth. So there isn't much time to gain their trust. Once I'm in the saddle I can sense if the horse is tough or if he is sensitive or fragile. It only takes a few seconds to know. For me a horse is the same whether it is owned by the Queen or from a minor stable. What matters is its behaviour.

From the moment we set eyes on each other in the paddock we have perhaps five minutes to form a relationship. It helps that I've been around horses all my life and had good teachers, but to be a good jockey you need race-sense, too, and some of the great horsemen in the game have no race sense at all. The trick is to combine the two. There are great work riders who can't do it on the track in the afternoons. It's the same in motor racing. There are so many decent test drivers but only a handful of great racing drivers. In a way I am a bit like a Formula 1 driver too, in that I'm in control of a fantastic machine. The difference is that a driver has only to turn the key to fire the engine into life. I'm working with an animal and I've got a sixth sense.

Horses are like human beings. You can bully colts and they will respond. As for the fillies, they are moody, like women. You are dealing with equine characters from all walks of life, Spice Girls and housewives, MPs, rascals and policemen. Now it all comes naturally to me. I've been doing it for eighteen years but it wasn't always straightforward. In my days as an apprentice with Luca Cumani a sprinter called Be Fresh got the better of me at home every time by running away with me. I couldn't hold one side of him. Yet when Luca's wife Sara sat on Be Fresh he'd canter along happily without a care in the world, not pulling at all. Perhaps he responded to a woman's touch. Of course Luca did it to teach me a lesson.

He drummed into me that if I wanted to be a decent jockey I had to find the key for every horse, not just the good ones, or the well-behaved ones. His words are printed in my head. At least I listened, though it took me an age to handle Be Fresh who was a right villain. I came to understand that the balance between having a horse relaxed and having one run away with you is the edge of a razor blade. I swallowed my pride, dropped my leathers, learned to humour Be Fresh and eventually won a decent sprint on him at Goodwood.

twenty-five

An Emotional Night in New York

News of my MBE in the New Year's Honours List in 2001 made all the headlines. I was thrilled to join a select band of foreigners to be recognised including Manchester United's Danish goalkeeper Peter Schmeichel. I've always felt Ray Cochrane was a far more suitable case for honours and I was the first to applaud when he collected several awards for his bravery. Early in January he received a Silver Medal, the Royal Humane Society's top award, from Princess Alexandra after being nominated by Peter Amos, one of the first men on the scene after our plane crashed.

Amos explained 'So many people felt that Ray's actions deserved public recognition. He behaved in a way that was not only extremely brave, but actually put his life at considerably increased risk.' It could have been me speaking. Two weeks later Ray was presented with the Queen's Commendation for Bravery, the civilian equivalent of the Military Cross, for rescuing me from the burning plane.

I had my chance to pay a further tribute to him when he received the Special Recognition Award for a flat jockey during an emotional ceremony at the annual Lesters evening at the Hilton Hotel. We both struggled to hold back the tears on stage as he received a prolonged standing ovation. It was no more than Ray deserved. He insists everything he did that black day was by instinct but he still had to fight through the flames and do it. He managed to get me out and save my life and no-one could have tried harder to rescue the pilot Patrick Mackey.

Late in January I returned to Addenbrooke's Hospital with Leo in my arms to open a new development costing £2.4 million. It was good to be back among the people who had taken such brilliant care of me. There was barely time to be best man at Colin Rate's wedding before I was in the groove again in Dubai, riding out each morning shortly before the sun came up.

I wasn't as fit as usual because I'd been unable to train properly after having two screws removed from my right ankle at the start of the year. Because the ankle was still a bit weak I made a complete hash of two flying dismounts that spring. The first came on our hardy standard bearer Best Of The Bests. I jumped off as usual, my legs gave way and suddenly I was sitting on my bum. Saeed bin Suroor was in stitches as he asked. 'What are you doing down there Frankie?' The next time it happened was much more embarrassing. I flung myself into the air after winning on Give The Slip, but as I started to come down he moved. I struck his quarters and in trying to save myself ended up landing straight on top of Sheikh Mohammed. I can tell you, he wasn't amused.

Catherine stayed in England that spring as she was expecting our second child around the same time as the Dubai World

Cup later in March. It looked like being a photo finish so once again we decided the baby should be induced. I flew home to be with her a day before Ella was born on 19 March, weighing barely 5 pounds. We were both thrilled to have a little girl and this time I didn't make the mistake of trying to take over Catherine's bed afterwards. Once she was settled I drove home for a good night's sleep.

A month later my father's sixtieth birthday allowed me to pay him a long overdue tribute. In the past we've had our differences but he has always been there for me in my hour of need and now we are closer than ever. Liberation Day at Florence racecourse on 25 April, his birthday, offered the perfect excuse for a celebration of his life as Italy's greatest jockey. It was a national holiday, devoted to a local hero organized around the Premio Del Arno, Italy's oldest race. I persuaded jockeys Olivier Peslier and Yutaka Take to join in the fun at a big dinner the night before his birthday and took Dad to the hotel in a horse-drawn carriage with me on the reins. It was a hell of a party with three hundred guests and the highlight came late in the evening when I presented my dad with a new Mercedes.

I said 'Dad, I want to show you something', took him outside to the car park, gave him the keys and explained that the gleaming Merc was his birthday present. That was the first time I've ever seen him lost for words. He was absolutely gobsmacked. As he started with nothing and came from a generation that felt it had to save every penny, I bought him the more economical diesel version. I knew that if I'd chosen a petrol engine he'd have kept it in the garage. He checked over the wheels, lifted the bonnet and examined the engine. Then he opened the doors, jumped in behind the steering wheel, began playing with it and moved his seat up and down until he was comfortable. He was so overcome he would have slept in his new car that night if we'd let him.

My friend Paolo Benedetti has been booking my rides in Italy for years. He excelled himself on this occasion with the result that I won four of the five races the next day. All but one of the horses I rode jumped out, made all and won easily. Olivier and Yutaka gave me some serious stick about Jim'll Fix It races.

Soon after I returned to England I was devastated to hear that Dubai Millennium was dead. Twelve months earlier the sky had been the limit for him. Now he was gone, struck down by grass sickness. It was an awful way for a great horse to go, quite horrible. Grass sickness is a mysterious disease that paralyses the intestines. As a result he was unable to digest any food and would have wasted away.

Sheikh Mohammed hired the finest vets to try to save him. They operated three times in seven days, opening him up and removing some of the infected intestine and Dubai Millennium was so strong that he stayed alive longer than anyone expected. But the task was hopeless and they put him down, with the boss there at this side, so that he didn't suffer. When all avenues had been explored he was the one who decided that the horse shouldn't be allowed to come round from anaesthetic after the third operation on his intestines.

It was a tragic end to a horse who had transformed all our lives. He was the ultimate racehorse and hardly had a chance to pass on his unique talent at stud before he died. It was a huge loss. The boss had promised me a nomination to Dubai Millennium but I missed out on his only season at stud because I couldn't find a suitable mare at the right price. I'd always wanted to own one of his offspring but the chance had gone forever.

The mood at Godolphin has never been lower than in the days following his death. The light had gone out of our lives, but however miserable we all felt the show had to go on. After a quiet start that spring we began to make up for lost time with a conveyor belt of victories at the highest level around the world. Fantastic Light proved to be a superstar that year. He kicked off with a stylish success in the Tattersalls Gold Cup at the Curragh then got me out of the soup with a blistering display of acceleration in the Prince of Wales's Stakes at Royal Ascot.

It was a championship race, I was drawn inside riding the Ferrari and I found myself trapped on the rail two furlongs from home with nowhere to go. The boys stitched me up like a kipper. Kieren Fallon had me locked away tightly while the others did me no favours either, so I just had to sit and suffer hoping a gap would appear. I was annoyed but that's race riding. I'd have done the same to them given half a chance. This time I got lucky by coming round them on the outside after being forced to pull back. Once I switched Fantastic Light sharply left he shot forward and won with plenty to spare. He was the real McCoy.

The Royal meeting wasn't all plain sailing. I should have

taken the Coventry Stakes on Sheikh Hamdan's two-year-old colt Meshaheer, but we had a shocking run from a bad draw next to the fence, and we were hampered several times in a huge field of runners before finishing third. We should have won by a minute but with so many horses in the way what was I supposed to do? Put wings on Meshaheer's back and make him fly? Afterwards I held up my hands, but Sheikh Hamdan wasn't amused. The next day he told his jockey Richard Hills in the paddock 'If you had ridden Meshasheer like Frankie you would be hanging from this tree above us. By your balls!'

Soon I was involved in two monumental clashes with Galileo, that year's outstanding Derby winner. The three-year-old was going to be tough to beat in the King George VI and Queen Elizabeth Diamond Stakes, particularly as my mount Fantastic Light as a four-year-old had to concede 12 pounds to him. Tactics played a crucial part in the result. As Mick Kinane tracked the pacemakers on Galileo on the rails, I followed close behind on Fantastic Light on the basis that if he didn't get out, neither would I.

It was looking so crowded in front that I eventually switched Fantastic Light to launch my run towards the outside. The moment I'd done it the field opened up ahead of Galileo like the Red Sea, they all let him through and he cruised into the lead cutting the corner, going the shortest way with Mick barely moving a muscle. That gave him the advantage. In contrast I'd probably wasted two lengths getting out and then had to burn Fantastic Light earlier than I wanted to attack Galileo.

Mick was sailing along in the lead in the straight, oozing

confidence, and I'll never forget the shock on his face when we ranged alongside him and looked him in the eye with just over a furlong to run. I could see that he was physically shaken that another horse was as good as his, but because I'd been forced to use up vital energy to get to him Fantastic Light then began running out of petrol.

When Mick asked Galileo for a final effort he gave him two smacks with the whip in his left hand. The first one caught me hard across the knuckles. I thought he'd cut my hand but the real pain came from knowing he was going to beat us. If I'd ridden out to the line we'd have failed by a length. With the cause already lost and my horse exhausted I eased up in the closing stages so that we were two lengths behind at the line.

I knew there would be another day to set the record straight and it came in the Irish Champion Stakes at Leopardstown early in September. Fantastic Light had the pace to go and pass any horse but once in front he tended to idle. This time we only had to give Galileo 7 pounds. My game plan was to stalk him the whole way like a shadow, then pull out inside the last furlong and nail him on the line. But all that changed after a call from Simon Crisford urging me to fly to Ireland the evening before the race for a summit meeting at the Kildangan Stud.

I remember arriving around 9 p.m., sitting down between Sheikh Mohammed and his brother Sheikh Maktoum and being offered champagne by the butler. It had been a long day and I was ready for a glass of bubbly. So you can imagine my feelings when Sheikh Maktoum swiftly changed my order to a pint of orange juice. It was not a request, more an order. Clearly there was serious business to discuss.

There followed a prolonged discussion with the boss and his brother on the tactics I should employ on Fantastic Light. So much for my plans. Instead they wanted me to jump out in front of Galileo and steal first run on him when the race came to the boil. I thought it was madness, said it would play to the strengths of Galileo, and outlined my fears that Fantastic Light would pull himself up in front. I kept fighting for the right to do things my way but my argument fell on deaf ears. On this occasion my views didn't count. I was losing the battle and since they owned the horse and I was their employee I had to do what I was told. I got the message and went off to bed fearing the worst.

I remember ringing up my dad the next day telling him that the race would turn out to be a disaster. In the paddock at Leopardstown I asked the boss one final time if he really wanted me to set off in front of Galileo. There was no late change of mind. Thank goodness there wasn't. It helped that Richard Hills, who rode a blinder on our pacemaker Give The Slip, agreed to stay a little off the rail so that I had the choice of passing him either on the inside or outside once I got to him.

Ice Dancer, a 200–1 outsider, took us along at a spanking pace for the first mile but it was Richard who controlled the race on Give The Slip in second place with my horse tracking him and Galileo behind us. As the pacemakers weakened,

Richard stayed far enough out from the rail to allow me to dive through on his inner into the lead with just under two furlongs left to run.

The next moment Galileo arrived on our outside. When I first saw him I thought we were beaten because I was still convinced that my horse would pull up in front. The pair of us then hooked-up for the best part of 400 yards, two great champions going hammer and tongs for one of the greatest prizes in racing. We raced head to head, nostril to nostril, a bit like one of those famous duels between Seabiscuit and War Admiral in the film that came out in 2003.

Fantastic Light was just too brave for the younger Galileo. He relished the battle more than his opponent and when Galileo couldn't get past him I think it broke his heart. I'd done my job to the best of my ability by trying to keep him going to the line, but if the horse doesn't want to do it too you are wasting your time. You have to give the credit to Fantastic Light who was a hero that day. I knew we'd won but was so drained mentally and physically I didn't have the strength to punch the air. As we came back Richard rode alongside asking if we'd beaten Galileo. When I nodded wearily, he kissed me then asked why I wasn't celebrating. I explained that I felt totally knackered.

I was also hugely relieved that all the pre-race planning had worked out. In the middle of frenzied scenes in the winner's enclosure Sheikh Mohammed and Sheikh Maktoum looked happier than I've ever seen them. No wonder. They had plotted the downfall of Galileo with clinical intent, yet I still can't believe the tactics worked so well. What would have happened if I'd been allowed to ride the race I wanted in Ireland? We'll never know the answer to that one.

A break for over an hour between races at Newmarket late in September gave me the chance to attend the wedding of my long-time friend and driver Andy Keates in the town. I had a couple of rides before slipping into the back of the church for the service with a jacket over my breeches and silks, posed for photographs with Andy and his bride Donna outside the church, then rushed back to work.

Late summer and autumn proved to be a wonderfully fruitful period for Godolphin in Europe. We scooped a hatful of Group 1 prizes thanks to Noverre, Kutub, Slickly and Sakhee – who continued his comeback from injury with a tremendous triumph in the Juddmonte International at York. But you can't get it right all the time and I didn't know whether to laugh or cry as Richard Hills added to the haul on the 33–1 shot Summoner in the Queen Elizabeth II Stakes at Ascot late in September while I finished fast but much too late in second place on our chief hope, Noverre. What made it worse was that Summoner had given me no feel at all when I had been called back from Goodwood a few weeks earlier to ride him in a solo piece of work.

I probably should have won on Noverre, but heavy rain turned the ground against us and, in keeping an eye on Bach, the one I thought we had to beat, I let Summoner pinch a decisive lead. Of course I gave Noverre too much to do, but you try what you think is right at the time and I made the mistake of not taking the ground into my calculations. Once I gave Summoner too much rope I was never going to get it back. Afterwards I took plenty of stick. It wasn't my finest hour.

The Ascot meeting began with the unveiling of a bronze statue of me to mark my seven winners there in 1996. It was generous of the course executive to commission the work but unfortunately it doesn't look anything like me. It was done by an artist who cannot know what I look like and has an uncanny resemblance to Paul Gascoigne. The worst thing is that, in years to come when I'm no longer riding, people will think what an ugly bastard Dettori was. That hurts.

Before racing I rode my old ally Fujiyama Crest alongside Jamie Spencer on Decorated Hero in a gentle canter in front of the packed enclosures. Fuji was a bit frisky. He gave a buck and a kick as he came out onto the course and wanted to go a lot faster than I let him. It was great to be back together again at the scene of our unforgettable triumph. We got a tremendous reception. I entered into the spirit of the occasion by announcing that I'd be giving all the money I earned that day to DAFA, the charity run by my friend Barney Curley which helps children in Africa. As it happens I didn't win anything so I donated £10,000 to the cause anyway. One day I'd like to go to Zambia with Barney to see for myself the scale of the problem.

Normal service was resumed on Sakhee the following weekend in Paris. He had given Sinndar a fright in the previous year's Derby before injuring his knee. A year on he felt like a champion in trouncing Grandera by seven lengths at York, and as the countdown to the Arc began I wouldn't hear of defeat. Ten days before the race he did one of the best pieces of work

I've ever had anything to do with. It was sensational. Afterwards I rang up my dad and explained that although I didn't want to tempt fate, the only way Sakhee could be beaten in Paris was if I fell off. He replied that no big race was a formality.

On the big day, I arrived at Longchamp early, sat in the sauna with a few of the French jockeys and told them all that I would leave them for dead three out on Sakhee. I said 'Boys, this one is the real deal, I am not kidding.' They all looked at me as though I was nuts, but on the soft ground he encountered in the Arc, Sakhee was every bit as brilliant as I predicted as he trotted up by six lengths. Only Ribot and Sea Bird have matched that huge margin of victory in the race. That sure was a nice way to bring up my century of Group 1 winners.

So now, for the first time, Godolphin had two big guns going into the Breeders' Cup – though there was a long debate in the camp about which races they should target. Nobody was sure until the last moment. In the end Fantastic Light tackled the Turf race over a mile and a half, which was probably stretching his stamina, while Sakhee was held back for the Classic for which Galileo was second favourite.

The 2001 Breeders' Cup at Belmont Park in New York was the first international sports event in the city since the terrible events of 11 September. Catherine and I enjoyed a few days in Manhattan beforehand and were welcomed with open arms by everyone we met. The sense of togetherness was overwhelming among the people of New York. Walking through Time Square at midnight we've never felt so safe.

On raceday, stars and stripes fluttered from every vantage

point and the racecourse crackled with emotion during the singing of the Star Spangled Banner by Carl Dixon, a serving officer in the New York Police Department. As part of a moving opening ceremony the leading riders – including myself, Mick Kinane, Jerry Bailey and Pat Day – handed over our countries' flags to policemen and firemen. Barely a dozen miles away colleagues of these officers were still working through the terrible remains of the twin-towers.

It proved to be a famous afternoon of achievement for 'team Europe'. I finished a close second on an early ride in the Juvenile Fillies, and Banks Hills won for France before Mick took the Juvenile with a blistering run on Johannesburg. Then it was my turn on Fantastic Light who'd been campaigned for two years like a grizzled old heavyweight boxing champion. He had a great draw and travelled through the race like a dream, but all the time, aware of the doubts over his stamina, I was concentrating on not making my move too soon. He was still cruising coming off the bend, hard on the bridle, different class. When I asked him to go half-way up the straight he took four lengths out of the field and, though he was dying under me in the last fifty yards, he still held on cosily by three-quarters of a length from Milan.

Forty minutes later I came tantalisingly close to achieving a second success on Sakhee. When we took a narrow lead from the previous year's winner Tiznow just over a furlong out the dream double looked on. Remembering what happened with Swain three years earlier, I changed my hands, got hold of Sakhee and maintained my rhythm, determined not to lose it.

At that stage I thought we were going to hold on. The race couldn't have gone any better until he faltered a hundred yards from the line.

Without warning he stumbled, his head dropped and he came back underneath me. I'm sure that's where he hurt his knee and where the race was won lost. Sakhee kept on bravely but the momentum was gone and Tiznow pipped us by a nose on the line. It wasn't a case of the winner pulling my horse back, more that mine stopped. I don't regret anything about the race apart from that injury to Sakhee. In my eyes he was still the champion, a priceless jewel for Godolphin.

That night in New York I was as happy as a pig in shit. Catherine and I celebrated with a lovely meal in an Italian restaurant on Long Island. It was one of those rare times when I was able to enjoy a big meal and a few glasses of wine without worrying about the consequences. I felt proud of my day's work. I'd ridden well with two seconds and my sixteenth Group 1 success of the campaign on Fantastic Light, the most I've ever achieved in one year. The nightmare on Swain in Kentucky back in 1998 seemed a lifetime away.

twenty-six

A Question of Sport

Being in the public eye has its disadvantages, as I discovered the morning I called on George Best's ex-wife Alex at her home in Epsom late in 2003 on the way to Lingfield races. It happened during the time the couple were fighting a war of words in the tabloids. So the papparazi photographer lurking in a tree nearby thought he'd struck gold when Alex stepped out of the house, sporting a black eye, and welcomed me with a warm kiss. The snapper was so busy taking photos he almost fell out of the tree with excitement. Then a reporter appeared and asked me if I was seeing Alex. Apparently they'd been shadowing her for two months. It was all entirely innocent and soon I was on my way to Lingfield. But how the hell was I going to explain it all to Catherine?

I'd stayed in London the night before after recording *A Question of Sport* late into the evening, and planned to travel to Lingfield by train until Pete Burrell offered me a lift since he was going to see Alex, another of his clients. End of story. But the picture duly appeared in the *Daily Star* two days later. It just shows you can't be too careful.

My role as team captain on *A Question of Sport* was a bundle of laughs. There was never a dull moment with Ally McCoist around, but after fifty shows I was happy to call a halt. I was amazed when they asked me to be captain and wasn't sure about taking it on because I knew that I'd struggle on lots of questions, having lived in Italy until I was nearly fifteen. That was a massive disadvantage even before I had to translate some of the quick-fire questions into Italian. Then I thought, why not, I'm not there to show off my knowledge. Let's have a crack.

I took over as captain from John Parrott who is incredibly quick-witted. I think it had got to the point where John and Ally had virtually taken over the show. It had become a bit of an ego trip for them because they were so fast at answering the questions the other guests weren't able to get involved. That's when the BBC turned to me. I hit it off at once with Ally who is game for anything, while Sue Barker made it all go smoothly.

Usually we recorded three programmes during each marathon session, which at first I found incredibly tiring. I'd arrive at the studios early in the afternoon with three sets of clothes, have a cup of tea with Ally, record the first show at 4 p.m., take a short break, record another session at 6.30 and the last one at 9.00. The first time I did three in one go I felt so drained I slept for half an hour between each recording. I had to have a nap because my brain was out of control. Later I tried to freshen up between sessions by taking a short walk outside.

I was never going to match Ally's encyclopaedic knowledge of sport. How could I? Because he'd hardly kicked a football in the previous five years, he was free to follow every sport day by day while I was riding all week. To help balance things up I recruited Kevin and Dave, two of Colin Rate's friends from Sunderland, to coach me on some of the more obvious facts on each week's guests. They travelled to the studios in Manchester or London, filling in a few gaps for me and eventually became part of the furniture at the show. On the odd occasion they didn't turn up the crew felt something vital was missing.

I didn't mind making a fool of myself most of the time but was embarrassed when I struggled to answer some of the racing questions. Like lots of people watching at home, you know the answer but sometimes your mind freezes in the few seconds that you have to come up with the correct response.

The best part of my long spell on the show was meeting all the famous sports stars I'd only seen on TV until then. I've forged lasting friendships with guys like Ally and Michael Owen and enjoyed getting to know Kevin Keegan, David O'Leary, Harry Redknapp, Peter Reid, Paul Merson and Ian Rush. Most viewers would give anything to meet all these soccer stars. It's been brilliant for me too, because I am as big a fan as anyone. I spoke to Michael most days, until he moved to Spain, and usually stayed with him when I was riding at Chester. I love watching him play. He has speed to burn and terrifies defences when he runs at them. If he was a racehorse he'd be a champion sprinter, no question. I think it's because he's so lightning fast that he pulls his hamstring sometimes. It's the same in racing. The quickest horses are usually the ones that hurt themselves because the slow ones don't have the pace to do any damage. Luckily Michael owns a pretty fast one called Purple Heights who will make a lovely brood mare.

I've also got to know Sir Alex Ferguson quite well. He loves a day at the races and famously had a stake in the brilliant miler Rock of Gibraltar. I've also ridden the odd horse for him over the last few years. When we meet he always wants to know what I fancy, while I usually tease him about Arsenal's superiority over Manchester United. It's been an expensive friendship because we have an annual £100 bet between the two sides in the Premier League. The first time Arsenal won Alex gave me a cheque for £100. I've still got it tucked away as a memento. Being a Scot, Alex would love the fact that it's never been cashed. Apart from one season, I seem to have been giving the money to him, but not last year. I couldn't wait to catch up with him for my big pay day. And this time I definitely cashed the cheque!

Appearing on TV comes naturally to me. I relish new challenges, don't suffer from nerves and am happy chatting away, whatever the subject, though I didn't know where to hide when Noel Edmonds caught me out on his programme.

During a radio interview I was invited to choose between two horses, red or blue, for people betting on an internet game. The first one won £100 for the lucky punter. Next time the stake was raised to £5,000. That won too. By the time they upped the bet to the value of a house I didn't like the feel of it. What if I picked the wrong one? Where was the exit? I was so terrified of the responsibility I couldn't wait to end the interview but they twisted my arm to make one final selection. I picked blue. The red horse won and a massive guy suddenly appeared, purple with rage, ranting that I'd just cost him his home. 'I'm going to knock your head off Frankie' he shouted, closing in for the kill. As I took to my heels, Noel popped up smirking like a cat that had just got the cream and said 'Gotcha!' I didn't appreciate the joke.

This Is Your Life was much more fun. I almost throttled Michael Aspell when he appeared with his red book while I was launching a new video in London. Several of my family and old friends from Italy were on the show, and the best surprise of all came at the end when my mum walked through the curtains to greet me. Because she hates flying, she'd travelled by car from Italy over the previous two days just to be there. That was a wonderful surprise.

When I began appearing on television on programmes like *The Parkinson Show, Friday Night with Jonathan Ross, Clive Anderson Talks Back, They Think It's All Over*, and Chris Evans' *TFI Friday*, there was a backlash from a section of racing people. It was the same old story. They didn't like what I was doing, moaned that I wasn't concentrating on my riding and began hinting that I was a part-time jockey.

Trainers were the worst culprits. I could see a degree of jealousy in their reaction to what I was doing. Yet often they were unaware that a TV programme shown in June had been filmed out of season in December. My business manager Pete Burrell and I learned to tread warily with my outside commitments so that people couldn't point the finger. I am a jockey first and foremost. Everything else has to fit around my racing schedule.

In all the years we've worked together I've only had one row with Pete. It blew up over the arrangements for *OK* magazine to take pictures of Leo's birthday party. On the day the photographers were driving me mad, and when Leo began crying I boiled over and took it out on Pete. Within an hour we'd made up again. Catherine and I turned down quite a few offers to cover our wedding, partly because we didn't want to have the *Hello!* voodoo on it.

One or two big promotion companies have tried to lure me away from Pete but I've never been tempted. They weren't interested in me as a person. All they wanted was to market me like a piece of meat. Anyway I'd trust Pete with my life. We talk at least twice a day, he puts all the deals to me and then we make a joint decision. When we started together back in the late 1980s he found the responsibility of the challenge terrifying. Both of us were new to the idea of how an agent works so I let him get on with it and we learned together. From the start we had this trust in each other. I knew he was on my side and wouldn't rip me off. If I'd gone to a multi-million pound agent who didn't know anything about racing he would probably have taken me for a right ride.

I had a brilliant time the night I appeared in the Royal Variety Performance late in 2001 where I shared a dressing room with Vinnie Jones and Dale Winton. Dale wasn't around when a butler appeared with a magnum of champagne for him from Cilla Black. It seemed a shame to wait so we popped the cork, jammed open the door with a fire extinguisher, and invited Claire Sweeney and Denise van Outen to join us with some dancers for a glass of bubbly. Naturally it was all gone by the time Dale turned up. Cilla gave me a right telling off.

When it was my turn to go on stage I wore the Royal silks in a sketch with Julian Cleary who played the part of the entire Royal Canadian Mounties. Whoever dreamed that one up? After the show we all lined up to meet the royal party, but just as the Queen appeared I spotted Jennifer Lopez, looking absolutely gorgeous, towards the far end of the parade. The temptation was irresistible. Ignoring protocol I broke ranks, shot down behind the line to Jennifer, tapped her on the shoulder, introduced myself, gave her two big kisses on the cheek because she couldn't run away, and raced back to my position in the middle of the pack with seconds to spare.

Later that evening Vinnie and I arranged to meet up with Ronnie Wood at a party given by Andrew Lloyd Webber. We arrived to find a guy singing some boring song as he played the piano. I remember saying to Vinnie, 'Get that idiot off. Even you could do better than him.' Vinnie looked shocked. So was I when he explained that the crooner on the piano was Donny Osmond. How embarrassing is that?

Sometimes I have to pinch myself at the lifestyle I lead. One night Catherine and I ended up at Tramps in a group including Rod Stewart, Ronnie Wood and his wife, Caprice, Prince and various other stars. I can remember thinking 'What am I doing here with these guys?'

For sheer, sustained, excitement my trip to the British Grand

Seldom out of
the headlines –
for one reason
or another.

RACING POST

www.racingpost.co.uk

Monday, October 8, 2001

£1.05

FOOTBALL BETTING SPECIAL

Who will be England's World Cup top scorer?
Who will take over in Scotland? Worthington Cup preview

SPORTS BETTING, BACK PAGE

On top of the world

Frankie storms to a
century of Group 1
victories on super
Arc hero Sakhee

Longchamp reports: pages 2-11

TODAY PONTEFRACT (2.20) 46, SEDGEFIELD (2.10) 70, WINDSOR (2.00) (Inspection 6.15) 24, Roscommon (2.20) 38, Results 58, Greyhounds 77, FULL CONTENTS 3

Dettori refused licence in HK

FOX ON THE LOOSE

Frankly, Frankie's one of the best

PHILIP ROBINSON'S
late father, Peter, once
sold me the father on ... , The 1930s

RICHARD

2·12 RACING

5 JUNE 1994 · THE SUNDAY TIMES

Classic first for delirious Dettori

John Karter sees Balanchine, who wintered
in the sun of Dubai, blossom at rainy Epsom

A RAY of dazzling Italian sunshine pierced the leaden gloom

challengers ranged alongside
Balanchine with a quarter-of-a

The Sporting Life, Thursday, September 23, 19...

THE SPORTING LIFE PROFILE

The Face of the Nineties

FRANKIE DETTORI
is today's Face of
the Nineties: many,
sharp, talented, and about
to be very rich.

GARY NUTTING on the making of
racing's new star

A kiss for my Leo, a pageboy at Colin Rate's wedding.

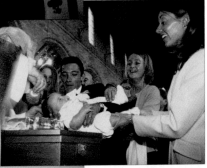

Ella's christening at Newmarket with Father Paul.

Leo doesn't seem very impressed by my new toy.

Just like Dad. Leo shows off in style on his pony Angel.

Six weeks after 9/11 I stand beside Pat Day at the moving opening ceremony after the 2001 Breeders' Cup at Belmont Park, New York.

In the paddock with David Loder.

Kazzia completes a Classic double in the Oaks at Epsom.

Happy days. The party starts after Sakhee wins the 2001 Arc de Triomphe in Paris.

Above: Marienbard
lands the 2002 Arc
from Sulamani.

Moon Ballad
captures the 2003
Dubai World Cup
(right and below)

Auditioning for the lead role in *The Hustler*.

Leo eyes up the cake at Ella's first birthday party at the beach club in Dubai.

Just like old times. Preparing to ride Fujiyama Crest at home.

Falbrav romps away with the Hong Kong Cup in December 2003.

Back in harness with Luca Cumani as we celebrate in the winners' enclosure.

Refuse to Bend, one of six winners for me at Royal Ascot 2004.

Move over, Tiger!

Catherine makes her
winning debut as a jockey
on Cristoforo at
Newbury in June 2004,
and promptly retires.

My 2000th UK
winner – and an
unforgettable ride on
Doyen at Ascot in July
2004. One of the finest
horses I've ridden.

Joy unconfined as I
ride 26-1 outsider
Wilko to victory in the
Breeders' Cup Juvenile.
I always love beating
the Americans on their
home turf.

Romping with Leo.

Proud parents
with Mia.

Happy family. Leo, Ella and Mia,
with baby Tallula.

Our new son Rocco, born in
January 2005, definitely thinks
he should be our last child!

Prix at Silverstone in 2003 will take some beating. Talk about VIP treatment. Bernie Ecclestone's right-hand man, Pascuale Lattunedu, who comes from Sardinia, hung about eight passes round my neck and introduced me to Arnie Schwarzenegger. I playfully challenged him to a fight and told him that if I was a foot taller I'd have him. Almost the only thing I wasn't allowed to do on the day was drive in the race. During the walk around the grid just before the start Arnie and I found ourselves on pole position beside the Ferrari driven by Rubens Barrichello.

We were still down there when a loud siren sounded and the cars set off on the warm-up lap. We found ourselves backing up to the concrete wall and watched in a daze as the cars shot past, two feet away. They seemed to be going at 200 mph. Pascuale led us onto a narrow footbridge over the road where we had a sensational view of the start. I felt as though I was suspended in the air barely thirty feet above the cars as they roared away making the most terrifying sound. It was so exciting to watch, but frightening too, as they hurtled at breakneck speed towards the first corner within inches of each other.

That was the day the race had to be stopped after a lunatic carrying a plastic bag wandered onto the track in some sort of protest. When the safety car came out Michael Schumacher was forced to wait while better placed drivers received priority in the pits. The delay cost him dear and it was his team-mate Rubens Barrichello who won. Michael clawed his way back up to fourth with some fabulous driving, but he was in a filthy temper when he walked back in, black with anger, just like me when I've lost a big race I should have won.

For me the party was far from over. I was given a guided tour of the Ferrari pits, chatted to Eddie Jordan and Brian Taylor, the drummer from Queen, and then met Carol Vorderman who I used to fancy like mad in my younger days watching TV. Of course she's a bit older now, but she's still a cracker. Just to top up the day, as I was leaving Michael Schumacher gave me his driving gloves in return for one of my whips. By the time I reached home I had a smile as wide as a river. It was an unforgettable day.

Four years ago I was tongue-tied for once when I found myself walking round a golf course in Dubai with Tiger Woods. It happened after we had a tip-off that he was about to hit a few balls before the Dubai Desert Classic tournament later in the week. I jumped into a car with the Hills twins, John Carroll and Kieren Fallon and made it to the Emirates course in record time. Tiger's opening salvoes on the practice ground made us all feel better. He topped the first one like a 28 handicapper and hooked his next one into the driving range, but his third shot disappeared over the horizon. We shadowed him for the first few holes of his practice round, chatting with him and Mark O'Meara and having our pictures taken. I doubt if we could have got so close to him anywhere else in the world. There we were, five little midgets pursuing the greatest golfer of modern times. I'll never forget it.

I was thrilled to do a cereal advertisement for Kelloggs with one of my heroes Frank Bruno, because I remember crying with emotion watching on TV when he won the world heavyweight title. I was so excited, jumping up and down on my chair as he bravely struggled to hang on over the last three rounds against Oliver McCall. I love watching the big fights.

Late in 1999 I flew to Las Vegas for the rematch between Lennox Lewis and Evander Holyfield. That was the night I was mistaken for the great champion Oscar de la Hoya as I arrived with three big guys who looked like bouncers. I played the part to perfection, bobbing and weaving as I walked in, even though his left jab wasn't as sharp as mine! Despite paying $1,000 for my ticket I was so far away from the ring I needed binoculars to see the action. From that distance it looked to me that Lennox was losing and it was a surprise when he got the verdict on points.

I was lucky to be given a second chance with Yves St Laurent. It started when I met a guy called Mike Morris flying back from Hong Kong seven years ago. He talked about racing with enthusiasm, mostly in the old days, and obviously knew some of the jockeys who once used the Turkish baths in Jermyn Street. Mike then gave me his business card as we touched down at Heathrow. Assuming he was looking for tips, I tossed it straight out of the window after jumping into my car. It was a mistake that could have cost me hundreds of thousands of pounds. Six months later I walked into the office of Yves St Laurent looking for sponsorship and there was Mike, the main man, sitting behind a big desk. I came clean about dumping his card and by the time I left I had clinched a three-year deal to be the face of Yves St Laurent's new collection 'Pour Homme'. One of my best paydays came from DFS, the furniture people. I earned £100,000 for eight hours of filming, jumping around on some couches and chairs stored in a big hanger. It was hilarious. I was also asked to turn on the Christmas lights in Regent Street. I think I followed the Spice Girls twelve months earlier.

A much tougher challenge was talking to the boys at Eton College. After a cup of tea with the headmaster, I was astonished to see youngsters hanging from the rafters and radiators when we arrived at the conference hall. The place was heaving, packed out with more than 600 just to listen to me talking a lot of nonsense. I'd imagined there would be fifteen or twenty boys there. I stood on a big pedestal on the platform, said my piece over the next half hour, then gave them a demonstration of my flying dismount by launching myself towards the floor far below. I seemed to be in the air for a week before I landed.

I also addressed the Oxford Union, four years ago. That was more a question and answer session than a debate. At the end, Luca Cumani's son Matthew snookered me by asking if winning the Derby was better than sex. The rascal sneaked that one in knowing perfectly well that I'd never won the Derby!

One of my favourite ways to relax is to spend time cooking, a hobby I picked up from my dad who is a wonderful chef. Though I say it myself I'm handy around the kitchen, too, despite the scandalous comment of my friend Olivier Peslier on *This Is Your Life* that I burn everything I put in the oven. For visitors at home my favourite dish is Melanzana alla Parmigiana, which is layers of aubergine cooked in tomato sauce topped with parmesan cheese, washed down of course with a nice bottle of wine. It was fun to take my turn on Ready Steady Cook, though I expected to be more involved. Because they have their own chefs on the show you are there mainly to talk, not waste time on cooking, so all I got to do was chop up a tomato and drink a glass or two of red wine.

I take more of a professional interest in food these days with my own branded pizzas, ice-creams and tinned tomatoes selling in shops around the country. I wish I could eat more of them. By using my name and always concentrating on quality, I'm attempting to bring the best Italian food into England. We package it ourselves but all the ingredients come from Italy. I am also working on plans with my neighbour Clive Garrard to expand our little empire into other products, including pastas, olive oil and maybe, one day, wine. It's looking good, but everything we've made out of it so far has been ploughed back into the business.

Over Christmas and the New Year I try to go hunting with Jason Weaver, which has led to some crunching falls. Once, when I was bored, I jumped a point-to-point fence the wrong way round without realising it was protected by chicken wire. The horse put the brakes on and sent me flying into the wire.

Another time, at a meet near Lord Archer's home at Grant-chester, I ended up in the bottom of a deep 'coffin' – a horrible fence with a hidden ditch – after my horse Elvis, bought for me by Catherine, spooked at the last minute and dumped me. Catherine warned me about it beforehand but I still didn't see it and neither did Elvis. As I lay in the coffin like a vampire, shocked and winded, Jason soared over the top of me on his hunter. I was so angry with Elvis that I remounted once Jason had caught him, jumped the fence again, this time without mishap, and rode for another hour. That was the end of my brief partnership with Elvis. More recently I've taken Fujiyama Crest hunting on Boxing Day and enjoy all the nonsense of dressing up and drinking our hip flasks dry to give us courage.

My bruising experiences in the hunting field increased my admiration for all jump jockeys, and in particular Tony McCoy, the nine-times champion. For me he is right up there with sporting legends like Muhammad Ali, Lester Piggott, Tiger Woods and Michael Jordan in being ten or even twenty years ahead of the others in their sport. He even makes the bad horses run faster. In his best season Tony won 289 races. That's incredible, better even than Sir Gordon's record of 269 on the flat. I don't think we give Tony the credit he deserves. He is doing everything I tried to do in my first two years as champion and also has to take all the injuries that come his way knowing that his next fall could be his last. He is superhuman, totally crazy.

While Tony was risking life and limb at places like Wincanton and Plumpton early in 2001, I was busy in Dubai on a photo shoot for my Christmas calendar. One picture involved me posing bare-chested, showing off my rippling muscles and washboard ribs. I saw myself as a rugged film star, a smaller version of Arnie Schwarzenegger, but the photographer swiftly shattered my illusions. 'This is hopeless Frankie. Go round the corner, pump yourself up and at least try to look the part when you come back.' Talk about a put down. 'This is pumped up', I protested lamely.

twenty-seven

Slow Boat to China

The dangers of racing are not exclusive to jockeys, particularly in the Orient. Shortly after I won the Macau Derby early in 2002 on Royal Treasure, his trainer, my friend Allan Tam Man-Chau (known to everyone as MC), was kidnapped. Perhaps it was just as well that I left for home after the race. The gang who snatched him were obviously impressed by the amount of money earned by Royal Treasure. They thought MC must have just picked up a fortune, caught him unawares in a taxi, and beat him up before demanding a ransom of 10 million Hong Kong dollars. He was later rescued by police from a flat in the Macau Peninsula. That spring I also won the Centenary Sprint Cup in Hong Kong on Firebolt, trained by Ivan Allan. He was lucky to be alive after being shot several times in the stomach in Singapore years earlier.

Riding in the Orient at the start of the year put an edge on my game, but I still ended up on the wrong one for Godolphin in the Dubai World Cup as Jerry Bailey claimed his fourth success in the race in seven years on Street Cry. It must seem like a benefit to him. In the build-up to the big night, Street Cry was bombing along on our gallops. He was obviously going the best, but how could I desert Sakhee after what he'd done for me the previous autumn? In the mornings he wasn't giving me a great feel but we were all hoping that he'd come alive on the racecourse.

Once Street Cry surged into the lead early in the straight there was only going to be one winner. I tried desperately to mount a challenge on Sakhee but the fire had gone out and we were well beaten into third place. I was disappointed my horse failed to spark and that I could have ridden the winner, but you can't have it both ways. That wasn't the Sakhee I knew so well. I suspect the injury he sustained in New York was troubling him again and he only ran once more before heading off to stud.

Spending each spring in Dubai gives me a chance to regroup before jumping on the treadmill at the end of March. Catherine usually comes out to stay with me for a couple of months, but the ages of our children mean that we can't always be together. When I'm on my own I get so lonely I end up ringing home four or five times a day, I miss them all more than I can say. I'm such a noisy person I can't stand the quiet that comes with sitting in my hotel room. There is work to be done every morning with Godolphin before I try to help the rest of the day pass quickly by surrounding myself with people, maybe on the beach or the golf course.

Once I was back in the swing in England in 2002 I experienced one of those crazy weekends which make my job so exciting.

I flew out to Louisville in time to ride Imperial Gesture, our big hope for the Kentucky Oaks at Churchill Downs late on Friday evening. We really fancied her but it was so hot that she seemed to melt, started to wobble, and suddenly slowed down. Afterwards she was badly dehydrated.

I flew back through the night in Sheikh Mohammed's private plane in time to partner Naheef in the 2,000 Guineas on the Saturday at Newmarket. I arrived home at around seven in the morning, took the dogs for a walk and had a sweat before heading for the races. I needn't have rushed because Naheef seemed more interested in trying to bite lumps out of another horse rather than taking a hand in the finish.

The many hours of overtime I clocked up that long weekend finally paid off when I raced to a narrow victory on Kazzia in the 1,000 Guineas on Sunday. It was the first Classic success for Godolphin in England since 1999. We were all a bit surprised because some of the team thought she had a better chance in one of the less-competitive Guineas contests in Europe. Sheikh Mohammed, however, wanted to go for gold. He was the one who spotted Kazzia's potential in Germany the previous autumn and moved swiftly to make her his own.

Aidan O'Brien ran four in the 1,000 Guineas, including Lahinch who appeared to be there as a pacemaker. So the other jockeys were shocked to see me up there with the leaders from the start, just about making the running. I thought 'Let's go, why not?' Kazzia was a fine, strong filly, hard as nails and stayed well. I ignored everyone else, jumped out quickly and let her run the whole way. In the closing stages I could feel them coming at us from all sides, but Kazzia was brave as well as talented and held on stoutly by a neck from Snowfire in a blanket finish. The boys in blue were back.

Next stop on my spring world tour, six days later, was Singapore where the tricky old character Grandera finished like a rocket with me from an unpromising position on the bend to take the first prize of £663,000 in the International Cup at Kranji. Grandera was one of the most difficult horses I've ever ridden. He carried his head awkwardly to the side, sometimes pulled, sometimes hung and occasionally didn't want to go at all. In addition he used to stop the moment he hit the front. Quite straightforward, then! He was brilliant on his day too, as he showed at Royal Ascot in high summer by thumping the best around in the Prince of Wales's Stakes.

If Grandera was human he would be like Hannibal Lecter, extremely smart but nasty too. If he wanted to kick you he didn't miss. He wasn't the type to take any prisoners. Once in Australia, he tried to eat one of the local vets as he attempted to take some swabs in the quarantine barn. The guy was a typical Aussie, straight out of Crocodile Dundee in his bush hat, khaki shorts and Timberlands. When our lads warned him that Grandera could be a handful, he replied that he'd been doing the job for thirty years and didn't need advice from any Pommies. He'd hardly finished speaking when Grandera darted forward, seized him by the shoulder, dragged him back into the box and started to devour him. There was blood all over the place.

Racing suddenly seemed irrelevant when I heard that my

great ally Mattie Cowing had died. I was shattered at the loss of the man who'd helped me so generously down the years. I couldn't have asked for a better agent than Mattie in my turbulent early days as a jockey. At least his heart by-pass operation had given him another five years and he enjoyed every minute of it. But he retired in 1999, at my suggestion, because he wasn't well enough to cope with the demands of the job.

We'd talked about it before agreeing he should step down. I think he was relieved that the decision had been made and I continued to look after him until his dying day. Despite constant medication Mattie had been going downhill for a while and needed major surgery to save his life. He almost made it through the long operation, survived for eight hours and fifty minutes then slipped away.

It was so tough on his wife Rita and their two children Steve and Julie who miss him badly every day. We all do. The least I could do was pay for the reception at the Rutland Hotel after his funeral. We all had a few drinks before I stood on a table and made an emotional speech from the heart about the friend who had guided my career so astutely. I did it for myself as much as for Mattie and Rita. We gave him a right old send off, a bit like an Irish funeral with lots of laughs and stories. Long before he died he told me that's what he wanted. He would have loved it.

Mattie shared my ambition to win the Derby but once again I finished out of the money at Epsom on 8 June. Nor did I hold out much hope of Naheef ending my drought in the race that continues to elude me. I chose him in preference to Moon

Ballad who, I was confident, wouldn't stay one and a half miles, particularly when the ground turned testing – but of course I ended up on the wrong one. Aidan O'Brien's classy duo High Chaparral and Hawk Wing finished miles clear of Moon Ballad in third, while I was a distant spectator on Naheef.

Some jockeys don't appreciate the media frenzy during Derby week but giving interviews has never been a problem for me. They keep me busy and take my mind off the demands of the day. Even if I want to have more time to myself I don't like knocking people back because I think it shows a weakness, that the occasion is getting to me.

The Derby is the one glaring omission in my CV. I've won Derbys from Macau to Hamburg but the one I crave the most keeps passing me by and it is beginning to irritate me. I want it for so many reasons, not just to get the monkey off my back. There are plenty of races around the world that are more valuable than the Vodafone Derby, but they aren't at Epsom and they don't provide that special atmosphere. I appreciate all the tradition that goes with the race. For me the English Derby still carries the most prestige even though it is held on such a peculiar track. Just look at the great horses and jockeys that have won it. I want to be on that list.

I remember explaining the course to the Japanese ace Yutaka Take who was shocked when he rode there for the first time. I told him it was just like climbing Mount Fuji. First you race up a steep slope. Then you sprint down the other side. Nor in the straight are you ever running on a level surface. From twenty runners, eighteen will have a problem, unable to handle the twists and gradients, but the first two finishers tend to be the ones that cope. They are the best. Most of them go on to frank the form and there's no denying the quality of recent winners like High Chaparral, Galileo and Sinndar. They were all outstanding.

Although Sir Gordon Richards was champion jockey 26 times it worries me that he didn't achieve his great ambition at Epsom until the twenty-eighth attempt. He was 49 by then. I'll be in trouble if I have to wait that long because I'm not planning to be riding at that age. I've been second on Tamure and third a couple of times, but I've never woken up on the morning of the race thinking I was definitely going to win it. There's been no cause for sleepless nights on that account.

Lester Piggott had the happy knack of ending up on the right one in the Derby. That's the main reason he won it nine times. Some of them were not far short of penalty kicks. Even so, nine . . . that's indecent! I'd settle for one. It's all I ask and with any luck I'll get there. It will happen one day, maybe when I least expect it, but it's not going to change my life if it passes me by.

The legacy of Lester's record adds to the difficulties of Epsom every year. The problem is caused by so many trainers telling their jockeys to take the position Lester made his own, sitting fifth coming down the hill, one off the rail. So we end up with everyone leaving their brains in the weighing room, riding like lunatics, all trying to be in the same place at the same time. With so many bad horses getting in the way it's not easy to ride a waiting ride, though Kieren Fallon and Walter Swinburn have shown that you can come from well off the pace.

I've always thought that Epsom is very much a front-runner's track. Jockeys like Steve Donoghue, Sir Gordon and more recently Steve Cauthen were prepared to make the running in the Derby on a horse with speed and stamina. Steve won it twice from the front and I wouldn't hesitate to try it on the right horse.

The fillies' Oaks over the same course and distance is one of my luckiest races. I won it for the third time on Kazzia in 2002. We set out to make all the running in a downpour, got the better of a battle with Kieren Fallon and Islington for the favoured stands rail turning for home, and had just enough left to hold on grimly by half a length from Quarter Moon in a tense finish. By being so positive I maybe pressed the accelerator a bit too soon. Kazzia was running on empty in the final fifty yards but she was as brave as they come and refused to surrender. No wonder I was singing in the rain afterwards.

By now Catherine and I were old hands at planning the birth of our children. With Royal Ascot looming and the arrival of another baby imminent, we took the decision that Catherine should be induced the previous weekend. On Saturday 15 June 2002, our third child Mia was born without complications. Suddenly, Leo and I were outnumbered at home by the girls.

When you ride as many horses as I do each season you are bound to be in trouble at some point. Suspensions have become part of the job. You learn to take your medicine and move on. Some jockeys even welcome a few days on the sidelines at the height of the season. I've managed to keep my nose clean most of the time, but things turned ugly for myself and Ed

Dunlop over the running of his colt Lobos at Newmarket in June after the local stewards referred the case to the Jockey Club disciplinary committee.

It was ridiculous that it got that far because neither of us did anything wrong. Perhaps the Jockey Club was suffering at the time from paranoia from the much publicised Panorama investigation into corruption in racing. I think, maybe, they called in their troops and wound them up to make a bit of a show, so Ed and I ended up in front of the firing squad. It was a sick joke. We were the first ones to cop the backlash from Panorama – all over Lobos having the second race of his life in a maiden race.

I made the running on him but he felt half crippled and dropped away tamely in the closing stages. We could have finished ninth. Instead, by easing up five yards before the line, we ended up tenth. Suddenly faxes were flying round the world reporting that I was involved in an inquiry for not trying. It was rubbish, of course, so unfair and damaging too. I don't normally make a fuss, but I felt it reflected very badly on my image. The disciplinary committee accepted my explanation that Lobos went freely to post, and that I was unable to find cover because he broke smartly from the stalls. Yet they still blamed me for easing the gelding just before the line and cautioned me about my future conduct. It was laughable. Talk about a storm in a teacup. Ed escaped with a fine of £240 for failing to report that Lobos was lame after the race.

The Irish Champion Stakes provided a nail-biting re-run for the teams involved in the previous year's clash between Fantastic

Light and Galileo. This time Godolphin had two darts to throw at the board in the shape of Grandera and Best Of The Bests. Galileo's trainer Aidan O'Brien relied on Hawk Wing who'd won the Coral-Eclipse after finishing runner-up in the Derby. Hawk Wing was odds-on favourite, but team tactics gave us two chances of overturning him. If he chased Best Of The Bests he'd set the race up for Grandera; but if he waited for Grandera to make his challenge he might not catch Best Of The Bests.

In a storming finish there was barely a yard between the three horses but once again it was Godolphin who prevailed. We needed nerves of steel, waiting to play our hands, as Sholokhov took the field along at a furious gallop. I was still eight lengths behind on Grandera two furlongs out, tracking Mick Kinane on Hawk Wing as, ahead of us, Best Of The Bests began to close on the leader. With two hundred yards to run I was only fourth and beginning to panic because when I first asked Grandera to quicken he preferred to stay where he was. I couldn't get him off the rail and time was rapidly running out because he didn't want to know.

By now Hawk Wing had come through to head Best Of The Bests, but just as the cause seemed lost my frantic efforts on Grandera paid off. He grabbed hold of the bit, made up two lengths in fifty yards and nailed Hawk Wing by a short head with Best Of The Bests a neck away third. Poor Mick. For the second year running I'd mugged him on the line. To claw back two lengths in such a short distance is almost impossible in a championship race, but Grandera managed it that day. I had to make up his mind for him and received a severe caution for my use of the whip.

By that time Grandera was a nightmare to ride, so complicated and temperamental because you never knew what he'd do next. Really he was a rascal, such a difficult character, one in a million and enormously talented. Going into that last furlong at Leopardstown he seemed to give up. Even when I got him out he wasn't sure about going. He looked at the crowd, he looked at Hawk Wing in front of him and then he put his head down and flew. I still don't know how he won but win he did. It was my day and my race, the fourth time I'd taken it in five years.

That summer Simon Crisford and Saeed bin Suroor never stopped talking-up just about the largest horse we've ever had. Marienbard was so huge we used to call him the slow boat to China. The more they rammed his name down my throat the more I laughed at them. With horses like Grandera and Moon Ballad around I thought they were crackers to be so keen on Marienbard, who'd campaigned for us the previous season over extreme distances but was not in the A team.

After two months lobbying, I finally agreed to sit on Marienbard in a piece of work. I couldn't have been more impressed. What a difference a year makes. For weeks and weeks I'd been ignoring him, but from that moment he became my best friend and I started riding him at least once a week. In the past he'd had one or two problems. That season, for the first time, nothing was hurting him and thanks to an uninterrupted preparation he had improved out of all recognition. In the autumn we picked off two Group 1 prizes in Germany with ridiculous ease. The second time he showed a blistering turn of foot. Although he looked like an elephant, he raced like a machine and deserved his chance in the Arc in Paris.

Catherine flew over with me as usual for the weekend but was feeling below par on Sunday morning, and decided to fly home early. Maybe she didn't fancy a long day at Longchamp by herself waiting for me to ride a horse that was dismissed as a no-hoper in many of the papers and started at 16–1 on the pari-mutuel, the French tote. Whatever the reason, Catherine missed my third victory in the race. I was quietly confident and felt that with a decent draw and a smooth run I could nearly win because in those few months Marienbard was out of the top drawer. I worried about the start because you need a good position early on in the Arc above all and he was such a great big thing he took an age to find his stride.

I jumped him out as quickly as I could, but he was still last in the early stages. We eventually wriggled our way into a useful position not far behind the leaders. Just as I spotted High Chapparal in trouble early in the straight, a gap opened in front of us. We squeezed through an instant before it closed and shot into the lead with barely a hundred yards left. Then it was just a case of hoping we could hold on. I could hear something coming at me fast and late and thought 'Where's the line, show me the line, bring me the line.' Luckily we got there just ahead of Sulamani, the French-trained favourite.

It was fabulous landing the Arc for the second year running. It doesn't come any better than that. I ran around like a lunatic, kissing everyone in my path, before being driven down the Longchamp straight in a horse-drawn carriage punching the air with both fists and shouting something daft like 'I love you all. I'm the daddy.' Of course it was crazy but that's what winning the Arc does to me because it's one of the great traditional races in the calendar. Best of all, my sister Sandra was there to enjoy it with me. That was a massive bonus because she doesn't get too many chances to see me in action.

Some people tended to question the value of the form that day but they were out of order because the pair we beat, Sulamani and High Chaparral, were superstars with three Derbys between them, while other outstanding horses like Islington and Aquarelliste finished on their heels. Marienbard won entirely on merit. It was anything but a fluke.

The European season was already over when I received a call, out of the blue, to ride the Italian colt Falbrav in the Japan Cup. He'd enjoyed a fruitful campaign until running below par in the Arc and, at first, I doubted if he was up to the task in Japan in November. At that time of the year I didn't want to travel half way round the world on a fool's errand. A phone call to my dad soon put me straight. He had no doubt that Falbrav was a serious horse and said I would be mad to turn him down. As I looked at the race more closely I realised it was wide open. Golan wouldn't appreciate the firm ground and there were question marks about the other leading contenders. My dad, I concluded, was right as usual. Falbrav had as good a chance as any.

In the days when Futoshi Kojima was a jockey, he took me

under his wing on my occasional visits to Japan. He's a flamboyant character, full of fun and in our younger days we got up to a fair bit of mischief in the clubs whenever we met up. I must have made an impression on him because he named his dog after me! Later, when he started training, he also named a couple of horses after me too. Once Futoshi heard I was coming over he booked me for four of his horses over the two days, including Eagle Café, an outsider in the Japan Dirt Cup. I was in the mood for anything after a double on the opening day on his pair Cat's Pride and Eagle Café. The prize money in Japan makes our purses look like peanuts and Eagle Café alone scooped £700,100 for his owners. That was some spare ride.

First up the following day was Falbrav, a wonderful specimen of a racehorse, a powerfully built, classy individual with bags of speed. The meeting was switched that year to Nakayama while the course at Tokyo was being renovated. That was a big plus for Falbrav, since the distance of the Japan Cup for that year only was a furlong shorter than usual. He jumped out handily, cruised round the tight bends travelling beautifully for me, then struck for home inside the final furlong. The distance of the race was probably still a bit far for him at that point of his career and as he began to tire Sarafan came rushing up to join us right on the line.

At first I thought we'd held on but I've been wrong before, so when Sarafan's jockey Corey Nakatani began celebrating I feared the worst. An unbearably tense delay of twenty-five minutes followed before the result was announced. Then Falbrav was announced the winner by a nose and I immediately burst into tears. It was too much to win a major race like the Japan Cup on a horse owned and trained in Italy, so important to me to give a little bit back to my own country. Before the day was over I rode yet another winner on Precious Café for Futoshi Kojima. My dad's advice to go to Japan had proved gilt-edged. But for him I might well have stayed at home and missed all the fun.

I thrive on the challenge of riding abroad, particularly in the key period when there are so many major races around the world between September and mid November. Normally I am bored by the demands of the domestic routine by then. Given the choice, I'd always prefer a long haul to Hong Kong or America to a dreary drive up the A1. I think it brings out the best in me.

At home we are still slaves to the numbers game. That's crazy. If you don't do it every day people start having a go, saying you're not interested any more, you're lazy and all that crap. I blame that stupid list of winning riders in the back of the *Racing Post*. It doesn't mean anything, it's just numbers but I have to go along with it because everyone expects me to. All jockeys are slaves to racing, yet half of them are charging around the country breaking even or losing money. What is the point of spending six or seven hours in a car for one ordinary ride? Everyone does it because they are too frightened to turn trainers down in case they don't get asked again. That's mindless. I am in the fortunate position of being able to say no when it suits me.

It's as if you have to burn yourself out to look good. So

I walk or run five kilometres a day, ride out four mornings a week, starve myself, spend hours in the sauna, race at least five afternoons, cover hundreds of miles a day, then dash off to evening meetings and spend a lot of Sundays working abroad. Yet if I end up with only two rides on a card I can hear the whisperers suggesting that I'm a part-time jockey. That's absolute bollocks. These people have no idea of what we go through. The workload we have today is totally different from that of previous generations. Once they only raced on the flat in England for just over seven months. Since I gave up the all-weather in the winter I start in Dubai at the end of January and usually finish in Hong Kong in the middle of December. Nobody riding has a longer season. I am the most travelled jockey in the world without a doubt.

Many of the best days have come abroad. I've relished them all, from racing on a frozen lake at St Moritz, to the delights of Tralee in Eire, the barracking in Australia and, most memorably, the amazing atmosphere in the final few minutes before the Kentucky Derby. As an outsider on his first visit I loved the build-up to the 2,000 Derby when I finished sixth on China Visit at Churchill Downs in Kentucky. I was able to take a step back and really enjoy it with the place awash with tears as 150,000 people sang My Old Kentucky Home. The noise of the anthem is so overwhelming I expected the horses to go berserk but they took it in their stride. China Visit could be quite frisky but he was as quiet as a lamb as we were led to the start – maybe the singing overwhelmed him too. It seemed to me that all the jockeys reacted just as we do at Epsom by leaving their brains in a box in the weighing room. We all went out there like headless chickens.

I had a ball at St Moritz without riding a winner. After a late night, I woke up to a blizzard outside my hotel window, but there was no question of the meeting being off. I changed with the other jockeys in a freezing Portacabin with one little heater in a corner and wore every bit of protective clothing I could find for my two rides. Racing on snow you go as fast as you can for as long as you can. Afterwards I almost passed out from lack of oxygen.

Tralee was a riot. When I walked the course beforehand it thought it was unbelievably sharp, as I discovered to my cost on my first mount in the sprint. I shot into the bend too fast, about eight lengths clear, but my horse didn't handle the turn and ended up on the wrong side of the track. Later my good friend Johnny Murtagh gave up one of his best rides for me and I managed to win on it late in the evening. Everyone at the course seemed to crowd into the winner's circle. From the reception we got you'd have thought we'd just won the Cheltenham Gold Cup. I gave them all a flying dismount, and came down on some Irishman's head because there was nowhere else to land!

Afterwards, I changed ready for an early night. Not a chance. We stayed at the course until midnight having a right old jolly with lots of singing and drinking. Nobody wanted to leave. I was starving but by the time we reached a restaurant in the town it was one in the morning. I thought they were bound to be closed, but when we walked in it felt like New Year's Eve, with the band going flat out and the tables all full. The whole night was utter madness and I didn't get to bed until dawn.

My day trip to Madrid in 1991 wasn't so funny. Wise old hands like Pat Eddery, John Reid and Ray Cochrane restricted themselves to one or two decent mounts. Not me. I was like the village idiot with eight rides in the burning sun. There were two weighing rooms – one for the local jockeys, the other for the visitors – and by the time I'd finished I was in danger of igniting a full-scale brawl between the two camps. It started when I tightened up one of the Spanish jockeys without knowing it. After the race about eight of them surrounded me, intent on revenge. As they closed in for the kill I rushed for the sanctuary of our weighing room, urgently calling for reinforcements. What happens? They all disappeared behind the door and slammed it in my face. I could hear Pat and Ray laughing as I faced up to my own Spanish inquisition.

The reception I got on my first visit to Australia for the Melbourne Cup in 1993 wasn't any better. The way the boys reacted when I appeared in the weighing room you'd have thought I'd come from another planet. Every one of them stood up and stared, looking daggers at me. It felt as though they hated me. It was so intimidating I almost wet myself as I ran into a corner. The atmosphere was horrible. Luckily I knew Brent Thompson from his days in England. He and Greg Hall helped break the ice, but the Aussies didn't really like Brent either because he came from New Zealand! The next day Mick Kinane received the same unfriendly treatment when he sat next to me, but he put them all well and truly in their place by winning the Melbourne Cup for Ireland on Vintage Crop. Did they not like that!

A few years later the Aussie press tore me to pieces after I finished fourth on Annus Mirabilis in the Mackinnon Stakes at Flemington. They were like a pack of dogs with a large, juicy bone. I hope they enjoyed the meal. One of them came up to tell me that my horse Faithful Son had no possible chance in the Melbourne Cup a couple of days later. Foolishly I fell into the trap by asking why. He replied: 'Your horse can't win with a c*** like you in the saddle.' Cheers guys.

The most painful trip of all was to South Africa over Christmas and New Year at the end of a lengthy world tour. I was worn out by then and although I managed a few winners I also developed a serious case of piles. It was agony. Desperate measures were required, so Pete Burrell spent one morning scouring the township of Soweto for a shop that sold cream to ease my discomfort.

By the time I'd ridden in seven races on New Year's Eve and another seven the following day my backside was on fire. I flew to Cape Town, squirming uneasily in my seat, and retired to my hotel bed with a high temperature, unable to continue. However the local racing authority didn't accept Pete's explanation when he rang to say I was crying off my remaining commitments.

Lester Piggott then stepped into an unfamiliar new role as my medical adviser. As he was staying in my hotel they sent him to my room to check on my condition. I bent over so that Dr Piggott could thoroughly inspect the problem area. He took his time and to his undying credit kept a straight face as he muttered the immortal words 'That doesn't look very nice Frankie. Not nice at all. I think you should get help.' What a carry on. He's probably been dining out on the story ever since.

A retired surgeon with Frank Bruno knuckles eventually appeared in my room to settle the matter. As he prepared to make his examination I nearly collapsed with fright as he pulled on a pair of surgical gloves over his massive hands. Once I'd calmed down he took the decision to lance the abscess. Afterwards I was in absolute agony. It felt like someone had slashed my bum with a razor. As soon as I was able to travel I headed home to England. What a way to start the New Year!

twenty-eight

Summer of Despair

I set off in 2003 with the irresistible force of a hurricane. On World Cup night alone in Dubai I earned around a third of a million pounds from three winners with the help of a horse who had been running wild in the desert twenty-four hours earlier. Little did I know that it would be pretty much downhill for the rest of the year. That was the peak of our season. We started and finished it in one evening. Soon, disturbingly soon, I was drifting like a crippled yacht heading straight for the rocks. Godolphin was desperately short of contenders in England and the other stables I rode for weren't firing. It was the start of a summer of despair that left me feeling more depressed than at any other stage of my career.

None of this was apparent on World Cup night which took place against the backdrop of a war in Iraq somewhere over the horizon. The atmosphere was a bit unreal all week. Obviously everyone around the world was watching hourly TV bulletins from Baghdad. We were doing the same in Dubai. It felt strange that a war was going on, but the difference for us was that we were much closer to it, with the fighting only a few hundred miles away. At one point there was a question mark about the World Cup meeting going ahead, but Dubai is a neutral country, we all felt safe and just had to carry on with our lives.

I started the most rewarding night of my life with a hard-earned triumph on Firebreak in the Godolphin Mile. That was a bit of a surprise. Next I finished third on Inamorato in the UAE Derby before a fabulous ride on Sulamani in the £750,000 Dubai Sheema Classic. It's fair to say the horse hadn't been thrilling us in his work since he was bought by Godolphin a few months earlier. Six days before the race the boss took him away from Al Quoz to his own stable in the desert so I didn't know if he would be running until I saw his name among the entries.

In the paddock Sheikh Mohammed looked concerned. He explained that I was to look after Sulamani at all costs because he'd got loose and disappeared the previous day. Obviously I was to give him a chance, but if he felt tired after his unscheduled excursion and was not going forward in the race, my instructions were to mind him for another day. At first I thought it was all an extravagant joke. Then the boss told me the full story. Apparently, after breaking loose, Sulamani had galloped flat out for more than three kilometres through the sand dunes with Sheikh Mohammed in hot pursuit in a jeep. Here was one of the most valuable racehorses on the planet running like the wind through the desert. Once he slowed to a walk, the boss jumped out of the jeep, caught him by his tail, and held him, before he was led back to his stable without a scratch on him. I'd never heard anything quite like it.

For the race itself I dropped Sulamani out towards the rear to let him find his feet, but he didn't feel very comfortable and I'd given up hope as we started into the bend at least twelve lengths behind the leaders. As he was hanging a little right-handed, I eased him to the outside and when I pressed him to take a closer look the response was electrifying. Down the straight he sped past horse after horse until we bounded to the front with a hundred yards to run.

It was a stunning victory given Sulamani's antics the day before. I asked him the impossible and he did the impossible. He got down and flew, quickened three times and took my breath away. Until then I'd never ridden a mile and a half horse who could do that, and the boss was clearly excited and surprised by what he'd just witnessed.

Finally it was the turn of Moon Ballad in the Dubai World Cup, the richest race in the world, which offered a first prize of £2.25 million. Godolphin ran two, which left me in the tricky position of having to desert my favourite old bruiser Grandera. It broke my heart to let him go, but Moon Ballad's home work forced me to side with him. I knew, beyond doubt, that he was the one to go for gold. For some reason he'd turned inside out that spring. Previously he tended to sweat up and usually wore blinkers but he was transformed at the age of four.

Moon Ballad was drawn widest of all in stall eleven. He had the speed and I was very confident, so I let him do his own thing in front and we were pretty much in control even before I turned the screw. He was a little bit like Dubai Millennium that night, though not, of course, quite in the same league, so

I had to be careful not to burn him out in the early stages. Yet he was always in charge and won unchallenged by five lengths from the American challenger Harlan's Holiday. I was overcome at such an unbelievable performance and came back shouting 'Show me the money! Where's the money? Give me the money!'

Then it was back to grim reality in England. I suppose the crisis started when our early Classic contenders all ran below par, with my mount Lateen Sails last in the 2,000 Guineas. Soon it became clear that Godolphin's horses were not as good as we'd hoped. Maybe I was to blame for taking a back seat after such a brilliant start on World Cup night. I was just waiting for us to clean up, anticipating a fantastic year with winners appearing from all directions. So I let most of the spring go, not bothering to get off my backside to chase opportunities elsewhere.

It was a shocking summer for me. The way I felt, I couldn't have been confident in a one-horse race. All my stables were out of form and – I'll be honest – I wasn't riding well, though maybe I was putting myself down. One thing led to another, and the more that things went wrong the worse I felt. I seemed to lurch from one crisis to another.

I tried like hell to dig myself out, but the more I persisted the larger the hole became. With Godolphin struggling for runners, John Gosden having a quiet time too, and not many chances from David Loder, I was under increasing pressure and began to take a lot of stick. I was having my own trouble with David who'd been such a big support down the years. As the weeks passed I ended up falling out with him.

We were like a couple whose marriage was going wrong, loving each other one minute and hating each other the next. It began when he started to prefer Jamie Spencer to me on his horses. That hurt after working so closely with him for ten years. David is very ambitious. We have our similarities and we have our arguments because we share the same goals. Early in 2003, after a period working solely for Sheikh Mohammed concentrating on his two-year-olds, David decided to become a public trainer again. He wanted results at all costs and ended with the best of both worlds by playing Jamie against me.

I didn't like being in that position one bit; it was unwanted pressure on me to produce the goods. And of course when you try to force things you never get the results you want. I had more seconds for David in 2003 than any other trainer, mainly because of that pressure, of being forced to do something that I didn't agree with.

It reached the point where he was accusing me of not giving his horses a ride in ordinary races. There were days when he didn't want me to go to places like Southwell for him because he thought my heart wasn't in it. I could detect sarcasm at the other end of the phone when we spoke. So Jamie ended up on quite a few winners for him. Obviously I disagree, but perhaps David had a point. It was just that I found myself desperately trying to prove him wrong, and when you push for something as hard as I did it just won't come. I was unlucky in races whatever I did, and when I got off a 20–1 shot to ride a better horse the outsider won. I kept thinking that this couldn't be happening to me.

It left me in turn depressed, lethargic, moody and angry. I felt that everyone was trying to jump on my back at the same time and squash me. As I'm not deaf I could hear the rumours in the background. It was the usual stuff. Frankie's had it too easy. He's got so much money he doesn't care anymore. They gave me loads of shit and threw the bait at me. It just shows how swiftly you are forgotten in this game.

I got really angry with people in the industry jumping on the bandwagon – trainers, jockeys, lads and owners all making out that I wasn't interested in riding day after day. Okay, I do some advertisements on TV, and on *A Question of Sport* I try to be myself and have a joke. But I care like mad about my riding. I love racing and I love my job and it hurt like hell that people couldn't see it. Everyone was blaming me. I was the scapegoat but why didn't they look at the whole picture? Godolphin only had a handful of runners last summer and most of my other teams were quiet, too. Who was I supposed to ride for?

At the height of my despair there was bleak consolation in the knowledge that Sir Gordon Richards twice suffered from depression at the height of his career. At least I was in good company. At one point he locked himself away in a room for a week in the middle of the season. He couldn't eat or sleep, and stayed in bed for several days in a swirl of self-pity. Apparently he wanted to give it all up and wouldn't speak to anyone for a few days. Sir Gordon was naturally a cheerful man but he couldn't cope with the pressure. He didn't know why and he was frightened by his reaction to it. His doctor persuaded him to go away for a short break and he came back at Glorious Goodwood with eleven winners.

Ours is a very unpredictable job. You never know what's coming next. I can leave home full of beans and come back spitting fire after a bad day at the races. Catherine has to pick up the pieces. She is the stable one. A lot of times she ignores me or shouts at me to put me back on the straight and narrow.

There were a few precious moments of sunlight for me that summer. One came on the day my victory on Vintage Tipple in the Irish Oaks gave her trainer Paddy Mullins his first Classic winner at the remarkable age of 84. Paddy is a legend of Irish racing, long on deeds but short on words. It was only later that I was told he trained the great mare Dawn Run whose stirring triumph in the Cheltenham Gold Cup left me in floods of tears as a teenager. I wish I'd had the chance to talk to him about that.

In the paddock I waited for instructions from Paddy, but he didn't say a single word to me. Hello, I thought, this is a bit strange, until his son George passed on a few hints about the filly. Nor did Paddy speak after Vintage Tipple all but raised the roof off the grandstand, though he was grinning from ear to ear when I jumped into his arms. I think his lips moved for a moment but, then again, it might have been my imagination.

The much needed lift from that success didn't last long. It was Thomas Castaignede, the former French rugby fly-half, who did the damage a few moments before we recorded a session of *A Question of Sport*. 'How long have you been retired, Frankie?' he asked in all innocence. That set the alarm bells ringing in my brain big time. It was a brutal shock to my self-confidence, the final straw which made up my mind to get stuck in again as a jockey. But how could I turn round my fortunes?

I was in urgent need of help when I flew over to Deauville with John Gosden on 9 August. Aware that I am a lot more sensitive than people realise and that I have a habit of withdrawing into myself like a crab under its shell when things go wrong, John listened to my tale of woe before advising me to stand back and look at myself. I was giving one-hundred percent, he suggested, but it wasn't working. Why? Was it me, was it the horses or was it something else? If the horses weren't right, he said, that was hardly my fault. Nor should I shoulder the blame if the horses were inadequate.

He added that I seemed to be putting myself under severe pressure by the way I was reacting to my bad run of form. He also stressed that there is only so long you can crouch in a corner feeling sorry for yourself. You must force yourself to come out again, so I had to get out there once more and ride flat out every day. It was a relief to share the burden with John because I knew he was on my side.

I sank to the lowest point of my depression the following weekend, when Sulamani landed the Arlington Million in Chicago on the Saturday night in controversial fashion. With some fast flights to help me I could have ridden him before rushing back for Deauville the next afternoon. But for some reason, probably because the horse was going to stay in America, Godolphin chose to use a local jockey, David Flores. That hurt as well but it was beyond my control. I stayed up late that evening, watching him finish a close second in a dramatic finish in which the winner, Storming Home, shed his jockey Gary Stevens a few yards after the line. But for mayhem in the final few strides Sulamani would have been fourth. I turned off the TV and went to bed.

You can imagine my feelings when I tuned into teletext in the morning to discover that Sulamani had been promoted to first place after the disqualification of Storming Home. It showed that when fate is set against you nothing can turn the tide. Later that day at Deauville people kept coming up to congratulate me on my triumph on Sulamani. That was hard to take.

Suspensions at Salisbury and then York later in the month gave me the chance to confront the demons haunting me. It was time for straight talking with my greatest supporter. I flew to Sardinia to see my dad in the hope that he could straighten me out. He made it clear my selective policy wasn't working. I had to kick arse and prove myself again. I also took the opportunity to consult a special person, a bit like a guru, with the insight to spot the doubts deep inside me. He, like my father, pressed me to be more positive and get rid of the negative thoughts that had been dominating my mind for the past four months. I was a champion jockey with the best job in racing, they both insisted. It was time to show that I was still the tops.

Back home in Newmarket my mate Colin Rate had been saying much the same but in blunter terms. He told me that people were saying I was riding like a plonker. What's more, he added, they were frigging right. He didn't need to spell it out because I wasn't blind to my failings. Ray Cochrane also tried to motivate me. They both urged me to get back on the road six days a week and ride more. That's what I did.

I returned from Sardinia a new man. I thought, 'Right, you bastards, I *am* going to prove you all wrong', though I had to prove it to myself as well. By the start of September I'd managed barely fifty winners. I set a target of a hundred for the season even if it finished me, and racked up thirty by the end of the month.

If you suddenly wake a dog when he is sleeping he is going to bite you. When it happened to me I was biting and kicking as hard as I could because all the doubters had touched a raw nerve that hurt deeply. I'm normally a nice person but they made me come out fighting for my life. I could see them pointing the finger and saying, 'Frankie is no good, he was just a flash in the pan. How come he got that plum job with Godolphin?' And I wanted to cry out, 'Don't kill me, don't try to kill me!' That was why reaching a century was so vital.

During the first week of September I managed a winner on most days, clocked up a treble at Lingfield and was suddenly riding the wave again. All my old confidence came flooding back. The big black cloud hanging over me all summer had drifted away. It was like going from zero to a hundred miles an hour in a flash. I started winning on horses that had no possible chance, notched up five wins over two days, and maintained an astonishing level of form for weeks on end. Crisis, what crisis?

At home Catherine was expecting our fourth child at the same time as the Melbourne Cup. Since she wanted me to be with her for the birth, we decided to have the baby induced, just like the first three. Catherine is a star. Not many wives would bring forward the date each time just to fit in with their husband's busy schedules. I flew back from the Breeders' Cup in California on Sunday, took her to the film premiere of *Seabiscuit* in London on the Monday night, then Tallula was born the next day. So all my babies have arrived close to a big race date. Tallula is a little darling but I didn't have much time to get to know her. The following morning I was on my way to Australia.

By November the final curtain had fallen on Pat Eddery's fabulous career as a jockey. Only Sir Gordon Richards has won more races in this country. What a loss to racing, because day in day out for over thirty years Pat was the most reliable man in the business. I feel sad that he is no longer beside me in the weighing room because we became very close over the last few years. He was a big influence on me.

Kieren Fallon is the one jockey at the moment that I can't work out. He's so hard to read I never know how much he has kept up his sleeve for the finish. Several times I've sat behind him, convinced I could take him when I chose, and he's found more than I expected and beaten me. I've given away several races to him like that. Kieren is a bit like my dad in that he came late to racing at eighteen but he's been making up for lost time ever since. He's determined, fearless, ice-cool and has a unique style that can't be copied.

As racing becomes more international, an eager new

generation has come through, very good boys like Olivier Peslier, Christophe Soumillon and Mirco Demuro. If I had to choose one jockey above all the others it would be Mick Kinane. He's the ultimate professional with no weaknesses, wise from years of experience, unbelievably strong and tactically very cute. Nobody intimidates Mick, that's for sure. He's at the peak of his career and would be the number one right now, but it could be somebody else next year.

Most of the top riders had eased right off the throttle by the time I reached my first century of winners in a season since 1999, on Rendezvous Point for John Gosden at Lingfield on 13 November. It was a relief to get there after the roller-coaster of the previous eight months and I celebrated in grand prix style by rushing round the winner's enclosure spraying champagne in all directions. I felt I deserved a glass or two of bubbly after turning down my usual night out at the annual Cartier awards in London the previous evening. With Rendezvous Point in the 12.20 I didn't fancy going straight to Lingfield from Annabel's nightclub!

Once my century was secure, I stole a short break with Catherine in Dubai. I was in charge of the children at the Beach Club when I realised the Rugby World Cup final between England and Australia was about to start. I dropped off the kids at their own club, which they love, said I'd be back in five minutes, then watched the game in the bar. What a fantastic final. I support Italy at soccer but we've only been playing rugby seriously for five minutes – that's why we are crap at the moment. As the match came to that amazing finish I shouted for England as if I'd lived here all my life, mainly because I'd got to know so many of the players on *A Question of Sport* – including Martin Johnson who is the biggest monster I've ever seen. When it stretched into extra-time I screamed myself hoarse and forgot all about the children.

Back in November I was still on holiday in Dubai when Luca Cumani rang. I sensed immediately that he was going to ask me to ride Falbrav in the Hong Kong Cup, though, he explained, he would have preferred Darryll Holland to keep the ride. Changing jockeys was not his style, but his hand was being forced because the horse's owners insisted on using me. Before he put the phone down he asked me to ride work on Falbrav a few days later.

You could say I lent Darryll the horse for most of 2003, though I doubt if he saw it that way. Falbrav's owners had wanted me to ride him all season but I was never free, so it was Darryll who enjoyed a brilliant campaign on him culminating in a narrow defeat in the Breeders' Cup Classic. I rode Falbrav in his final piece of work in thick fog on a freezing December morning in Newmarket. The way he pulled readily clear of his galloping companions left me tingling with anticipation. I hadn't had a feeling like that since World Cup night. He felt just like my Ferrari, all power and class. And for such a big horse he was surprisingly light on his feet.

I was totally confident going into the race and settled him a fair way back, at least eight lengths off the pace. When I pressed the button he was so explosive I nearly peed myself. The way he shot up to the leaders and sped clear took my breath away.

Without doubt he was the top middle-distance horse in the world that year, up there with the very best I've ridden. I was so excited I gave the huge crowd two flying dismounts for the price of one – the first when we came back to unsaddle and another when we paraded down the course.

Luca, too, was beside himself, suggesting that Falbrav reminded him of Muhammad Ali in his prime. For Luca and me the wheel had gone full circle. Years before he'd backed me to the hilt in my early days as an apprentice. Now we were triumphant together once more as he supplied me with the one-hundred and twenty-first Group 1 success of my career. Sometimes I look at the statistics and wonder: how on earth have I won all those big races? It was a hell of a way to end the most testing season of my career.

twenty-nine

Top Dog Again

Two thousand and four was an amazing year for the Dettori family, though nothing I achieved matched the brilliance of Catherine winning on her debut as a jockey at Newbury early in June. She promptly announced that was the end of her racing career, sensible girl. What no-one realised at the time was that she was already expecting our fifth child. I don't know which of us was more nervous in the day's leading up to the charity race, me or Catherine. She trained long and hard riding out for Barney Curley on Cristoforo. She'd ridden well in her days working for David Loder but being pregnant so often had affected her confidence when she started riding out again. With four children at home in the back of her mind, she was a bit frightened that something might happen. But once she agreed to race for charity, she wouldn't back down.

On the day, Catherine raised £30,000. What a star. Watching her in the long preliminaries was nerve-wracking. I thought if she beat one or two and finished the race on Cristoforo, she would have done well. For her to win the race looking so good and tidy was wonderful. I was shell-shocked and the proudest man in England as I rushed out to lead her back into the winner's enclosure. It was a fairytale.

During the previous winter Godolphin's racing operation made some significant changes. They came in the wake of our poor season in England. This time round, it was decided hardly any of our best horses would be trained to the minute for the Dubai World Cup meeting in March. Instead we would be more patient and keep our powder dry for the many challenges that lay ahead later in the season. The policy was to concentrate on England with a strong team and not spread the jam so widely abroad. In addition, for the first time in years, we would have our own powerful team of two-year-olds under the care of Saeed bin Suroor in Newmarket.

Riding out each morning as the sun came up over Dubai, I began to realise the strength in depth we possessed in all departments, particularly the two-year-olds. And for the first time I dared to think that maybe, just maybe, I might have a chance of being champion jockey again. Six months earlier I'd been in the depths of depression, wondering where the next winner was coming from. If anyone had suggested that I might be challenging for the title once more, I'd have told them they were mad. Now as each day passed I began to believe that I could claim the crown again after a gap of nine years. I'd need luck of course. The horses had to stay healthy all year and I'd have to avoid suspensions and injury. Even then I couldn't be sure of beating Kieren Fallon, an outstanding champion.

I call him 'The Assassin' because of his habit of coming fast and late to pinch a race when you think you've got him beaten. In truth he is a competitor from hell, a man who rises to the challenge every time. He pursues you all the way. He puts the marker on the table and you have to take it. I knew it would be hard, incredibly hard to beat him. But in those first few weeks back in Dubai in February 2004, I decided to give it a crack. At that stage it was just a plan in the back of my mind and there it would stay for a while. Saying what you are planning months in advance is tempting fate, and I didn't want to invite bad luck. I'd had enough of that in 2004. But I was always going to give it a go with the enthusiastic support of Catherine, who was delighted to hear I would be back on the championship treadmill after the dark days moping around at home the previous summer. She said I'd been a pain in the butt around the house with all my moaning.

I knew I'd miss quite a few winners at home while riding for Godolphin abroad. But as my confidence grew in the spring, I felt that given a good roll of the dice only injuries or suspension could stop me from knocking on Kieren's door. It helped that I made a flying start. I was in the firing line pretty much from the day the tapes went up and notched up five winners in one day at Folkestone early in April. In racing you find that once you're hot, everything goes your way. You feed off the momentum. That's how it was for me in 2004.

After my last ride at Folkestone I dashed to London to present the prize for the Sports Book the Year at the British Book Awards dinner. I remember stepping onto the stage, opening the envelope and announcing 'The winner is the autobiography of my twin brother, Martin Johnson'. The sky seemed to go dark as he marched up, looking at least nine feet tall, and I had to stand on tiptoe to reach up to shake his massive hand. He had fingers like bananas. What a giant!

While I set off at a smart gallop at the start of the season, Kieren Fallon was already in trouble with the stewards for his riding of Ballinger Ridge at Lingfield early in March. At a delayed inquiry he was suspended for three weeks, which prevented him riding on the turf here until 9 April. That ban set the pattern of a turbulent campaign for him. All year he seemed to be finding choppy waters.

The championship is not a sprint. It is a stamina-sapping marathon and you have to take it month by month. My plan was to try to stay in touching distance of Kieren until the end of the evening meetings late in August. If I could do that, I knew I had a big chance of beating him once we were back to one meeting a day. Things were going every bit as well as I could have hoped until I broke the little finger on my left hand in a bizarre fall at Goodwood on 18 May. I was cantering quietly to the start on Chinkara when a pheasant suddenly flew up in front of us. The horse whipped round in alarm and stumbled as he tried to run away from the noise. Caught by surprise, I ended up on the floor. Somehow I landed on my feet but in clinging onto the reins I damaged my hand. I knew I was in trouble when I heard a nasty cracking sound. At first it wasn't too painful but Chinkara was withdrawn, and soon I was on the way to hospital in Chichester where X-rays confirmed that I had a displaced fracture of the shaft of the little finger on my left hand. It doesn't sound much but a jockey's hands are as precious as a pianist's; you need full movement of your fingers on the reins and whip.

With only 17 days to go to the Derby some people were already ruling me out of Epsom. But I had every intention of being there for Snow Ridge even with one hand tied behind my back. I flew to Sardinia for a brief holiday at my father's home but returned to England after four days ready to start riding work a week after the fall. I've always healed quickly and with the finger strapped up there wasn't too much discomfort when I rode to victory on Masa at Lingfield exactly a week before the Derby.

I had such high hopes of Snow Ridge after he finished full of running to take second place behind Haafhd in the 2,000 Guineas on his first run for Godolphin. It looked a brilliant trial for the Derby, and in weeks days leading up to Epsom I really did believe that I was about to end my hoodoo in the race. It was the first time I'd gone there with a serious chance.

Snow Ridge was almost too laid back, so quiet and placid, a real professional. He had a high cruising speed, which is important for Epsom, and a great turn of foot. Just what you look for in a Derby winner. But he also needed the stamina to stay twelve furlongs and the jury was out on that one. I was pretty confident that he would get the trip, and it was all beginning to look a bit too straightforward, and too good to be true.

So much for my dreams. The reality left me wondering if I will ever win the Derby. I dropped out Snow Ridge in the early stages and made a bit of progress running down to Tattenham corner. Early in the straight things looked promising and we

403

did briefly challenge for second place, but just as my hopes were rising he began to falter before emptying on me. For some reason he didn't pick up like he had done in the Guineas. In the end Snow Ridge finished seventh behind Kieren Fallon on North Light. That was my Derby over for another year. Months of hope and planning blown away in little more than two minutes. I'll just have to keep coming back until I win it.

The night before the Derby I'd flown by helicopter from Epsom with boss Sheikh Mohammed, Simon Crisford and Saeed for one ride on Dubawi in a six-furlong maiden at Goodwood's evening meeting. It was a hugely important landmark for us because the colt was the first of Dubai Millennium's offspring to set foot on a racecourse. The Sheikh had unshakeable faith in his ability to be a great stallion. Naturally we already owned quite a few of his offspring, so after his tragically premature death, Godolphin's agents were instructed to acquire as many of his foals as possible from the only crop that he sired. I think we ended up with at least half of them.

Apparently Dubawi had been giving the boys the right signals at home. Everyone in the paddock was excited, but I can't say I was hugely impressed on our first acquaintance. He was cheeky on the way down to the start, slowly into his stride and ducked and dived through inexperience before edging to the front a furlong out and keeping on for a comfortable victory.

Okay, he won all right, but I didn't think it was a special performance. But I knew that the horse had more to give by the way he behaved, and the other jockeys in the race were impressed by him.

The fireworks came later in the season. At Newmarket he overcame a poor draw and had to do it the hard way. He was very tough and gutsy that day and showed the right spirit in the way he wanted to get to the front. On his final outing, Dubawi looked like a superstar at the Curragh where his easy triumph in the Group 1 National Stakes saw him catapulted to the head of the market for the 2005 Derby. Is he the real deal? Could he be the Derby horse I've craved for so long? I've been fooled so many times before by promising two-year-olds. This game tames lions. You can spend all winter dreaming about one horse and then you come down to earth with a bump when they run. What I will say is that Dubawi has got a lot of ticks in the right boxes.

In Ireland I could have done with a decent lead for longer. But he was going so easily I had to let him stride to the front. There is plenty of stamina in the dam's pedigree, he's got a high cruising speed, a good turn of foot and loves a scrap. I like his cheekiness. He wants to be involved but will only do what is required of him. Here's hoping.

There was a shocking postscript to the 2004 Derby. Four months later Snow Ridge was dead. He was a sick horse after Epsom with a respiratory problem. What started as a cough turned into pneumonia. He then developed laminitis, a horrible condition that causes inflammation of the bones around the foot.

The vets did everything possible to help him but laminitis can be fatal and in the end the decision was taken to put him down humanely to save him from further suffering. Never mind his ability. Snow Ridge was such a kind horse, the sort you could take home with you. He deserved a better life.

Royal Ascot was a riot for me and Godolphin. We had a ball. I had a winner every day, six in all including the Gold Cup on Papineau, the Queen Anne Stakes on Refuse to Bend, and an effortless victory on one of our new recruits, Doyen, in the Hardwicke Stakes on the Saturday which sealed another London Clubs trophy for me as leading rider at the meeting. I was pretty much speechless with excitement after Doyen smashed the mile and a half course record set twenty-one years previously by Stanerra. The way Doyen won took my breath away. When I asked him to go, he took off with me. He is a magnificent looking horse, just about the perfect specimen of a thorough-bred, and luckily his ability matched his looks.

Our rich summer harvest continued at Sandown with Refuse to Bend who just pipped Warrsan in a spine-tingling finish to the Coral-Eclipse Stakes. I loved Refuse to Bend from the moment I first rode him and was scratching my head when he fired blanks in his first two races of the year. Maybe he'd had one dance too many for his previous connections in Ireland. The Queen Anne was the making of him, and I was confident that he would cope with the step up to ten furlongs. That's why I was pretty aggressive on him.

I knew he would run to the line. I had a big smile on my face when Rakti ran off in front with Philip Robinson. That was one danger out of the way, and by the time we reached the straight we had the others covered. Once we hit the front we were always going to win, even though Warrsan pressed us hard in the last half furlong.

I arrived at Ascot on 26 July knowing I was on the brink of my 2,000th winner in this country. It came with an unforgettable ride on Doyen in the King George VI and Queen Elizabeth Diamond Stakes. No wonder I love the place so much. My afternoon's work began with a silly fall from Nightfall as we cantered to the start for the opening race. He jinked and I fell off. We were soon re-united, though, and made all the running to take my score to 1,999.

After two more rides it was the turn of Doyen, a red hot favourite on the day at 11–10. Early that morning I'd told Catherine I couldn't see how he could be beaten. Happily I was right. I settled him just behind the leaders and he was running away with me on the last bend. Beside me, Martin Dwyer was driving the ears off his mount Phoenix Reach. It was just a case of waiting for them to drop back before easing Doyen out to make his challenge. I was itching to let him go but Phoenix Reach, although flat out, was keeping us in. I was so impatient that I shouted, 'Martin, if you don't move over I'm going to knock you over!' Luckily for him his horse dropped away, beaten the moment I spoke. I threaded my way into the clear on Doyen and set sail for home. His response was electrifying and the race was over in less time than it takes to tell. Doyen surged clear in a matter of strides and strolled home by three lengths from the American raider Hard Buck. It was a fantastic way for me to reach such an important landmark and a perfect place to do it.

I'd been nervous all week because I thought so much of Doyen, and the way he won was devastating. I rode him like a favourite, sat fourth, then kicked on and said 'Come and get me if you can'. With the crowd screaming I was trying to look at the big screen on the inside of the course to see how far he was ahead. What I saw confirmed what I felt. That day he was one of the finest I've ridden. No question.

The championship battle ebbed and flowed all summer. A purple patch took me back into the lead on 5 August. Later that month, I was still ahead when I set off for a long weekend that included riding in America on the Saturday night and at Deauville on the Monday. Kieren Fallon took full advantage of my absence to seize back the lead. In the space of a few days he was in front once more with a useful advantage. That's how it was for weeks on end. Neither of us took anything for granted. Kieren remained the bookies' favourite, but aware of the depth of firepower provided for me by the Godolphin two-year-olds I was increasingly confident of coming out on top in our marathon duel.

Of course there were setbacks along the way. Looking back now I'm surprised to see that I collected a total of twelve days' suspension for various minor offences during 2004. It felt as though both Kieren and I were walking on a thin piece of string. If you want to ride all the winners, you have to keep your cool, too. Sometimes I didn't. All the time I knew that a single stupid mistake could lead to yet another forced holiday and that could be enough to give Kieren the edge.

One of my bans came at York for using my whip with excessive frequency during Sulamani's gutsy victory in the Group 1 Juddmonte Stakes in August. I couldn't really complain about that one as I needed to be harder than usual on him to make sure of victory. Because he'd had his problems in the past, he was wary of stretching out even though the easier ground was in his favour. After the wear and tear of a busy racing life, he probably needed a cushion under his feet. Horses remember experiencing pain from running on firm ground, so sometimes you have to be even more aggressive than usual to help them produce their best form. That's how it was with Sulamani that day. In the end he dug very deep to catch Norse Dancer in the last fifty yards with the subsequent Arc winner Bago a close third.

Summer was drawing to a close when I took delivery of the winning post that stood for years in the unsaddling enclosure at Ascot. It has been the scene of many of my best days, so I put in an early bid for it when I heard that the course would be closing down for almost two years for a massive re-building programme. Many historical items have been auctioned for charity. Others were given away or disappeared under the onslaught of a fleet of bulldozers that reduced the famous grand-stand to rubble.

Ascot means everything to me. I've got a phenomenal record there; achieved so much. Maybe I was their clerk of the course in a previous life. I'm so grateful it is my lucky racecourse. Imagine if the best days of my career had come at Folkestone! I am touched that Ascot gave me the prize that I wanted most. I think maybe they were almost obliged to do so after all the winners I'd ridden there.

Naturally I was keen to land the last race there, too, before the builders moved in. In the end I had to settle for second place on Swift Tango behind Johnny Murtagh on Defining. Afterwards I asked Ed Dunlop's travelling head lad Robin Trevor-Jones if he could transport the post for me. He popped it into the back of his lorry and delivered it to my home that night. Within days the winning post was standing sentry in the middle of our stableyard.

It's nice to see a bit of history first thing every morning through the kitchen window. It's close to the box where Fujiyama Crest lives when he is not turned out in the paddock. He was the one who made me famous as the last winner of my magnificent seven. He is part of my history and so is the winning post which greeted so many great horses and jockeys down the years. I will treasure it for the rest of my days. One thing's for sure, it won't be leaving here because it is set deep in concrete.

The battle for the championship was just coming to the boil when Kieren Fallon was one of more than a dozen people arrested in dawn raids by police on 1 September as part of a major investigation into race-fixing. Other jockeys were arrested, too, both that morning and subsequently. It was a sensation at the time and I was as shocked as everyone else when it happened. I didn't know what to think but Kieren was eventually bailed, and I admired his strength of character in turning up to ride at Salisbury the next day. If I'd been in his position, I wouldn't have had the courage to step out of the house. I felt it was extremely brave of him to show up at Salisbury. But then Kieren is unbelievably tough.

There must have been five camera crews and a pack of fifty photographers and newsmen following his every step throughout the afternoon. There seemed to be more media than racegoers. Whatever the sport, at the top level you need as clear a mind as possible to concentrate on the job in hand. You must be relaxed and at ease with yourself. If there is something bothering you, then you can't perform to the best of your ability. The atmosphere that day at Salisbury must have affected him. It would definitely have affected me. No question.

I like Kieren very much. We are good friends. All right, we battle really hard all the time, but we respect each other and I think even more of him after seeing how he buckled down after all the distractions that followed his arrest.

It was still quite tight between us when he had a bad fall at Leicester early in October. By then I was favourite to come out on top, partly because Godolphin's horses were flying. So the fall may not have made any difference. At first Darryll Holland and Seb Sanders were also involved in the title race. Then Kieren and I were left in the final push for the summit. I knew I could never relax because Kieren is so unbelievably competitive. He even rode at three meetings one day to give himself an advantage.

Once I had a cushion after his fall I was keen to have the championship in the bag towards the end of October before I left for riding engagements in Canada and America. Nobody expected me to be champion again. I'm not sure I expected it myself. Even the bookies had me as an outsider in March, but once I made a quick start I became addicted to the chase. It was going down to the wire until Kieren had that nasty fall. Being champion again took a while to sink in because for several years I thought it would never happen again.

Now I am the top dog and want to remain so. That doesn't suit Kieren one bit because he is obsessed with the championship. The challenge was set again for this year until his decision to move to Ireland to ride for Aidan O'Brien. It will not be quite the same without him pushing me to the limit.

Away from the races we both like playing golf but Kieren is much more professional about it than me. He often plays before and after racing. In fact he would play golf in the middle of the night if he could find a course that was open. I think golf helps keep his weight at a sensible level. Eating is part of surviving for him. He is not a big eater and happily gets by on a small sandwich, a bit of chocolate and a can of Coca Cola. In contrast, eating is one of the great pleasures of my life. I love preparing and eating food, preferably with a glass or two of good wine. You could say that eating is part of surviving for Kieren, while for me life comes with eating.

Late in October Kieren and I flew together to Canada for the Pattinson International at Woodbine in Toronto and then on to America for the Breeders' Cup in Dallas. We ended up dominating the finish in Toronto with Sulamani winning comfortably from Kieren's mount Simonas. Then it was on to Texas for the Breeders' Cup, though for over an hour at Toronto airport I wondered if Kieren would be coming with me. Later, as we boarded the flight to Dallas, he gave me the full story.

Seasoned international travellers will know that the formalities of customs and passport control can take an age in North America. It was just as well we gave ourselves extra time to travel to the airport. I passed through all the controls without incident and waited for an age for Kieren to come through. Ninety minutes later, I eventually spotted him queuing to board the flight. How had I missed him? He couldn't wait to tell me what had happened. Apparently the computer in the immigration area had lit up like a Christmas tree when his passport was examined. As a result, Kieren was immediately escorted into a back room and a uniformed officer arrived with a pen and notepad.

The first question went straight for the jugular. 'Mr Fallon, have you ever been arrested?'

It was so unexpected that Kieren 'ummed' and 'ahhd' before saying no. It must have been terrifying for him.

The officer pointed out: 'That's a camera filming you and a microphone is recording your every word. So shall we start again, Mr Fallon? Have you ever been arrested?'

This time he reluctantly admitted that yes, he had been arrested almost two months previously.

The officer's eyes narrowed with suspicion. 'Tell me why you were arrested,' he asked.

Kieren replied: 'Well, allegedly for race fixing.'

The officer immediately relaxed. 'But you're a jockey aren't you?'

'Yes,' answered Kieren, sensing an escape route.

'Well, that's part of your job, isn't it?' concluded the officer, the interrogation obviously at an end. He then stamped Kieren's passport and with a broad smile sent him on his way!

We had a great week together before the Breeders' Cup, riding work at Lone Star Park in the morning, playing golf some days and taking part in the International Jockeys event at the start of the weekend. I am not saying we work as a team but if I can help Kieren, I do, and I like to think he does the same for me. On the big day Kieren had just the one ride on the brilliant filly Ouija Board in the Filly and Mare Turf. And after taking part in the mile turf race on Diamond Green, I was able to pass on one crucial piece of information. It had been a wet week and a lot of the moisture had rolled towards the inside of the track. I could see that the horses closest to the rail were leaving a decent hoofprint while the ones further out were not even making a mark. So I said to Kieren if he had the choice to be sure to stay out away from the rail. Sure enough, entering the straight he left his filly drift away from the fence and she took off with him on the way to a great victory.

Then it was my turn on Jeremy Noseda's Wilko in the Juvenile. In the betting we were dismissed as 26–1 no-hopers. I was encouraged that Jeremy gave me positive orders. Actually I was very surprised that he wanted me to be bold. He explained that since we knew the horse stayed I should try to kick on half a mile from home. Easier said than done. Three furlongs out things did not look promising. I was flat to the boards in fourth place on Wilko with the three in front of us apparently going much better.

Two furlongs out, I was still pushing and shoving behind the leaders thinking that we would only be fourth at best. But the horses in front of us didn't go anywhere and then began to tire. Suddenly we were closing them down and as they struggled we sped past on the outside to snatch the prize.

I can't tell you the sheer excitement I felt when I knew I would win. I haven't been so carried away since Markofdistinction gave me my first Group 1 success at Ascot back in 1990. What followed was just the same.

Everything seemed to happen in slow motion. Then it went dark. I think it was the sheer joy of knowing I would win, yet when I passed the post I had the strange feeling that it wasn't for real. As I waved like a lunatic to the crowd, I was wondering if I had really won or would I be waking up from a dream at any minute.

It was almost surreal and all the better for being unexpected. Don't forget I still had the scars of Swain's defeat on my heart. Once again I wanted to show the Americans that I could beat them. It was an amazing day. Our two lone English raiders had both won in cowboy country in Texas. Everyone involved with the two horses had mixed in and helped each other. After racing we all met up in the bar of our hotel The Four Seasons for a celebration. There was Lord Derby, the happy owner breeder of Ouija Board, his trainer Ed Dunlop, Kieren, Jeremy and the lads involved with the horses. But after a couple of hours I had to rush off to the airport for my flight to Australia for the Melbourne Cup. Within days I came crashing down to earth with a hell of a bump.

What happened was very weird. With twenty-four runners in such a valuable handicap there will always be a bit of trouble in running. But when I left the track at Melbourne after finishing seventh on Mamool, I didn't know that anything was wrong. The first hint came at seven that evening with a call on my mobile from the stewards asking me to attend an inquiry the next morning. Apparently the press had picked up something from the television sky view.

That was when I made a slight manoeuvre half a mile out. It didn't impede anyone or cost anyone a place or prize money. But they wanted to have another look and several other jockeys were asked to give evidence.

Perhaps I should have seen what was coming because I remember my agent Ray Cochrane being hit with a four-week ban and a huge fine for causing interference in winning the Caulfield Cup on Taufan's Melody in 1998. The Australians can be overexuberant about these things and I was working for Godolphin. Maybe they wanted to make an example.

I knew I was in trouble when two camera crews and ten press guys turned up at the inquiry. During a short hearing I pleaded guilty because I had made a slight manoeuvre, though the interference was minimal. If it had happened in England, I might have got two or perhaps four days maximum for careless riding. Or I might have been let off with a caution.

So I was flabbergasted when they hit me with 31 days. If you put all my suspensions together over the years they wouldn't add up to much more than a month. I was that shocked at the severity of the sentence it made me laugh. The stewards did ask me if I would miss anything apart from the last days of the season at home, so maybe they took that into consideration.

There is one thing more I want to say about my long suspension. Now that they have laid down the guidelines by hammering me, I hope the local stewards adopt the same tough approach with their own people in the race in the future. I've ridden in quite a few Melbourne Cups. It is always a really rough race with horses getting knocked sideways. Let's see what they have to say in November this year.

The press wanted to know if I was going to appeal. But I had a flight to catch a couple of hours later and had no intention of flying half way round the world and back again just to appeal. I might have reacted differently if it looked like costing me the championship in England, but that was already won. November is always a quiet month, I wasn't missing anything important, so I decided to take the ban on the chin and spend a month on the sidelines. But if it had come in the middle of the English season, I would have felt like killing myself.

There was just time to take in the last day of the flat season at Doncaster before the suspension took effect. Catherine, Leo and the girls travelled up to Yorkshire with me for a memorable day. None of my children had been born the last time I'd been champion. It was lovely to have them with me this time round, a special day because I'd forgotten what it felt like to be champion. I realised how much I missed it. There's nothing like walking around as the King Cock in the pen. The Championship was exciting for everybody, especially me after I stopped being Frankie the star and started being Frankie the jockey again.

After rushing around at a frantic pace for month after month from dawn until midnight, I struggled at first to settle down to the rhythms of domestic life. Having time on my hands was a novel experience and it was hard to find my role in the house. It took me the best part of two weeks to adjust, but I spent a lovely month with Catherine and the children and over-indulged myself eating and drinking. I helped out with the cooking at home, took Leo to school in the mornings and also took him to a couple of football matches including Arsenal at home to West Brom. We travelled by tube from Knightsbridge. After the game I kitted Leo out in the full Arsenal strip, plus duvet cover, pillow slip, clubs badges, gloves, tee shirt and hat. I hope he enjoyed the experience. I think he did because he says that he is definitely an Arsenal supporter now. For me it was all very emotional because from the day he was born I couldn't wait to take him to a game at Highbury.

I also took Leo to watch our local club Norwich at home to Liverpool. As the tickets were provided by my good friend Didi Hamann, we sat in the middle of a lively group of away fans chanting Liverpool songs. Poor Leo was very confused. After the game, Didi gave Leo his shirt. He took one look at it, said it was too big for him and handed it to me!

I also took the whole family to Frankie's Italian bar and restaurant, the place I opened in Knightsbridge in partnership with Marco Pierre White in September. It all started from a chance meeting between us the previous winter. I remember lecturing Marco about *carpaccio*, one of my favourite Italian dishes. I also moaned about the lack of suitable family restaurants in London. I think Marco was surprised at my passion for food. One thing led to another and now Frankie's is catering for 1,600 customers a week.

Marco is in charge while I am a 'sleeping partner'. It is an interesting sideline which could lead to other projects. One night Catherine and I travelled to Birmingham with our friends John and Amanda Duffy to see Ronan Keating in concert. He couldn't have made us more welcome. We spent the evening in his dressing-room and dancing on the side of the stage.

Then it was time to get back into shape for the Hong Kong International meeting shortly before Christmas. That's where the equisizer in my gym is so useful. Pumping away on it for ten minutes at a time really makes me sweat. Most flat trainers in Newmarket are almost closed down in December, with the horses ticking over with gentle canters. My old pal Barney Curley helped out by letting me ride out on his team of jumpers for ten days. It was a bonus that he did not expect me to turn up at dawn on freezing cold December mornings. Instead he was quite happy for me to appear at a civilised hour for second or third lot. That way I could ride out and still have a nice lie-in every morning. What a luxury.

I needed to be fit for four rides on the day in Hong Kong. They were all important races for Godolphin and winning on Firebreak was for me the icing on the cake of a memorable year. I'd done as much training as I could in a short time, but you count your fitness by the speed you recover your breath after each race. I don't mind admitting that after my final ride Ancient World had finished a close fifth, it took me a while to explain to Saeed how it had gone because I was gasping for air. I was fit to ride but not to talk to him for long.

A momentous year ended with a big jolly to celebrate my birthday and my third championship. I invited most of the jockeys in Newmarket and we had a great time. The next morning I felt every day of my age 34. Early in the New Year I fulfilled a long-time invitation to ride at Siracusa, the only racecourse on the island of Sicily. It was a public holiday and a crowd of over 12,000 turned out to greet me at the meeting, which finished under floodlights early in the evening. The reception I got after winning on my first mount Mister Personal took my breath away. It became even more emotional when I completed a double in the final race named in honour of my seven wins at Ascot in 1996.

Normally in January I like to switch off completely on holiday with Catherine and a few friends in Barbados. But with our fifth baby due early in February that wasn't possible. Anyway, thanks to the Melbourne stewards, I'd already had an extended winter holiday. After my trip to Sicily I was ready for action again. So we decided to leave for Dubai earlier than usual so that I could ride at the opening meeting of the International Racing Carnival at Nad Al Sheba late in January.

The time was getting a bit tight for Catherine to fly. With three weeks to go before the baby was due, British Airways were the only airline prepared to take us to Dubai. They seemed quite relaxed about it. So were we at the time because the flight lasts less than seven hours. Four days later, our little son Rocco James was born. He weighed in at 5lb 7oz.

It was great to have another boy for Leo's sake. With three girls in the family, Leo and I were being overrun in the house! Rocco has balanced things up a bit and will be spoilt by all of us. You should never say never, but this time Catherine and I agree that Rocco will definitely be our last child. Five is the limit. I think.

Catherine may have retired undefeated as a jockey, but giving up riding is the last thing on my mind. What drives me on is the certainty that there is nothing I'd rather be doing than riding horses, above all in the big races. It started out as just a job but soon moved far beyond that. I do it simply because I love the buzz and the pressure of being a jockey. Days last year like Doyen at Ascot, Wilko in Dallas and Firebreak in Hong Kong make you want to go on riding for the rest of your life, because you know you will never get the same highs from anything else. I'd settle for another ten years. That would give my kids the chance to see me ride and appreciate what I can do, just as I was able to see my dad at the very top and be proud of him. I'd like them to experience the same feelings. I don't need the money any more and yes, I'd probably do it for nothing – but please don't tell Sheikh Mohammed!

Since I enjoy racing more than ever, I want to carry on for as long as possible. I'd be mad to give up what I have, but all good things come to an end and I don't want to overstay my welcome. If something goes wrong before then, I'll probably walk away. I have the best job in racing with the best boss and the best team of horses in the world to ride. It's like having the fastest seat in Formula 1. I am the one riding the Ferraris and our horsepower was stronger than ever in 2004. After the sort of Group 1 results I've enjoyed, dropping down a league or two would be too painful for me. If Thierry Henry left Arsenal after being knocked off his perch, you wouldn't expect to see him finish his playing days in the second division or the Conference. It's the same for me. I've been so spoilt with the horses I've ridden that I couldn't settle for second best.

And after that? Who knows. Several years ago Michael Parkinson looked shocked when I told him on his chat show that I was planning to take over his job when I retired from riding. There are already offers on the table for work in TV and other media, but I don't want to think of them just yet. My strongest ambition is to win the Derby at Epsom and keep riding for as long as I enjoy it. *Come on me!*

Career Record

PERSONAL DETAILS

Born: Lanfranco Oscar Dettori, 15 December 1970, Milan

Parents: Gianfranco and Iris Maria

Sister: Alessandra

Family: Wife Catherine, sons Leo and Rocco, and daughters Ella, Mia and Tallula

Height: 5ft 4in

Weight: 8st 5lb (53kg)

CAREER HIGHLIGHTS

1986   First winner on Rif, Turin

1987   First UK winner on Lizzy Hare, Goodwood

1989   Appointed stable jockey to Luca Cumani. Crowned Champion Apprentice

1990   First Group 1 winner on Markofdistinction, Ascot. Reaches 100 winners in the season (first teenager since Lester Piggott to achieve this feat)

1991   First Derby win, on Temporal, Germany

1992   French Derby Win, on Polytain

1993   Appointed retained jockey to Sheikh Mohammed Al Maktoum

1994   Rides 233 winners. Champion Jockey.

1995   Wins the Breeders' Cup Mile and the St Leger. Champion Jockey

1996   Goes through the card at Ascot for an unprecedented 'Magnificent Seven'

2000   Survives plane crash with fellow jockey Ray Cochrane

2001   Awarded an MBE

2004   2000th UK career win on Doyen, Ascot. Champion Jockey

WINNERS IN UK

1987 – 8

1988 – 22

1989 – 75 (Champion Apprentice)

1990 – 141

1991 – 94

1992 – 101

1993 – 149

1994 – 233 (Champion Jockey)

1995 – 216 (Champion Jockey)

1996 – 123

1997 – 176

1998 – 132

1999 – 132

2000 – 47

2001 – 94

2002 – 69

2003 – 101

2004 – 195 (Champion Jockey)

GROUP 1 RACE WINS

BRITISH CLASSIC WINS (9)

Oaks – 1994 Balanchine, 1995 Moonshell, 2002 Kazzia
2,000 Guineas – 1996 Mark Of Esteem, 1999 Island Sands
1,000 Guineas – 1998 Cape Verdi, 2002 Kazzia
St Leger – 1995 Classic Cliché, 1996 Shantou.

UK (44)

King George – 1995 Lammtarra, 1998 Swain, 1999 Daylami, 2004 Doyen.
Eclipse Stakes – 1998 Daylami, 2004 Refuse to Bend.
Sussex Stakes – 1991 Second Set, 1999 Aljabr, 2001 Noverre.
Ascot Gold Cup – 1992 & 93 Drum Taps, 1998 Kayf Tara, 2004 Papineau.
St James's Palace Stakes – 1997 Starborough.
Queen Anne Stakes – 2003 Dubai Destination, 2004 Refuse to Bend.
QE II Stakes – 1990 Markofdistinction, 1996 Mark Of Esteem, 1999 Dubai Millennium.
Juddmonte International Stakes – 1996 Halling, 1997 Singspiel, 2001 Sakhee, 2004 Sulamani.
Juddmonte Lockinge – 2000 Aljabr.
Coronation Cup – 1996 Swain, 1997 Singspiel, 1999 Daylami, 2001 Mutafaweq
Prince of Wales's Stakes – 2001 Fantastic Light, Grandera 2002
Nunthorpe Stakes – 1993 Lochsong, 1995 So Factual, 1998 Lochangel.
Haydock Sprint Cup – 1999 Diktat
Yorkshire Oaks – 1994 Only Royale.
Nassau Stakes – 2001 Lailani

Ascot Fillies' Mile – 1990 Shamshir, 1997 Glorosia, 1999
  Teggiano, 2000 Crystal Music
Cheveley Park – 2000 Regal Rose, 2003 Cool Kat Katie
Middle Park Stakes – 1996 Bahamian Bounty, 1998 Lujain.

FRANCE (26)

French Derby – 1992 Polytain.
French 2,000 Guineas – 1995 Vettori, 2000 Bachir.
Prix de l'Arc de Triomphe – 1995 Lammtarra, 2001 Sakhee, 2002
  Marienbard
Prix Vermeille – 2003 Mezzo Soprano
Prix Ganay – 1995 Pelder
Prix Lupin – 1995 Flemensfirth
Prix d'Isaphan – 1996 Halling, 2002 Best of the Bests
Prix Jacques le Marois – 1999 Dubai Millennium, 2000 Muhtathir.
Prix de Moulin – 2001 Slickly
Prix Jean Prat – 1995 Torrential, 1997 Starborough, 1998
  Almutawakel.
Prix Maurice de Gheest – 1999 Diktat
Prix Morny – 1996 Bahamian Bounty
Prix de la Salamandre – 1995 Lord of Men, 1998 Aljabr.
Prix de L'Abbaye – 1993 & 94 Lochsong, 2004 Var
Prix Marcel Boussac – 1996 Ryafan, 2001 Sulk.

UNITED STATES & CANADA (7)

Breeders' Cup Turf – 1999 Daylami, 2001 Fantastic Light
Breeders' Cup Mile – 1994 Barathea.
Breeders' Cup Juvenile – 2004 Wilko.
Canadian International – 2000 Mutafaweq
Beverley D – 2004 Crimson Palace.

ITALY (14)

Derby Italiano – 1999 Mukhalif
Oaks d'Italia – 1997 Nicole Pharly

Gran Premio d'Italia – 1992 Masad

Gran Premio di Milano – 1997 Shantou

Premio Vittorio di Capua – 1999 Muhtathir, 2001 & 2002 Slickly,
    2004 Ancient World

Gran Premio del Jockey Club – 1993 Misil, 1996 Shantou, 2001 Kutub

Premio Roma – 1990 Legal Case, 1992 Misil, 1996 Flemensfirth,
    2002 Sunstrach

IRELAND (12)

Irish Derby – 1994 Balanchine.

Irish 2000 Guineas – 2000 Bachir.

Irish Oaks – 2001 Lailani, 2003 Vintage Tipple

Irish St Leger – 1999 Kayf Tara.

Irish Champion Stakes – 1998 Swain, 1999 Daylami, 2001
    Fantastic Light, 2002 Grandera

Phoenix Stakes – 1992 Pips Pride

Tattersalls Gold Cup – 2001 Fantastic Light

National Stakes – 2004 Dubawi

OTHERS (19)

Dubai World Cup – 2000 Dubai Millennium, 2003 Moon Ballad

Dubai Sheema Classic – 2003 Sulamani.

Japan Cup – 1996 Singspiel, 2002 Falbrav

Japan Cup Dirt – 2002 Eagle Cafe

German Derby – 1991 Temporal

Deutschland Preis – 1997 Luso, 2002 Marienbard

Bayerisches Zuchtrennen – 1995 Germany

Grosser Preis Von Baden – 1995 Germany, 2002 Marienbard,
    2003 Mamool

Grosser Dallmayr Preis – 2001 Kutub

Europa Preis – 2001 Kutub, 2003 Mamool

Hong Kong Cup – 2000 Fantastic Light, 2003 Falbrav

Hong Kong Mile – 2004 Firebreak

Singapore Airlines International Cup – 2002 Grandera

FRANKIE'S CAREER WINS WORLDWIDE

	UK	Dub	Fr	Ger	HK	Ire	It	Jap
1986							5	
1987	8						12	
1988	22							
1989	75						9	
1990	141						6	
1991	94		1	1			2	
1992	101		2		4	1	11	1
1993	149		5	2			11	4
1994	233		2	3		4	2	
1995	216	1	11	3		1	2	
1996	123	6	10		4	1	10	3
1997	176	7	6	1	2	1	8	
1998	132	4	9			3		
1999	132	7	5		3	6	3	
2000	47	5	9		1	1	3	
2001	94	14	8	3	1	4	3	
2002	69	9	4	3		1	6	3
2003	101	18	3	2	1	1		
2004	195	9	1		1	1	1	
Total	**2,112**	**80**	**76**	**18**	**17**	**25**	**94**	**11**

Statistics supplied by Nick Higgins at www.jockeysroom.com up to 9 January 2005.

Nor	Sng	Mau	SA	Aus	Esp	Swe	USA	Total
								5
								20
								22
								84
1							1	149
					1		9	108
							1	121
	1							172
								244
	4						1	239
			4			1	1	163
								201
								148
				1			1	158
	2						1	69
		3					2	133
	1	1						97
								126
							3	211
1	**8**	**4**	**4**	**1**	**1**	**1**	**20**	**2,475**

Index